THE
FRONTIERS
── OF ──
FORTUNE

Predicting capital prospects
and casualties in the markets
of the future

JONATHAN STORY

 Prentice Hall
FINANCIAL TIMES

An imprint of **Pearson Education**
London • New York • Toronto • Sydney • Tokyo • Singapore • Hong Kong
Cape Town • New Delhi • Madrid • Paris • Amsterdam • Munich • Milan • Stockholm

PEARSON EDUCATION LIMITED

Edinburgh Gate
Harlow, Essex CM20 2JE
Tel: +44 (0)1279 623623
Fax: +44 (0)1279 431059
Website: www.pearsoned.co.uk

First published in Great Britain in 1999

ISBN 0 273 63166 7

British Library Cataloguing in Publication Data
A CIP catalogue record for this book can be obtained
from the British Library.

10 9 8

Typeset by Northern Photosetting Co Ltd
Printed and bound in Great Britain by
Biddles Ltd, King's Lynn, Norfolk

*The Publishers' policy is to use paper manufactured
from sustainable forests.*

ABOUT THE AUTHOR

Jonathan Story is Professor of International Political Economy at INSEAD. In the past he has served as a consultant to governments and international corporations, banks and service companies, on European and world politics and markets. Prior to joining INSEAD, he worked in Brussels and Washington, where he obtained his PhD from The Johns Hopkins School of Advanced International Studies (SAIS). He has written widely in professional reviews, and his latest book, co-authored with Ingo Walter of New York University, is entitled *The Political Economy of Financial Integration in Europe: the Battle of the Systems*, and was published in 1997–8 by Manchester University Press in Europe and MIT Press in the US. Some of his cases on EU public policy appear in Olivier Cadot's edited volume, *Industrial and Trade Policy Cases*, Prentice Hall, 1996. He also has a series on country studies, which is updated regularly and useful for crafting corporate strategies to local conditions.

CONTENTS

....

LIST OF TABLES AND FIGURES

....

LIST OF ABBREVIATIONS

....

ANC	African National Congress
APEC	Asia Pacific Economic Community
ASEAN	Association of South East Asian Nations
CEE	Central and Eastern Europe
CEO	chief executive officer
CIS	Confederation of Independent States
EU	European Union
FDI	foreign direct investment
G7	Group of Seven
G16	Group of Sixteen
GATT	General Agreement on Tariffs and Trade
GDP	gross domestic product
GNP	gross national product
IBRD	International Bank for Reconstruction and Development
IISS	International Institute for Strategic Studies
IMF	International Monetary Fund
ISI	import-substitution industrialization
IT	information technologies
MERCOSUR	Mercado Común del Sur (The Southern Common Market)
MPT	Ministry of Post and Telecommunications
NAFTA	North America Free Trade Agreement
NATO	North Atlantic Treaty Organization
OAS	Organization of American States
OECD	Organization for Economic Co-operation and Development
OPEC	Organization of Oil Exporting Countries
UK	United Kingdom
UN	United Nations
US	United States of America
USSR	Union of Soviet Socialist Republics
WIR	World Investment Report
WTO	World Trade Organization

FOREWORD

························

Human society has, from its beginnings, been in a constant state of transition. Transition obviously impacts upon the opinion-leaders and decision-makers in the business environment, for whom the challenging questions are, 'From what point are we in transition? When did the transitionary phase begin? Where will this transition lead?' To answer the last question one needs to possess the ability to determine the key global forces and critical players.

Conventional wisdom until mid-1997 was that the world was in transition from Atlantic dominance to a new Pacific Century. This view of the world held that the transitionary phase began with the Japanese 'economic miracle' of the 1960s. It was confirmed when, in the 1970s and '80s, the emerging Asian tigers achieved spectacularly high growth rates. It was also perceived that, in continuation of this trend, the reform programme undertaken by Deng Xiaoping would propel China, and with it all of East Asia, into the uncontested global driving seat during the 21st Century. The '80s and '90s witnessed an enormous literary output explaining this extraordinary phenomenon.

Even after the Japanese economy stagnated in the early '90s, global enthusiasm for Asia was not doused – quite the contrary. European bankers literally fought over each other to lend more and more money to East Asian enterprises – a phenomenon which in good part lies at the heart of the crisis that subsequently ensued – while Western multinational corporations focused a great deal of their energy and resources in building up robust long-term positions in Asian markets.

In early 1999 it is clear that the 'Pacific Century' has, at best, been postponed. Indeed it could be argued that the Atlantic territories, combining the twin powers of North America and Western Europe, have never been stronger. This is most emphatically not the scenario we would, until recently, have forecast!

The problem with the 'Pacific Century' vision was that it was conceived exclusively within parameters defined by business and economics. Politics was left out of the equation. Although there can be no doubt that East Asia provided a lot of excitement, it was by no means the only show in town in the last quarter of the twentieth century. While a lot of attention had been focused on East Asia, relatively little was paid to the series of critical political transitions which had occurred in Southern Europe. In the mid-'70s Greece, Portugal and Spain broke away from decades of fascist totalitarian regimes to embrace democracy. This, according to Jonathan Story, was the key departure point of late twentieth century transition. This transition manifested itself in a wave of democracy that, by the mid-'90s, had washed over a good deal of Latin America, Southern and Eastern Europe – and, indeed, stretched as far as East Asia, with Korea and Taiwan as prime 'Confucian' examples of democratisation.

It is politics that drives the world economy, not economics that drives world politics. Neither the Marxists nor the ayatollahs of neo-classical economic liberalism, according to Story, grasp this fundamental point. What should have become clear to them in this last decade is that, while the defeat of communism heralded the end of the Soviet Union, the post-cold-war era also witnessed the death of 'economism' (ie. economics is the only 'ism'), hence the rapid eclipse of Japan as a formidable global player. The defeat of communism and economism ultimately represents the political victory of liberal democracy.

Story provides a good deal of illuminating insight into his discussion of both the global theatre and its major actors. He has asked the right questions and set the correct parameters. As he says in his concluding chapter, Japan, in spite of all its amazing accumulation of wealth, 'missed the bus to world eminence', and, consequently, 'history passed Japan by'. Why? There is nothing desperately wrong with the economics in Japan: the country has lots of capital, state of the art production technology, and a large pool of highly skilled workers. At the root of the Japanese malaise is the political paralysis which has plagued the country. Analysts should not, therefore, ask the question, 'What are Japan's economic problems?', but, 'What are the Japanese political solutions?'. It is only when the latter question is asked that one can become aware of how desperate Japan's situation is. Japan has failed to come up with any political solutions not only in respect to its own problems, but in respect to the Asia Pacific region's many pressing challenges. On the global level, Japan's political insignificance stands in inverse proportion to its economic weight.

The eclipse of both communism and economism should raise some very serious questions regarding the People's Republic of China. Beijing may have thrown Marxism out the window on the economic front, but Leninism remains paramount in the political realm. With ideology buried China is a communist state whose sole legitimacy rests on material deliverables. China has done exceedingly well in the course of the last couple of decades, but there are nevertheless three points that should be kept in mind:

- The first is that if Story is correct and the key global trend driving humanity into the 21st century is the wave of democracy which has risen since the death of Franco and Salazar, this wave should ultimately reach Chinese shores. The idea that Confucian models of authoritarianism reject democracy has been bankrupted by the recent successful transitions to democracy of both Korea and Taiwan. Whereas in Japan democracy was imposed by the US Occupation, the Korean and Taiwanese people gained democracy through their own efforts.
- The second is that economic success and political tranquility do not necessarily go hand in hand. For example, in the case of Korea the violent student uprisings that ultimately drove out the military dictatorship occurred well before the Korean financial crisis – in fact at a time when the nation was on the crest of its GNP-growth wave.
- The third is the possibility of China learning lessons not from Korea, but from Indonesia. Suharto's Indonesia had also prospered, but when the party stopped and the economy crashed, Suharto and all his family and cronies became parasites.

China faces an uncertain future; one thing, however, is assured – its present course is unsustainable. By no means does this need to imply that disaster looms. There is an array of possible scenarios, any of which could prevail. What is both amazing and distressing, however, is the apparent unwillingness of the Western business community to contemplate change in China. For foreign investors, the only Chinese scenario is business as usual. As Story points out, this calls to mind a precedent set by pre-1979 Iran.

Story's wave of democracy will, I am quite certain, continue to gather momentum. In today's borderless world economy the wave of democracy will ultimately come to all shores. It is also almost certain that political shocks and transformations will occur sooner than might be expected. Two driving forces underpin this particular trend: the universal pursuit of liberty and happiness – history has shown repeatedly and emphatically that people the world over are prepared to die to be free; and the advancement of communication technology leading to a rapid and global dissemination of information – authoritarian governments can no longer rely on keeping their people ignorant.

However, the eclipse of communism and economism notwithstanding, it is not the case that a homogenous order of political market economy will prevail throughout the world. Cultures remain strong and diverse. It is impossible to dogmatically impose onto highly heterogeneous societies a single model of political orthodoxy.

Liberal democracy, it must also be recognised, is a strange and quite unpredictable thing. Freedom of speech and advanced communications technology provide means for spreading information and entertainment, but also for spreading hatred. Looking forward, one must take into consideration what Story calls the ancestral voices, which, as he writes in the beginning of Chapter Five, 'find the tools of modernity particularly congenial to broadcasting their particularistic messages of salvation and vengeance'. In periods of rapid transformation, ancestral voices easily become not only louder, but also more appealing.

Even when the whole world will be basking in regimes of liberal democracy, it will not be, *pace* Francis Fukuyama, 'the end of history'. By no means will global liberal democracy necessarily be synonymous with global peace.

Finally, three bold brush strokes by way of concluding this foreword and introducing this highly thought-provoking book:

Story ends *The Frontiers of Fortune* on an optimistic note. The victory of liberal democracy does not presage eternal peace and prosperity, but, to paraphrase Winston Churchill's dictum about democracy, it certainly beats all known contenders. The victory of liberal democracy is, in great part, due to the supreme political, military, economic, ideological and cultural power of the United States. Having won the geopolitical battle against the Soviet Union, it was able to get into quick economic shape to be able to take on Japan and its mercantilism. However, for the sake of longer-term global stability, American hegemonism needs to be challenged. Looking at the world, none of the traditional large powers are in contention. Russia is out of the running, so is Japan; India may one day have an interesting story to tell, but even the preface is yet to be written; China is in need of rationalisation, and Story's sense that it will be about 2070 before possible political solutions will merge with economic power is probably correct, give or take a decade. So it has to be the European Union. Story believes the EU will manifest itself more boldly on the global scene and that the first half of the twentieth century will be characterised by trans-Atlantic 'bi-gemonism'. This vision, though Story does not say so, would represent the Europeanisation of Eden's view of the Anglo-American special relationship, namely one whereby Britain (now Europe) will play Athens to the American Sparta. Sounds good, but an '*Inch'Allah*' may be in order.

Contrary to what he says, Jonathan Story's book is not a work of political science. In fact, what Story's book proves once again is how badly decision-makers and opinion-leaders are served by academe. Academic distinctions between economics, politics, the impact of the collective vision of the past (history), social psychology, etc. are virtually non-existent. A holistic view of humanity will become increasingly necessary as the world becomes more interdependent and interconnected. People increasingly need to work with the different disciplines, be knowledgeable about different cultures, and familiar with both the worlds of government and industry.

Companies must develop more sensitive political antennas. Very serious consideration needs to be given to investments in countries with murky regimes, not only for ethical reasons, but also for reasons of longer-term enlightened self-interest. There are many different types of ancestral voices which may return to haunt the investor. There can be no such thing as a totally politically neutral business decision. As Tony Jackson wrote in the *Financial Times* ('When work makes slavery', 27 February 1999), it is important 'to remind companies tempted to cross the ethical divide that the past can come back and bite them. And when it does, their record on shareholder value will be no defence'.

Jean-Pierre Lehmann
March 1999

PREFACE

....

How can we conceive of the world in a practical way? business people often ask. This book provides my answer. Politics drives the world economy, because history is made by humans, and we humans can choose between alternatives. What those alternatives are depends very much on the preferences of those who decide between what is significant and what is not. The significance of one factor or idea relative to another is difficult enough for individuals to decide, and much more so when two or more people seek to combine their wills to achieve some objective.

Politics occurs whenever two or more people seek to combine their wills. This definition enables us to place states and corporations centre stage. But it also allows us to populate our zoo of players on the world stage with business people, as well as professional politicians, media types, academics, financial market wizards, drug barons or the occasional saint.

The run-of-the-mill view is that economics drives politics. The world is what it is because 'the market' says so. This was the stock-in-trade of the average Marxist-Leninist: the infrastructure is composed of the production system, and the superstructure is religion, politics, law, the arts and culture.

It is surprising how many business people, lazily, tend to agree with this view. The predisposition is understandable. Business people are concerned on a daily basis to buy, make or sell. They are more than aware of how volatile consumer preferences may be in the light of alternative offerings on the market.

But business people are also dealing daily with very complex problems of organization, of choice between alternatives, and of people. They are permanently engaged therefore in what I have just referred to as politics. How they choose is in part a matter of personal judgement, in part a result of collective decisions, and in part the result of inertia or tradition. The results can be measured in the intangibles of corporate culture, or via corporate accounts.

That is where the market is so important both to business and to government. As von Hayek, the great Austrian liberal economist, teaches, the magic of the market is that it restricts the amount of information needed by buyers and sellers to one price. Participants in the market do not have to know how the product is assembled, transported, transformed and distributed. All they need to know is the present price. They can then decide to transact in the light of their preferences and their budgets.

The market is an extraordinary mechanism for collecting, conveying and synthesizing information. It follows therefore that if market price is to be unpacked, its contents have to be laid out on the table for examination. This is what *The Frontiers of Fortune* seeks to do. It tells the story of what is contained in the price. That includes the collective decisions of the peoples of the world, their whims, their greeds, their loves and their hates. The price mechanism is a cornerstone of world society. It also assimilates and conveys world politics.

States are participants in this world market. Without the price mechanism, they could not account for their activities, or make choices between alternatives. They are territorially bounded, varying in size, cohesion or wealth. They are members also of the international or world society of states, and pillars of the international or world system. Reference to a world society assumes that relations between states are conducted on some generally agreed principles, while the international system conveys a sense of impersonality, of hostility in relations between states.

Other major participants in world affairs are nations, or cultures and civilizations. Most states in the world contain a number of nations, whose members often spill out into surrounding territories. They may also be clustered in a wider nation, defining itself more as a civilization, and represented through the many diasporas which populate the world.

Currencies are state-produced commodities, traded in markets. They are the most visible price through which political affairs are conveyed. The general assumption of the 'rational expectations' school of thinking is that relative prices contain all known information. That is what von Hayek, too, seems to be saying. This is a circuitous argument. It says that what is known is known, or at least contained in the price.

But what of the vast areas of human life, let alone life on this planet and beyond, which are not known about, or the significance of which is not recognized even if they are known about?

This is why I introduce the concept of world and local time. World time is instantaneous, tied to the expanding reach of modern communications, future-oriented, and trade-off based. It contains what I call local time, the inherited sphere in which most people live. Most people are also parts of cultures and civilizations, with their own mental landscapes and holy places.

In 'rational expectations' language, such inheritances are 'irrational'. They are not. They contain their own, often terrifying rationalities. And they use the conveniences of modern communications to dispense their approval or to wreak their vengeance. These are the sources of the unpredictable in the luminous lenses of our Western rationalists.

So *The Frontiers of Fortune* proposes ways to think about the future, where corporate opportunities lie, and about how to conceive of change in the world, in politics and in corporations. We start at the turn of the nineteenth century, and look forward well into the second half of the twenty-first. The structure of the book flows from the years 1989–92, when four transformations came to a head simultaneously: the world state system; ideas about the world's future; world markets; and relations between states and corporations. All these four processes of transformation have been simultaneous, interactive but non-synchronized.

As someone educated in England and Ireland, Europe and America, I must end this short introduction by stating my point of departure. Edmund Burke preceded present-day institutional economists by a couple of centuries. Their important work is therefore harking back to an older tradition, whose elegance of prose they might well learn from. Burke lamented living in an age of 'sophisters, economists and calculators', and concluded that the glory of Europe was extinguished for ever.

Little could Burke have guessed what a prosperous future awaited this tribe. Shorn of any historical insight, and political neophytes, their modern descendants have dispensed their forecasts and advice to all four corners of the universe. Only a small minority, such as my late, lamented colleague Edith Penrose, was or are aware of the subtle and intricate links of politics to markets.

Burke's wrath was directed against you 'who lay down metaphysic propositions which infer universal consequences, and then [who] attempt to limit logic by despotism'. How full is the graveyard of unintended consequences from your ill-thought-out acts! When Brezhnev ordered Soviet troops into Afghanistan, Georges Marchais – France's Communist Party leader, good friend of Mr and Mrs Ceauçescu – opined that the invasion would bring to an end the feudal lord's *'droit de cuissage'*. Little did Brezhnev or Marchais know that the invasion lit a fuse across Islam, helped to precipitate the Soviet Union's collapse, and has still a long trail of destruction to run.

Similarly, our very own flat-earthers believe that economics drives politics, that the economic infrastructure 'basically' supports the 'superstructure', and that – to add another metaphor introduced in *The Frontiers of Fortune* – we all climb the great, progressive staircase of history. They are joined by Jeffersonian democrats (and republicans), who shout 'democracy, transparency, accountability for all, at once', intoxicated as they are, as Edmund Burke wrote, by 'the wild gas of liberty'.

Burke was a lover of liberties, and aware how fragile their enjoyment could be. For him, circumstances prevail always when glittering intellectual constructs, developed a priori, are applied to particular situations. They may absorb the intellectual constructs, use them, and then reconstruct them in ways which their originators never dreamed of. It is the circumstances and situations which we therefore look for. We value the fragile liberties of the world too much to leave them in the tender care of flat-earthers, and their ilk. The 1998 Asian meltdown is the most recent of their monuments.

I would like to thank Richard Stagg, Pradeep Jethi and Martin Drewe for their friendship and professional support in the preparation of this book. *The Frontiers of Fortune* is dedicated to the memory of Galileo, who declared notoriously that the world moved around the sun – to the horror of the *savants* of his age. It is also dedicated to my spouse, Heidi, and to our children, Henry, Christina, Nicholas and Big Alex.

Fontainebleau, Winter 1998

Chapter 1

THE GREAT TRANSFORMATION OF 1989–1992

A s the Cold War drifts into history, the contours of the new international system mock the long crusade made this 'short twentieth century'[1] for greater equality among nations and peoples. Nationalists challenged the inequality between states, and socialists attacked the inequality among people. Both onslaughts were levelled against world capitalism, initially championed by the British Empire and then resurrected after 1945 under the aegis of the United States: nationalists sought self-determination through statehood, and socialists aspired to create a just society without capitalism. Their fusion under Lenin, Stalin, Hitler or Mao created the greatest tyrannies in the annals of human history. In the 1990s the US stands as a lone great power in a world of unprecedented inequalities. We look first at the early decades of the twentieth century, then at the geopolitics and global economy of the second half of the century, and end with an analysis of the distribution of power capabilities in the 1990s.

The first half of the century

Throughout the twentieth century, a driving force of world politics has been nationalism; capitalism has had to accommodate. In the nineteenth century the revolutionary force which made thrones tremble, established a world market, forced nations to renounce their 'narrow-mindedness', and absorbed all human relations within its reach was capitalism. Marx and Engels wrote in admiration of the bourgeoisie as capitalism's agent in the Communist Manifesto of 1848:

> The bourgeoisie cannot exist without constantly revolutionizing the instruments of production … Constant revolutionising of production, uninterrupted disturbance of all social conditions, everlasting uncertainty and

agitation distinguish the bourgeois epoch from all earlier ones. All fixed, fast-frozen relations with their train of ancient and venerable prejudices and opinions are swept away, all new-formed ones become antiquated before they can ossify. All that is solid melts into air, all that is holy is profaned ... The need of the constantly expanding market for its products chases the bourgeoisie over the whole surface of the globe. It must nestle everywhere, settle everywhere, establish connexions everywhere.[2]

Capitalism's chosen institutions were free trade, representative government and the gold standard. Free trade was predicated on the doctrine of comparative advantage, which held that the location of production depended on different endowments in natural resources, and different proportions in the factors of production – labour and capital. Thus Portugal enjoyed a warm climate, a suitable soil and little capital per worker, so was ideally suited to specialize in the production of wine. England had a rainy climate, abundant labour and also abundant capital, and was therefore suited to the production of textiles. International trade benefited all countries because it enabled them to escape the limits of production from their own resources and mixtures of production factors. It also created the need for a cosmopolitan culture where peoples depended on one another for their prosperity.

Enlightened policy was to facilitate such a development. This was best achieved through representative government, where the propertied classes with a stake in good governance would be widened beyond the narrow confines of kings, courts and aristocracy. America had set the example of widening the franchise to all citizens within a constitution that ensured life, liberty and property. But it was the excesses of the French Revolution which haunted the Europe of the nineteenth century, and cautioned its various governments to limit citizenship to men of property. They favoured the extension of parliamentary rights to make laws and to limit the powers of executives to intervene in the freedom to innovate, produce and exchange. They required courts to enforce contracts and to ensure the sanctity of property rights. And their businesses required sound money, without which calculations about future business risks could not be made.

The gold standard was an international arrangement whereby enlightened governments agreed to facilitate international exchange by joint regulation of gold at a fixed price. All major powers had joined the gold standard by the 1880s. Countries running trade deficits exported gold in payment and thereby reduced money in circulation. This contracted domestic consumption, and prompted a rise in exports, returning the country to equilibrium in its external transactions. The adjustment was made possible by a temporary rise in unemployment as workers and companies supplying home markets were laid off or went out of business. Countries running trade surpluses would import gold and expand money in

States acted to preserve the balance because they were self-seekers.

circulation, thereby promoting higher consumption and imports. The key condition for countries to respect the disciplines of such an international regime was that their labour markets be equally flexible, and that unwanted production be cleared off the market by a rigorous application of bankruptcy law.

A fourth institution, inherited from earlier times, though, was the balance of power,[3] which free traders – such as Richard Cobden – abhorred as 'an incomprehensible nothing … barren syllables, which our ancestors put together for the purpose of puzzling themselves about words'.[4] Essentially, the phrase referred to the practice of European diplomacy whereby states tended to unite around opposition to the hegemony of anyone whose emergence would jeopardize the status quo. That could mean preserving the constituent elements of the system that might be threatened, or acting to preserve the system overall, i.e. the balance. States acted to preserve the balance because they were self-seekers, and knew that if they did not act to preserve their interests others would do so for them. In particular, the balance was kept by interactions among the great powers, differentiated from the rest not only in domestic structures or values but notably by the distribution of capabilities among them.

One by one, the institutions which preserved the general peace of the nineteenth century were undermined. Free trade was challenged by the rise of protectionism in the late 1870s, as producer groups mobilized to defend local production against the workings of international specialization. The idea of representative government threatened monarchical privileges on the Continent and the major powers' positions in their colonies. The development of divergent legal and financial practices with regard to bankruptcy and the extension of mass electorates ensured that the gold standard was more honoured in the breach: there was little political benefit for a government to preside over a recession while supply and demand adjusted through the markets. Company owners organized to reduce competition and trade unions mobilized workers to ensure greater security at work. They turned for protection to their governments first; international balance and trade came a poor second.

The European balance was upset, not for the last time, in Asia. Japan's defeat of Russia in 1904–5 was the first victory of a non-European state over a major European power, and the significance of the event was instantly appreciated by nationalists in the rest of Asia, in India and in Africa. Japan had meted out the same punishment to Chinese imperial arms a decade earlier – a defeat which led China's nationalists to overthrow the Manchu dynasty in 1911. Russia also sought to accelerate industrialization, but its efforts were cut short when the Tsar declared war in August 1914 on the side of France and Britain. In 1917 Russia's monarchy collapsed under the strain, and the Bolsheviks seized power. They proclaimed the Soviet Union in 1922 as a militant messenger of socialism to a world still under the rule of capitalism in its 'highest stage' of imperialism. The promise of a socialist world under Soviet leadership never seemed more probable than in the years following the defeat of Germany and Japan in 1945, and the entry of the communists to Beijing in 1949.

Germany's domestic organization and its place in Europe – the two central dimensions to the 'German problem' between 1870 and 1945[5] – were finally settled in 1949: the Federal Republic would pursue state unity through peaceful means and within the bounds of the Atlantic alliance. The Bundesbank was later set up to avoid the financial instability of the past. After the crash of 1873, following on speculation fuelled by the 5-billion-franc indemnity paid by France to Prussia for the war of 1870, Germans of all political persuasions never lost a powerful sense of anti-capitalism.[6] United Germany developed an organized capitalism, characterized by cartels and protection. In the 1920s war reparations, inflation and reconstruction kept the German financial system fragile. National Socialism derived much of its ferocity in the years 1933 to 1945 from the promise to deliver Germany and Europe from the tyranny of 'cosmopolitan' finance. European Jewry, along with gypsies, and other opponents of the National Socialists, were rounded up in the concentration camps and annihilated in the flames of the Holocaust.

Victory over Japan and Germany confirmed the United States as the world's leading power. The United Nations (UN) Charter encapsulated liberal ideals for a world based on the principles of self-determination, individual freedoms and access to world markets. US armed forces were deployed in Europe, the Asia Pacific, the Mediterranean and the Gulf. The US enjoyed a monopoly of nuclear weapons. It was the world's bread-basket. Industrial output had soared, making the United States the world's main producer of military and consumer goods. The dollar, convertible into gold at $35 an ounce, was the world's key currency. The US held two-thirds of the world gold stock. It was the prime world exporter, and the world's pivotal domestic market. US business interests were keen to open world markets to prevent a postwar recession. The US government believed the causes of the 1930s depression lay in trade protectionism, competitive economic policies and restricted access to raw materials.

None of the participants in the discussions on the postwar world economy, though, wanted to return to gold standard economics. Both world wars demonstrated that governments could organize national production and consumption on a grand scale, and the inter-war years of financial instability stood as a reminder of the dangers of attempts to return to the ways of the past. Not least, the Soviet Union continued to wage war on capitalism. The central idea of the Bretton Woods accords of 1944 was therefore to reconcile the best from the nineteenth century with the practice of the twentieth century: governments were to be held responsible for national economies in order to meet citizens' demands for higher living standards and high levels of employment. National economic expansion was a government responsibility, for which an extensive array of policy instruments was available. But governments were also beholden to co-operate among themselves to regulate jointly the markets of the world.

The second half of the century

What was the central conflict of the second half of the twentieth century? As the prime victor in the world war, the decision lay in US hands. Let us look first at world politics, and then examine the dynamics of world capitalism during the Cold War.

US foreign policy placed the Soviet Union's challenge centre stage: containment aimed to bottle up communism within the boundaries of the Soviet Union, and to contest its expansion abroad. There were two variants of containment:[7] one was expressed by Secretary of State Marshall in June 1947 as aiming to promote 'a working economy in the world so as to permit the emergence of political and social conditions in which free institutions can exist'. The other was defined in the years following the Chinese communists' entry to Beijing in October 1949, and the two major communist powers' apparent support in June 1950 for the invasion of the south by north Korean troops. President Truman announced military intervention in the Korean conflict, and in September 1951 the United States signed a peace and security treaty with Japan. The Korean war opened two decades of US foreign policy, predicated on global military containment. The US military positions in Japan, Korea, the Philippines, and then in Indochina, were supplemented by a network of alliances and military bases, complementary to the North Atlantic Treaty Organization (NATO), and strung around the periphery of the Soviet Union in Asia and the Middle East.

Geopolitics shaped the familiar structure of world politics and business during the Cold War; its main features were clearly drawn by the mid-1950s. The United States was a continental island, pre-eminent throughout Latin America and the Caribbean, with key positions in Germany, Japan and the Gulf. The US dominated the world seas and air traffic. US bilateral alliances with Germany and Japan formed the cornerstone of their domestic and foreign policies. Reconstruction of the port at Rotterdam tied Germany's industrial machine into world markets. Japan's raw materials needs were assured by US control of the Pacific sea-lanes. The US was firmly established in the Gulf, with its finger on the world's oil well. The Soviet Union, by contrast, was a continental power, with a contested position in Germany and central Europe and a rival communist party-state in Beijing. Its energy and raw material supplies lay within its frontiers. Soviet state socialism offered the world an alternative to the US formula of a 'working world economy'.

By the 1990s the world had matured from the unequal bipolarity of the mid-1950s to a dynamic multi-polarity, with the US at the centre. The heart of the great struggle between the US and its allies with the Soviet Union was over different ideas of political community and of economic organization. The Western allies stood on the belief of the necessary distinction between the sphere of public power and policy and the private domain of individual conscience and rights. Government could propose and implement, but the public would dispose through open elections, freedom of association, liberty to express opinions, recourse to the courts and constitutional guarantees of

> *The driving force of history was not nation, religion or technological progress, but class.*

property rights. Restraint on state powers and a wide arena for the pursuit of individual or collective goals meant enthroning markets as indispensable social institutions for the creation and distribution of wealth.

The communist party-states predicated their mission to free the world from capitalism on the primacy of class war. The driving force of history was not nation, religion or technological progress, but class. As the bourgeoisie established their hegemony over the working masses through their ownership of the means of production, communists expropriated and killed in order to exercise political hegemony in the name of the workers. The party-states tolerated no alternative to their rule, suspended the market and allocated resources by a plan. They thus erected a monopoly on political power, on economic resources, and on 'truth'. All economic decisions relating to production and distribution were centralized. Consumers had the limited freedom not to buy whatever was on offer, and to keep their opinions to themselves. Of all the brutal regimes spawned in the twentieth century, the communists bore no equal: 100 million people died at the hands of communist party-states between 1917 and 1991.[8]

This fundamental conflict over different concepts of political community was played out in the arena of international politics. Both sides invested heavily from the late 1950s onwards in the development of nuclear capabilities, which served as expensive instruments of psychological war and as incentives to restrict confrontations to conventional force. Britain, France and China acquired their own nuclear forces, in the face of opposition from Moscow and Washington. Both sides also sought to extend their coalitions in a race for allies in the post-colonial world. The Soviet Union established a position in Cuba, befriended India, entered the Middle East in alliance with Arab nationalism in the 1970s, and then expanded into Africa, Vietnam and Afghanistan. But the US established the alliance of convenience with China in 1971, and in 1991 destroyed Soviet military technology in the UN war against Iraq. In retrospect, victory in Iraq symbolized the massive Western technological lead over the Soviet Union, and its disparate coalition of poor-country allies.

The world economy in the Cold War

Over the years of the Cold War, the world economy came to be profoundly shaped by the initiatives of the US, the dynamics of capitalism and the struggle between the two powers, their allies and their ideologies. Let us examine this evolution in the form of ten major economic features of this global battle for supremacy.

1 Both the US and the Soviet Union fostered the demands for self-determination in the European empires. The trend had set in during the 1914–18 war, leading to the creation of the Irish Free State, the movement for India's independence and the break-up of the multinational empires of Austria-Hungary and Turkey. Marxist-Leninist ideology ensured the unity of the Russian empire until its collapse in the course of 1990–1. By then, the number of sovereign territories in the world had multiplied from the fifty-one which signed the UN Charter at San Francisco in 1945 to 185. US corporate interests were not hostile to newly independent states protecting their domestic markets, as they could simply hop over the tariffs and join the local oligopoly. But they were the target of the wave of expropriations which began with Soviet Russia's loud encouragement in the mid-1960s and reached its peak in the early 1970s, when the oil-producing countries extended ownership over their natural resources. National self-determination fragments the world market space.

2 US policies shifted the world economy on to oil as its primary fuel. Changes in US tax incentives encouraged the seven major Anglo, Dutch and US oil companies to increase their liftings from the oil-rich region of the Gulf and the Middle East. Cheap oil stoked world growth. The world became dependent on political conditions in the main supplier countries. This drew the two powers deeper into the affairs of the whole region, which became a war zone stretching from the Levant to Afghanistan. The worldwide rise in oil prices, initiated by Libya and Iran in 1970–1, lasted fifteen years. High oil prices encouraged Japan and Germany in their export drives and precipitated oil importers into debt. They also helped to disguise the severity of the economic crisis afflicting the Soviet Union. When oil prices fell in 1986, the Soviet Union lost $5 billion a year in export revenues between 1986 and 1989.[9] Falling oil revenues prompted Iran and Iraq to end their bloody nine-year conflict in 1989, but then stimulated Saddam Hussein to ask Kuwait to fund the debt which Iraq had incurred during the conflict. Kuwait's refusal sparked the Gulf war of 1990–1. Oil suppliers depend for their revenues on movements in world prices set by conditions of world supply and demand.

3 The conversion to oil extended the dollar's primacy, as the key commodity currency. This was confirmed by President Nixon's unilateral announcement in August 1971 that ended the dollar's convertibility into gold. Henceforth the US operated as world central banker and to its own benefit. The US economy financed its own growth by incurring $1 trillion in debt to the rest of the world by the mid-1990s. It ran federal budget and trade deficits on a permanent basis. The relative value of the dollar to other currencies was set as a function of US domestic requirements, and of the price of oil that OPEC could sustain on world markets. Abundant dollars on world markets fuelled the expansion of 'offshore' financial centres, which provided ready finance for multinational corporations and governments. US investment banks grew fat on a steady diet of US bonds, supplied by a US federal government eager for a growing slice of world savings. The world capital markets developed by leaps and bounds, breaking down the neat compartmentalization of the world into national economies. The dollar is emperor of world financial markets.

4 Both Africa and Latin America enjoyed positive growth rates in the 1950s and into the 1960s. In the 1970s buoyant primary goods prices sustained expansion, though at a lesser rate. African governments received a steady flow of aid, while Latin American governments paid for higher oil prices by borrowing on the offshore private dollar markets. But in October 1979 the US raised world interest rates to unprecedented levels. Latin America and Africa were precipitated into recession. Domestic expenditures were curtailed, as debts spiralled out of control. Exports were raised in order to pay interest on foreign loans. Net resources transferred by Africa and Latin America to the rest of the world amounted to 3–4 per cent of their GDP per annum in the 1980s. Foreign investors turned their attentions to the developed country markets and to East Asia. In the 1990s the pattern was reversed, as private capital returned to buy the assets that the cash-strapped governments of Africa and Latin America could no longer run. Establishing an autonomous national economy has proven a will-o'-the-wisp for most countries.

5 Japan's economy surged from 1 to 18 per cent of world GDP between 1960 and 1995. An 'iron triangle' of relations between politicians, bureaucrats and big business ensured pro-growth policies were pursued over decades. The nation's energy and resources were mobilized exclusively to win market share. Under the meticulous supervision of the Ministry of Finance, banks lent preferentially to carefully researched industrial sectors based on government perceptions of long-term international comparative advantage (industrial targeting). The system was fed by extraordinary levels of debt exposure by corporations. Capital controls kept Japan's high savings home, capital cheap and the yen undervalued. Japan's trade surpluses mounted so that by 1995 the country's foreign exchange reserves were over $200 billion. The rest of the surplus was recycled by Japanese financial institutions to purchase US Treasury bonds, by a surge in Japan's foreign direct investment, or by aid to China and Indonesia. Japan's economic nationalism provided the model for other East Asian states. Japan became the world's main creditor.

Japan's economy surged from 1 to 18 per cent of world GDP between 1960 and 1995.

6 East Asian countries rode on the coat-tails of the US and Japanese economies. The mid-1960s proved a crucial period. General Suharto seized control in Djakarta, and opened Indonesia to Western business; Singapore split from Malaysia; and further north, Taiwan and the Republic of Korea launched ambitious development strategies under authoritarian governments. Unlike Western Europe, where political systems accommodated left parties and programmes, East Asian governments remained aggressively pro-business and anti-communist. Accumulation proceeded apace, as they followed Japan up the value added chain of production and exports, along the model of the 'flying geese development paradigm' (see Box). Investors from Taiwan, Singapore, Hong Kong shifted their labour-intensive production to less developed countries in the region.

The Asian-Pacific regional pattern of industrialization came to resemble the 'flying geese development paradigm', originally devised by the Japanese economist K. Akamatsu in an article published in 1932 in Japanese, and entitled 'The Synthetic Principles of the Economic Development of our Country'.[10] In this process, leader countries would phase out production in areas of activity where they were losing competitiveness, and replace local production with imports from 'followers', which succeeded in building up a competitive industry in that product. Once a product matured on the market, the comparative advantage of producing it would pass to the follower country, while the leader launched into the production and sale of a new product.

East Asia's boom was further stimulated by the dollar's revaluation against the yen in the ten years following the September 1985 meeting of the finance ministers from the five leading industrial nations in the Plaza Hotel, New York. With their currencies tied to a low dollar, and foreign investment pouring in from Japan, East Asian exports grew by 20 per cent per annum. But currency co-operation broke down when in 1993 China devalued the yuan to join the export boom. Then, in 1995, the US Federal Reserve had the dollar rise against the yen to help the hard-pressed Mexican economy. East Asian exports slowed as their currencies rose against the yen. Matters were made worse by the relative closure of Japanese markets, and stagnant growth there. Savings flooded out of Japan, and a low-growth EU, in search of higher returns in the small East Asian economies. Boom abruptly turned to bust, when investors took fright at their current account deficits. Their currencies and living standards plummeted, while the region's massive production potential, built up in previous decades, was thrust on to US or EU markets in a desperate bid to export or die. Japan is the sick man of the Asian, and of the world, economy.

7 Soviet economics could not sustain competition with world capitalism. The heart of the Bolshevik experiment was to abolish the market. In its place, the state mobilized resources at terrible human cost. This served well enough to produce tons of steel and tractor parks full of tanks. Victory in 1945, and Soviet Russia's later delivery of arms to allies, ensured communism a seat at the world's top table. But the system failed to deliver goods in the shops and it stifled innovation. The 'plan', with its 200,000 lead prices and 24 million prices overall,[11] was a farce. It also proved resistant to Secretary General Gorbachev's efforts at reform in the late 1980s. Inflation rates soared. The loosening of state control over Soviet society awoke nationalist demands for independence across the Soviet Union. On 25 December 1991 Gorbachev resigned. Soviet communism and its dream of a socialist world were dead. For all its exertions, Russia's income per capita was one third of the US figure, much as in 1850. By the end of the 1990s Russia's economy was smaller than Indonesia's. Dependent still on the world oil price, Russia heads for social implosion as world oil demand falls away in the wake of the East Asian crisis.

8 Collapse of the Soviet Union deprived the Chinese communist leadership of their fraternal rival, and accentuated their drive to create a 'socialist market economy' under one-party rule. China's main relationship was now with the United States, with which diplomatic relations were re-established in 1978. As a result of economic reforms initiated in that year, China's economy became one of the most dynamic in the world. During the 1980s, GNP grew at an average rate of 9.2 per cent, average per capita income doubled, investment and

savings were maintained at high levels, and the incidence of rural poverty was reduced. By 1995 China's economy was about four times bigger than in 1978; if China achieved its growth targets, by 2002 the economy would be eight times bigger than it was in 1978. At this point, China would have matched the performance of Japan, Taiwan and South Korea during their fastest quarter-centuries of economic growth. China has declared its intent to inherit the mantle of the world's major power in the second half of the twenty-first century.

9 The collapse of the Soviet economy also accelerated India's move away from Soviet-style plans and import substitution introduced after independence in 1947.[12] Forty years on, India was the thirteenth largest economy in the world, roughly equivalent in real terms to the Netherlands, and it had become agricul-turally self-sufficient. But a plodding 'Hindu rate of growth' at 3.5 per cent was far too low to meet its huge popula-tion's needs, and its world market share was 0.5 per cent, down from 2.5 per cent in 1938. Government finances were in chronic deficit, and its reserves had dropped to just enough to pay for two weeks' imports. In 1991 India decided to accelerate integration into the global economy.[13] A $7 billion bail-out organized under US auspices was followed by a stabilization-cum-liberalization package. Growth rates doubled, and exports expanded at 25 per cent, as the direction of trade shifted from the Soviet bloc to Asia. Foreign trade rose to 10 per cent of GDP, and the composition altered visibly to higher value added activities. India has no option but to meet China's challenge.

China has declared its intent to inherit the mantle of the world's major power in the second half of the twenty-first century.

10 Finally, the long years of the Cold War had enabled the states of Western Europe to create an interdependent economy, equal in size to the United States. The habit of elaborating common policies had been developed over the decades within a dense fabric of institutions, with overlapping tasks and diverse memberships. The salient organizations were NATO, which bound the US and Canada into European security, and the European Union, which provided a broader setting to mediate the central relationship between France and Germany. EU growth rates, at 5 per cent in the 1960s, slipped to 3 per cent in the 1970s and to 1 per cent in the early 1980s, when a common programme was launched to open up the EU's 'internal market'. Growth rates picked up in the late 1980s, but ground to a halt in the early 1990s under the dual impact of the high cost attached to Germany's move to unity, and the conditions agreed to achieve monetary union by 1999–2002. The EU is thus positioned as the US's prime partner, and eventual rival, in the early decades of the twenty-first century.

Still a US-dominated world

In the dying years of the Cold War, Americans became worried that the country was in decline.[14] Many considered that the country was over-extended, and in retreat as a world power. *Business Week*, reflecting the general gloom in the US following the overthrow of the Shah of Iran,[15] declared that 'the colossus that emerged after World War II' was 'clearly facing a crisis of the decay of power'. The US had suffered defeat in Vietnam, an oil embargo and rising domestic inflation. Monetary rigour and a hard line on Moscow were the tonic provided. Once the euphoria of the Reagan years began to wear thin, the recommendations shifted to redefining US security policy in the light of changes in the global economy.[16] The US fiscal deficit was said to be due to its overspending on the military budget,[17] a root cause of underinvestment at home, and of the slide from being the world's largest creditor to net debtor. The US share of world product and world exports, respectively at 33 and 17 per cent in 1950, had slipped to 25 and 11 per cent by 1989. The US share of world monetary reserves had fallen from 50 to 9 per cent. As the saying went at the time, the US was one among equals.

There could be no doubt that the US disposed of fewer resources relative to the rest of the world by the end of the Cold War than at its beginning. But in 1945 major centres of industrial production in Europe were devastated by war, and Russia was bled white. Japan had lost 30 per cent of its industrial capacity and 80 per cent of its shipping during the conflict. As the world economy recuperated in subsequent decades, the US position of postwar pre-eminence declined to stabilize by the mid-1970s. Twenty years later, in 1995, as Table 1.1 shows, the US share of world merchandise exports was still around 11 per cent, and its share of world GDP was stable at 25 per cent. Both Europe and Japan were major markets for US exports and companies, and in turn their producers were major competitors for US companies in American markets and around the world. The US, to use George Orwell's phrase about the pigs in *Animal Farm*, was more equal than others.

Table 1.1
Shares of traditional power resources

	US	Russia	Japan	China	India	Brazil	Germany	Britain	France
Population (m)	263	148	125	1,200	929	159	82	58	58
Territory ('000 sq km)	9,364	17,075	378	9,561	3,288	8,512	357	245	552
GDP p.c. (\$ 1995)	26,980	2,240	39,640	620	340	3,640	27,510	18,700	24,990
GDP 1995 (% world)	24.9	1.2	18.3	2.5	1.1	2.4	8.6	4.0	5.5
Manufactures (% world)	21.4	1.8	20.9	4.5	1.0	2.8	13.3	4.9	4.9
Merchandise exports (% world)	11.6	1.3	8.8	3.0	0.6	0.9	10.1	4.8	5.7
Hi tech exports (share of OECD)	26.3	–	21.1	–	–	–	16.2	10.2	8.7
FDI outward stock (% world 1996)	24.9	–	10.4	0.56	–	0.02	6.4	11.2	6.5
Military expenditures (\$ billion)	278	82	50	32	8	6.9	42	34	48

Source: *IBRD, IISS, WIR, OECD (Total FDI stock in 1996 equals 11% of world GDP)*.

US declinists put a negative spin on this achievement by arguing that leaders tend to over-reach their resources. The United States, they lamented, was going the way of Britain – a stock-in-trade target for assorted axe-grinders. As defined by Paul Kennedy in his best-selling book, *The Rise and Fall of the Great Powers*,[18] 'the Great Power is likely to spend much *more* on defense than it did two generations earlier, and yet still discover that the world is a less secure environment'. The comment was intended as description and prescription: a description of America's over-extension in pursuit of the policy of containment; and a prescription for the US to retrench from commitments abroad. In fact, it was much better directed at America's rival. If there was a clear candidate for the title of champion in 'imperial over-stretch', it was the Soviet Union, not the US. In the late 1980s Soviet Russia devoted 80 per cent of capital goods production to military use in a desperate effort to stay within reach of the overwhelming resources of the Western allies, and without any evident improvement in its sense of security.

As Table 1.1 indicates, the US in the mid-1990s was clearly the world's leading power as measured in terms of traditional power resources – population and territory, and five measures of economic prowess. There were five major states in terms of territory and population – the US, Russia, China, India and Brazil. But China's and India's per capita income, below that of Africa, recorded their low level of development and the long way that lay ahead before they would be able to effectively activate their resources as world powers. Russia's territory, shorn of large chunks of the Soviet Union, was still nearly twice the size of America's, but its population was impoverished, with a per capita income well below that of Brazil and a rapid widening of the wealth gap that was speeding Russia to Brazilian levels of inequality – the highest recorded in the world. In terms of military expenditures, the world was unipolar, with US outlays over three times Russia's and five times those of Japan. Both the US and Russia were reducing their land- and sea-based ballistic missile capabilities. But the US was continuing to enhance its capabilities in munitions, battlefield surveillance, missile defence and advanced detection devices. In space, the investments of the Reagan years placed the US in undisputed primacy, while the Russian budget went largely to cover costs of operations and maintenance.

The distribution of economic power resources in 1995 showed a rather more complex pattern. It involved two major powers, the United States and Japan, and the smaller European powers seeking to move to 'ever closer union' within the EU. Japan's emergence as the world's second economy was measured by a population less than half of America's, an economy equal to 73 per cent of US GDP, and a per capita income 50 per cent more than that of the US. Japan's economy was visibly driven by domestic demand, as evidenced by its share of world GDP and world manufacturing exports: its near 9 per cent share of world manufacturing exports compared with Germany's 10 per cent, but its GDP stood at nearly 19 per cent of the world's, relative to Germany's 8.6 per cent. Germany, as Europe's prime industrial power, was heavily dependent on foreign, particularly other European, markets. Japan also held the third largest stock of foreign direct investment, and played a major role in terms of technological resources.

Another feature of the distribution in economic power resources was the pecking order among developing countries, and the gap between them and the European powers. The clear leader was China, with an economy well over twice the size of India's and Russia's, and similar to that of Brazil. China's share in world trade was already on a par with that of France and Britain, despite its low per capita income, and its military expenditures were significant. China's promise was indicated in the overseas expansion of its corporations, in addition to being a favoured 1990s target for inward direct investment. But it was far from being a contender in technological resources, and would remain essentially an inward-oriented country, whose prime task was to haul its 1.2 billion people into the world economy over the coming decades. By contrast, Britain – the smallest of the European three – held major assets abroad and a sizeable proportion of technological resources.

The shares of measurable power resources clearly indicated that only the United States ranked above all others in all five dimensions of economic prowess. No other power approximates the US. Japan's exiguous territory, and lack of natural resources, make it highly vulnerable in the military dimension. The sum of European powers' resources place them in the front rank of potential challengers to the US, but the political process of 'pooling' their capabilities and then translating them into effective use on the world stage remains problematical. China is a distant challenger, with a long tail of problems to overcome before entering its undoubted claim to status as the world's leading power. Russia, for the foreseeable future, is out of the race, as are India and to a lesser extent Brazil.

In other ways, too, the US disposed of formidable intangible means of influencing the world's evolution in a way compatible with its preferences. Its cultural values had wide appeal around the world, and ready access to peoples. By the 1990s the English language was unchallenged as the language of business, the sciences, the arts and literature. American universities attracted students from all over the world, and the US remained the prime target for immigrants. The US capital market lay at the heart of world capital markets, and the products engineered there to manage risk were eagerly absorbed by practitioners. No other country had the like of Hollywood, or enjoyed America's domination over fantasies and imaginations. It took Walt Disney to convert Victor Hugo's hunchback of Notre Dame into cartoon.

By the 1990s the English language was unchallenged as the language of business, the sciences, the arts and literature.

The major institutions such as the UN, and its family of organizations, were imbued with the liberal vision which inspired the foundations of the US. Other states' policies, and their peoples' preferences, were now filtered through the language of the UN Charter, however alien or abstract that language was to local conditions. The US participated in key institutions, and could use its veto powers in case of need.

The US was also the focus of a network of multilateral and bilateral alliances around the world. In the Asia-Pacific, US diplomacy had woven a string of bilateral relations with the states of the region, and then in 1992 was present at the creation of the Asia Pacific Economic Community (APEC), a broad umbrella grouping aimed at shepherding the states of the region to more open markets and to common discussions on security matters. In Latin America the Organization of American States (OAS), created in 1948, served as a conduit for US military, economic and political policies throughout the region. The new approach of Washington to Latin America was expressed by President Bush in the Enterprise for Americas initiative of 1990, that led to the signing of the North America Free Trade Agreement (NAFTA) in 1992 between the US and its two dependent neighbours, Mexico and Canada. Above all, NATO served to aggregate European policies and forces during the Cold War, and remained the only effective security organization in Europe after its end. The unequal distribution of power resources in NATO ensured that the US benefited disproportionately as the hub of alliance relations.

Finally, the US and the leading economies dominated the world military system through the network of US-centred alliances. Their corporations produced the products for and fashioned the tastes of consumers. Their currencies played the central part on foreign exchange markets and their financial centres in London, Chicago or Tokyo paced the innovations that affected all. Not least, their universities and research laboratories – public or corporate – made the discoveries that drove forward the new technologies. They, and the US in particular, held structural power, 'the power', in Susan Strange's words, 'to shape and determine the structures of the global political economy within which other states, their political institutions, their economic enterprises and (not least) their scientists and other professional people have to operate'.[19]

Conclusion

As the dust lifted slowly from the wreckage of the Soviet Union's collapse, and the Cold War drifted into history, the contours of the international system appeared in sharp outline. The US stood without equal, in a world of unprecedented inequalities of power and wealth. A key question for the century's end ran: how could the poorer countries and the poor people of the world gain access to the rich markets, on terms that the citizens of the rich countries could accept? That is a question for us to explore in the next chapter, and in a world where capitalism now rules unchallenged.

Notes

1 Eric Hobsbawm, *Age of Extremes: The Short Twentieth Century*, London, Little Brown, 1994.

2 From the Penguin Books version, with an introduction by A. J. P. Taylor, reprinted 1975.

3 The four institutions of the nineteenth century are presented in a brilliant essay by Karl Polanyi, *The Great Transformation* (1st edition,1944), Boston, Beacon Press, 1957.

4 Richard Cobden, *Political Writings*, London, William Ridgeway, 1868. Vol. 1, p. 259.

5 David Calleo, *The German Problem Reconsidered: Germany and the World Order, 1870 to the Present*, Cambridge, Cambridge University Press, 1978.

6 Fritz Stern, *L'Or et le Fer: Bismarck et son Banquier Bleichröder*, Paris, Fayard, 1990.

7 John Lewis Gaddis, *Strategies of Containment: A Critical Appraisal of Post-War American National Security Policy*, New York, Oxford University Press,1982.

8 Stéphane Cortois et al., *Le Livre Noir du Communisme: Crimes, Terreur, Répression*, Paris, Robert Laffont, 1997.

9 Ed A. Hewett, *Open for Business: Russia's Return to the Global Economy*, The Brookings Institution, Washington DC, 1992, p. 13.

10 K. Akamatsu, 'A Historical Pattern of Economic Growth in Developing Countries', *The Developing Economies*, Vol. 1, No. 1, March–August 1962.

11 Nikolai Shmelev and Vladimir Popov, *The Turning Point: Revitalising the Soviet Economy*, Doubleday, New York, 1989, p. 81.

12 Fancine R. Frankel, *India's Political Economy, 1947–1977*, Princeton University Press, 1978, p. 105.

13 Vasantha Bharucha, 'Policy Liberalisation in India with Special Reference to Trade and Investment', in K. Fasbender, O. Mayer and D. Chatterjee (eds), *Indian-European Trade Relations: Prospects of the Liberalisation Process in India and Europe*, Verlag Weltarchiv GmbH, Hamburg, 1992, pp. 16–21.

14 See Joseph S. Nye, *Bound to Lead: The Changing Nature of American Power*, New York, Basic Books, 1991.

15 'The Decline of US Power', *Business Week*, 12 March 1979.

16 'Strategic Shift: US Redefines Its Views on Security to Put More Emphasis on Global Economic Factors', *Wall Street Journal*, 11 August 1988.

17 David P. Calleo, *Beyond American Hegemony*, New York, Basic Books, 1987.

18 Paul Kennedy, *The Rise and Fall of the Great Powers: Economic Change and Military Conflict from 1500 to 2000*, New York, Random House, 1987.

19 Susan Strange, *States and Markets*, London, Pinter, 1988.

Chapter 2

THE CLASH OF EXPECTATIONS

Capitalism's predominance in the 1990s left the world looking two ways: back to pre-1914, and forward to the twenty-first century. Pre-1914 seemed in many respects a golden age of civilization, cut short and wrenched from its path by war and revolution. Was the world heading forward to a renewal of the golden age, or towards the disasters which overcame it in the past? The question was answered by a flood of contradictory prognoses,

Pre-1914 seemed in many respects a golden age of civilization, cut short and wrenched from its path by war and revolution.

from the contrasting ideas of 'One World' idealism or of a world of competing great powers, to a 'clash between cultures' or of a borderless, cosmopolitan world (see Figure 2.1). These are presented, and then contrasted, with a view to making a schematic presentation of the existing tensions in the world political economy.

Figure 2.1
CONTEMPORARY VISIONS OF THE FUTURE AND THE PAST

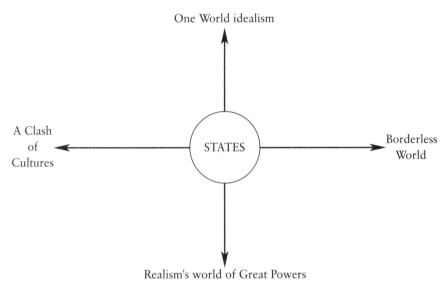

The pre-1914 analogy

The opening years of the 'long twenty-first century' in the 1990s witnessed a world economy in many respects more integrated than at any period of history. But celebrations of the victory of economic and political liberalism over all contestants was muted by memories of the breakdown of the nineteenth-century liberal world. There were enough parallels to draw from the years prior to 1914 for many to interpret present trends as a return to this earlier period of globalization. Trade witnessed a steady expansion, drawn along by the boom in primary-product exports, which represented 60 per cent of the total. Britain, Germany and France supplied funds for investment in primary products and raw materials, amounting to 55 per cent of the stock in 1914.[1] Industrial and infrastructure investments were financed through corporate equity and government bonds. Europe, India and China were the major source of migrant workers in the Americas, Africa, and South-East Asia.[2]

This economic interdependence was underpinned by intercontinental transport and communications, as well as by a series of regimes to facilitate the flow of cross-border transactions. The central financial markets of London, Paris and Berlin competed for business, but jointly held the golden threads of trust and mutual interest which bound the world market together. The flow of industrial investment fostered managerial exchanges, and cross-border trade union confederations. As Norman Angell wrote in his best-selling book, *The Great Illusion*, published in 1910, 'international finance is now so interdependent and tied to trade and industry that military and political power can in reality do nothing'. Henry Brailsford, the historian, hoped that the rising socialist parties would educate the public about the value of fostering an integrated Europe. 'My own belief,' he wrote in the summer of 1914, 'was that there will be no more wars among the six Great Powers.'[3]

One World idealism

It could have been no surprise that the varied streams of idealist think-ing should have converged around 1990 on a vision of a One World polity. Here was the chance to create a global society, whose progress had been interrupted in 1914. In 1917, and again in 1941, the US had gone to war in the cause of a liberal world order. The onset of the Cold War in 1946 undermined support in Washington to build a One World economy around the Bretton Woods institutions. Instead, the alliance was formed among the Western democracies, and the principles of an open world economy were applied in a more restricted sphere. Its premise was the promotion within the Western alliance of flexible domestic economies, open to mutual trade and investment, and co-operatively governed through international institutions.[4]

One World idealism had its roots in the idea of history as process and purpose. The German philosopher, Immanuel Kant, had envisaged the world as heading towards a perpetual peace, whose two pillars were republican government and international organization. The steady expansion of the rule of law within and between states would end the condition of war between them. Then, Georg Hegel conceived of mankind as progressing through various stages of social organization, to a culminating point when a rational form of state and society became victorious. History, he declared, ended in 1806, when Napoleon's defeat of the Prussian monarchy at the battle of Jena pro-claimed the victory of the ideals of the French Revolution and the imminent universal extension of the state incorporating the principles of liberty and equality. Karl Marx, half a century later, also conceived of history as purpose, proceeding through an interplay of material forces, and ending in the nirvana of a communist paradise.

It was the victory of liberal democratic ideals over Marx's commu-nist nirvana that prompted Francis Fukuyama, of the US State Depart-ment, in 1989 to celebrate a new 'end of history'. President Mitterrand, too, was staging the bicentenary of the French Revolution in Paris, and here was an opportunity to laud the spread in conscious-ness of the truths embodied in the American and French Revolutions.[5] One after another, Fukuyama argued, the major twentieth-century challenges to Western liberal ideals of individual freedoms, free markets and the self-determination of peoples had succumbed to defeat or had failed to deliver their promise. Fascism's creation of a strong state to forge an exclusive people demonstrably yielded disaster. Communist states had preserved inequality and failed to produce the cornucopia of Western capitalism. Neither religion nor nationalism was incompatible with liberalism, as a private sphere for religion was permitted in liberal societies, and nationalist demands for self-determination could be explained in terms of peoples who were forced to live in unrepresentative political systems.

Like Kant, Fukuyama looked forward to a peaceful and prosperous future. It would, he considered, take many years before Russia and China joined the developed nations of the West as liberal societies. War was obsolete between democracies which had abjured power politics for the dull round of technical discussions about standards, taxation and trade. Prosperity would spread consciousness of Western ideals as the world was 'common marketized', and developing countries were weaned from the various forms of despotism which afflicted their societies. The democratic wave that swept the world from 1974 to the 1990s, starting in Portugal, Greece and Spain, then spreading to Latin America, Eastern Europe and Russia, would expand into Asia. International organization would help to settle differences between the representatives of an ever wider sphere of enlightened peoples. Large-scale conflicts were passing from the scene, and future centuries stretched out ahead over an endless vista of post-historical boredom.

One World idealism's foundation was thus consciousness of liberal ideas and of representative institutions within the states, that created the presumption of favoured co-operation and commerce among them, and the preference for settling disputes through arbitration or through negotiation. In the wider scope of things, Kant's vision of a perpetual peace would be attained through a UN of global governance, agreement on collective and individual rights and duties, the elaboration of common rules and regulations to govern trade, investment or the environment, and the guarantee of equal access for all to world markets. Only with such a programme could the global village be secured for future generations.

Realism's world of powers

If One Worlders greeted the fall of communism with hopeful anticipation, realists feared disintegration of the Cold War structure which had contained war within limits since 1945. Without such constraints, the natural tendency of states to expand their dominion would resume, once the fears of nuclear war were ended, and the appetite for gain was whetted. Economic interdependence in 1914 had weighed less in the scales than Germany's bid for hegemony in Europe. Nor had Germany in the inter-war years been held down by arbitration procedures of the League of Nations or by the 'court of international public opinion'. The 'international community', beloved of One Worlders, had failed to keep the peace. After 1945 the US alliances had contained communism by a judicious blend of coercion, competition and conscription. Both world powers avoided war between them for fear of the nuclear consequences, and managed with more or less success to restrain war between their respective clients.[6]

Now those constraints were lifted, the many conflicts bottled up within the carapace of the Cold War would erupt anew. States were cold monsters, ready to adapt an argument to fit the circumstances, even to the extent of mouthing the platitudes of liberal utopians.[7] The words of their representatives were only one aspect of their actions, and it was these that realists had to attend to. This was the central insight recorded in the famous Melian dialogue, set down by Thucydides, the Greek historian of the Peloponnesian wars, where the Athenians declare, from a position of strength: 'The standard of justice depends on the equality of power to compel and that in fact the strong take what they can and the weak suffer what they must.' Morality proceeded from power, as Machiavelli taught. 'He who neglects what is done for what ought to be done sooner effects his ruin than his preservation.' Power struggles about different formulations of morality were a constant of international politics.

In its purest form, realism holds a deeply pessimistic view of human beings, as fundamentally flawed, incapable of self-restraint and in need of a strong authority to cage their inner passions and drives. As Hobbes argued, it required a Leviathan to tame greed and to instil fear into people. Without authority, people lived in a state of nature where life is 'nasty, brutish and short'. Once consent has been won by the Leviathan's use of force within its frontiers, an international state of nature is created, as no supreme authority exists to end the anarchy of relations between Leviathans. Indeed, states, as Leviathans, duplicate externally the greed and fears of their citizens within. All live in a system of self-help which keeps them divided and forever competing. They unite temporarily only if any one of them threatens to acquire such wealth and power as to impose its own morality on all. Peace is thus a truce which is kept by the balance of power, and not by covenants or international institutions.

The future would therefore not be different from the past, as the One Worlders preached, but similar in that the conditions for war had not been removed.

- First, there was no historical evidence to suggest that economic interdependence would reduce the vulnerability of states to dependence on supplies for vital materials from others. Indeed, interdependence created greater competition among states to ensure their own survival. If the latter was deemed to be endangered, prosperity would be sacrificed and the international economy with it.
- Second, neither was there evidence to suggest that democracies did not go to war with one another. It was the circumstances of the Cold War which kept the peace; without that peace, economic nationalisms would revive, aggravated by the differences between nuclear and non-nuclear powers.
- Third, war between great powers was not obsolete, only deadly. In a future world of multi-polarity and shifting coalitions between great powers with different capabilities, the possibility of nuclear proliferation or of nuclear miscalculation was higher, not lower than during the Cold War.

● Fourth, the rivalries among the multiplying states of the developing world over territory, prestige, religion or economics would be sharpened as the competition among the multiple poles of the emerging world structure took shape. Government collapses, and the claims of local peoples for self-determination, would bring in external powers to conscript the rival domestic chieftains as clients

In short, if, during the Cold War, war had been improbable, and peace had been impossible, in the memorable formula of the French political philosopher, Raymond Aron, in the post-Cold War peace was impossible and war was more probable. The conclusion for the United States was to 'maintain robust military forces to help keep the peace among the great powers'. For China, it was to accelerate economic growth and develop the muscle of a great power. For Europe, it was to end its state of nature and create a federation. That challenged the very security which the sovereign states of Europe valued so highly.

A clash of cultures

Cultures and civilizations, not the stage of economic development or the type of political system, are the relevant categories for grouping countries in the post-Cold War period.[8] The preceding five hundred years had been dominated by Europe and America, and it was their cultural preferences and political visions that had been transferred to the rest of the world. Western 'civil wars' between monarchs, states and then between the ideologies of capitalism and communism in the twentieth century were primarily about Western quarrels. But with 1990, world politics moved away from its Western phase, 'and its centrepiece becomes the interaction between the Western and non-Western civilizations and among non-Western civilizations ... the fundamental source of conflict in this new world will not be primarily ideological or primarily economic. The great divisions among humankind and the dominating source of conflict will be cultural'. This was the world which had to be incorporated into Western imaginations.

Civilization is defined as the 'highest cultural grouping of people and the broadest level of cultural identity people have short of that which distinguishes humans from other species'.[9] Civilizations imply basic differences among people in language, culture, tradition and religion, and in the past they have generated the most prolonged and violent conflicts. As the world becomes a smaller place, frictions between peoples from different civilizations will rise. Economic and social modernization separates people from their long-standing identities,

Cultural identification cannot be discarded like ideologies, or rise and fall like economic fortunes.

weakens the state as a source of identity and casts peoples back to their religious and cultural roots. Resistance to 'common marketization' takes the form of an assertion of an 'Asian', 'Hindu', 'Muslim' or 'Russian' identity. Cultural identification cannot be discarded like ideologies, or rise and fall like economic fortunes. But the trend to economic regionalism around the world will reinforce consciousness of belonging to a civilization.

If the new flashpoints for bloodshed are no longer drawn along Cold War lines, it is in 'Eurasia' that the great historic fault-lines between civilizations are once more aflame. European identity is drawn along the fifteenth-century boundaries separating Western Christianity from Orthodox Christianity and Islam. Conflict between the Western and Islamic civilizations has been going on for 1,300 years, and could become more virulent as the humiliation at the Western presence in the Gulf becomes unbearable, and Islamic movements benefit from demands for democratization. Arab Islam also confronts the spread of Christianity along the old Arab slave routes in Africa, from the Sudan to Nigeria. Turkic Islam confronts the Orthodox peoples in the Balkans, the Caucasus and Central Asia. In India, the destruction of the Ayodhya mosque in December 1992 signals the strains between Hindu and Muslim as India drifts away from its secular foundations. In East Asia, China has outstanding territorial disputes with all its neighbours, and relations between the US and Japan are tense.

In part, conflicts will take the form of kith rallying to kin. This pattern was most evident in the Gulf war of 1991, in ex-Yugoslavia, and in Azerbaijan where Muslims, Russians, Germans and Austrians sided with their own kin and co-religionaries. But the main clash is between the Western powers, disguised as 'the international community', and the rest. In the eyes of the rest, the West in effect is using international institutions, military power and economic resources to run the world in ways that will maintain Western predominance. Western efforts to propagate such ideas create reactions, which take three forms: costly isolation in the manner of North Korea or Burma; joining the West and adopting its ways; or modernizing, but not Westernizing. East Asia, Kishore Mahbubani has written, 'wants to succeed in its own right, without trying to become a member of a European Club'.[10] It does not want to be at the receiving end of 'human rights imperialism'.

Countries, such as Turkey and Russia, which are torn between their Islamic or Orthodox civilizations and their aspirations to join the West, are candidates in the future for dismemberment. Overall, Latin America and Eastern European countries may join the West without too many difficulties, but this will prove much more divisive for Orthodox countries, and even more so for Muslim, Confucian and Buddhist societies. For the West, the main focus of conflict will be over the mutual support offered by some Muslim and Confucian states to one another. In the short term, this means the promotion of unity within Western civilization, and in the longer term a unified West will have to come to terms with non-Western modern civilizations whose power will come to approximate its own. Civilization will not be universal, but the world will be composed of different civilizations.

A borderless world

Markets have broken free of states, and of politics, and now girdle the globe. Local tastes are becoming homogeneous, to the benefit of firms that produce standardized products.[11] A prime cause of this shift is technological change, which has been accelerating at an ever more rapid pace.[12] This has increased the cost of capital for innovations, and lowered the input of labour, raising the stakes for corporations and governments in the race to keep up with the competition. Abundant supply of credit has been provided through a mutual conspiracy between governments and corporations to allow the development of a private world capital market, beyond the regulation of any one state or even of a collection of states. The result is that the realm of politics now includes all players in the world market for goods and influence.

Power over outcomes is exercised by impersonal markets, and by those who deal in markets. Authority in society and over economic transactions is legitimately exercised by a multiplicity of agents, which operate alongside and often in disregard of states.

For a protagonist of the German right such as Carl Schmitt, such a trivialization of political authority is all that can be expected from liberalism. Liberalism segments political authority, allows competing power centres to emerge, and is too spineless to crush them when they challenge the state. Armed with such views, Schmitt embraced Hitler with enthusiasm, and wrote wildly anti-Semitic articles blaming Jews from Spinoza to Marx for the intellectual paralysis of the state.[13] David Ricardo, an Englishman who abandoned his Jewish faith and was one of Marx's favoured economists, elaborated the theory of comparative advantage, which suggests that the world's populations escape the confines of local resources, specialize in the production of goods for which they are specifically best suited, and jointly create an efficient world economy. A 'system of perfectly free commerce ... diffuses general benefit, and binds together by one common tie of interest and intercourse, the universal society of nations throughout the civilised world'.[14]

Fifty years after the end of the Second World War, such a system has been recreated, though with some notable differences. For Ricardo, the factors of production – land, labour and capital – would remain national, and global specialization would proceed through trade. Men of property would be satisfied, he declared, 'with a low rate of profits in their own country, rather than seek a more advantageous employment of their wealth in foreign nations'. Corporate behaviour has not borne him out. Corporations have expanded abroad, and have grown to be parallel authorities alongside governments 'in matters of economic management affecting the location of industry and investment, the direction of technological innovation, the management of labour relations' and the extraction of value from governments and shareholders.[15] In other words, they – alongside the mafias, insurers, accountants, 'econocrats' of the OECD or IMF – structure the outcomes that affect the lives of billions.

The forces driving towards a boundary-less world have made old nation states obsolete, and old civilizational fault-lines irrelevant. They have made capital immediately transferable, enabled managers to know in real time about their markets, products and organizational process, and altered what customers can know about alternative life-styles, about the products and services available to them, and about the relative value attached to such offerings. All around the world, consumer tastes are converging on a global norm, 'Californization'. 'Global brands of blue jeans, colas, and stylish athletic shoes are as much on the mind of the taxi driver in Shanghai as they are in the kitchen or the closet of the schoolteacher in Stockholm or São Paolo.'[16] And as income levels have edged upwards, these patterns of consumption have begun to eat into traditional culture. The process has been accelerated by the development of multi-media, making children more like one another than like their elders.

Ricardo's focus on trade as facilitating a universal society among the nations paints a generous vision of brotherhood among all people. It does not assume that all countries are equally endowed, but it does pre-scribe trade between rich and poor as mutually beneficial. In its modern form, this international society of peoples is filled out with a population of traders, scientists, consumers or sports *aficionados* whose common interests transcend boundaries. It welcomes the reduced powers that governments may have over their peoples, and seeks to liberate those who are still prevented from joining the multitude. It recommends market opening as a general prescription for policy, and places its hopes in the multilateral institutions. While recognizing that states are self-cen-tred, as the realists maintain, its chosen method is to appeal to the inter-est of states for reciprocity. A deal between two states for mutual access is extended through 'most favoured nation treatment' to all countries.

A critique

Each of these four visions adopts the same procedure of starting with an assertion, which serves as a statement of faith, and then proceeds to draw out the implications. Each of the visions may be questioned on its own terms, and the implications drawn from them challenged.

1 Fukuyama's vision of a Kantian perpetual peace assumes that it was consciousness of liberal ideals that emerged triumphant from the major conflicts of the twentieth century. This is a bold assumption to make.

Other ideals of very different complexion have survived, such as democracy and nationalism, the fascist ideals of the supremacy of political will in the ordering of human affairs, or the institutional innovations in economic policy from the 1930s introduced in Japan, Germany, Italy or France, and predicated on the idea of creating an exclusively national economy. Democracy and nationalism have never been easy bedfellows of liberal ideas, as nationalism often recruits its own rendering of religion in its service, while democracy notoriously threatens to override minorities in the name of a majority. The imbalances in the world economy bear testimony to the incompatible policies pursued by states in their permanent attempt to make relative or absolute gains over competitors.

Liberalism's failings in Weimar thus laid the ground for Auschwitz, as its triumph surely would for future disasters.

Fukuyama assumes that the triumph of liberal democracy brings Kant's perpetual peace closer. It is equally possible to maintain that liberalism's optimism about human beings and its suspicion of concentrated power are not a sound basis for the world's future. Liberalism liberated people from state religion, and allowed them the choice of pursuing their private religions, on condition that they inflicted no harm on others. The result was a multiplicity of faiths, and no means of discerning the value of one from another. This fostered the spread of secularism, with its attendant sense of loss and alienation. At the root of this sense of alienation is nihilism or the belief in nothing, that in turn opened the doors of human hearts to the tyrannies of the twentieth century, and notably to the preaching of Hitler. Liberalism's failings in Weimar thus laid the ground for Auschwitz, as its triumph surely would for future disasters. This is one of the central tenets of neo-conservatives in the US Republican Party.

Even if such a position is rejected, liberal internationalism holds serious weaknesses as a prescription for world order. It seeks to foster the spread of individual and collective rights, though the two are not necessarily compatible. A collective right to self-determination in a territory may be at the expense of the rights of a minority or of individuals. It favours open world markets and human rights for all, and thereby attracts opprobrium as an ideology promoting Western interests and values. It allows for the right of a state to self-defence, but also accepts the need for collective security. Liberal internationalism therefore has no means of judging which right to support when two or more principles come into conflict. As a predisposition, it tends to underestimate the appeals of nationalism or of civilizational identity, and overestimates the appeal of Western values embedded in 'market democracy' to non-Western peoples. It proposes co-operation between the great powers, but they are rarely so disposed.

2 Huntington assumes that non-Western civilizations will tend to clash with Western civilization, in other words with liberal internationalism, in its disguise as the 'international community'. There is much historical evidence to support the argument. The Western and Eastern Churches broke apart in the eleventh century, just as the conflicts between the Western Church and Islam may be dated to the battles in northern Spain in the ninth and tenth centuries. Competition in the 1990s between the two Churches in the Ukraine, events in Bosnia, or the civil war in the Sudan between the Islamic regime and the African Christian minority serve as a reminder of how deeply rooted these conflicts remained. Similarly, the severity of the fighting in the long civil war in Lebanon, and the barbarities perpetrated in ex-Yugoslavia, showed that the previous decades – when consumerism had spread and both countries had been in part 'common marketized' – did not make older cultural fault-lines obsolete.

Huntington exaggerates the homogeneity of his civilizations. Civilization, culture and race are categories that transcend political boundaries and are used to agglomerate widely dispersed peoples into a community whose identity is supposed to prevail over other claims on loyalty. Count Joseph Arthur de Gobineau wrote his *Essai sur l'inégalité des races humaines*, in 1856, claiming that the White, Yellow and Black races were of unequal value, and that all high cultures in the world had been the creations of the 'Aryan' ruling caste, now sadly interbred and therefore decadent. In *Mein Kampf*, Hitler presented his Aryans as 'culture-creating', the Japanese and Chinese as 'culture-bearing', the Slavs and Blacks as inferior and the Jews as evil. And just as Hitler's categories were pan-racial, so his conquests were supranational. He ignored state boundaries, as Huntington's thesis tends to do, and the absolute claims that states make on their citizens when security and survival are at stake.

Huntington writes with the US melting pot in mind, from a country where the motto *e pluribus unum* allows for a celebration of membership of the nation, without denying cultural roots and community affiliations.[17] Huntington's message of the necessary coexistence of civilizations in a pluralist world is thus compatible with American liberalism, and with the experience of recent decades where other civilizations and cultures have won acceptance, alongside predominant Anglo-American values. But the fault-lines which he traces are drawn on the Euro-Asian continent, as if to say that the aggravation of cultural conflicts in Europe, the Muslim world, in India or in East Asia could flood back into the US. The US, as a nation of immigrants, cannot afford to disentangle from world affairs, because it is bound to the four corners of the earth by its own population. Nowhere is this more the case than in the US's entanglement in Europe – the heartland of Western civilization.

3 Realism remains predominant in international relations. Its tenet that states are self-regarding and concerned more with security than with economic interdependence underlines the fragility of the international economic order. The lack of trust between states sets some limit to their readiness to depend on world markets, and draws an invisible ring of defences around their producers. The name of the game beyond achieving security on their own or collectively is to ensure that their own producers win more market access or hidden privileges than their competitors. If security between states is as near assured as possible, greedy states will seek to escalate their relative gains to absolute gains by continuing to tilt the market-place in their favour. Liberal internationalists deplore the practice and suggest international negotiations for mutual tariff disarmament, while the cosmopolitan mentality trusts that market forces prevail over the dense web of vested interests knotted into the heart of most states in the world.

Realists tend to assume that domestic differences between states, and the international conflicts which derive from them, are part of the daily round of international affairs. This has led them sometimes to underestimate the salience of ideological differences between the norms informing the policies of states. A realist view of the Western powers' relations with the fascist dictatorships, with the communist party-states, or with the theocracy in Iran would tend to assume that they could be dealt with as states, governed by fears and appetites, and therefore amenable to the calculations of reason. But Hitler was governed by a pan-national racist ideology, beyond the bounds of traditional state-craft; the communist party-states sought to be fully fledged members of the world system of states, while continuing to export revolution to its other members; and Iran is implacably opposed to liberalism's scepticism with regard to religion. Norms matter in interstate relations.

Democracy, as the liberal internationalists argue, is a necessary but not sufficient condition to maintain the peace. Modern democracies date essentially from 1945, so the time-scale for making confident assertions that they do not go to war is too limited. Attempts to take the argument back to the nineteenth century are obviously flawed, since universal suffrage was limited, arguably, to the US and to New Zealand. And generalizations from the long peace among the Western democracies during the period of the Cold War understate the importance of the Western security structure in providing the context within which old fears and ambitions could be slowly transformed into a degree of trust among the Western states which may enable them to build a peace after the Cold War's end. Furthermore, the peoples who suffered because of the World War were satiated by its violence, so that even the Soviet leadership had an interest in explaining their investment in armaments to the Soviet people as ensuring peace.

4 The cosmopolitan mentality argues that markets have broken free of states. This is indeed a bold assertion. It is generally father to a preference for inter-governmental co-operation or for domestic measures to liberalize further. Champions of both more and less government paradoxically use the same line of argument, that trade, foreign investment, currency flows or personal exchanges have grown at many times the rate of national economies. As the sphere of private choice has expanded, so the effectiveness of the public sphere to regulate the behaviour of citizens has declined. Governments should therefore band together to be able to reassert their powers over their citizens, or they should never aspire to the control that they seek to exert in the first place. In effect, states manage huge budgets, run extensive educa-

tional establishments, regulate access to capital markets and are engaged in a host of activities on a daily basis. They are co-participants in a world market, which none has ever controlled.

The vision of a borderless world holds that there is no single authority, but a host of competing public and private powers. The world political economy runs as a system, interacting between its parts, and distributing values and rewards according to a hidden hand of its own. This hidden hand is none other than the consumer, and the shareholder. All that has to be done is for producers of goods and services to satisfy the needs of both. Anything like tariffs, or government regulations, that stand in the way of the system operating according to its own inherent logic, is a 'rigidity' that has to be removed. Indeed, the policy of 'the inter-national community' should be to see that the markets are opened and that governments take back-seats, as regulators of the process. As John Locke, the founding philosopher of liberalism, suggested, a society of gentlemen was to live free of constraints, as long as the pursuit of individual passions and interests did not infringe upon the freedoms of others.

> *As politics is a struggle of cosmic forces between good and evil, all measures are permitted.*

The evident fallacy here is that if the system is self-driven, according to some mysterious inner formula which no one knows, then the states cannot fulfil their allotted liberal task as regulators if they do not know what they are doing and if other authorities contest their actions. One response is to reassert the primacy of politics, of human choice, over a blind system. In religious terms, this may mean that there is a sacred duty on the part of the faithful to smash the 'system', and to have God's injunctions obeyed in this life. As politics is a struggle of cosmic forces between good and evil, all measures are permitted. Alternatively, belief in the obsolescence of states and civilizations suggests the reformulation of political boundaries, either by a delegation of legitimacy from existing states to smaller regions, which act as ports into the world economy, or through the creation of continental Leviathans – the way of the EU. Religion, provincialism and empire-building are the responses to cosmopolitanism.

Contrasts

Each of these views on the world both describes and prescribes. None of them is immune from the barbs of the others, and all overlap. So, rather than choose one over another, it may be more to the point to ask which are compatible, and which are incompatible.

Liberal internationalism is not readily compatible with the 'clash of civilizations' view. Its prescription for the world's travails is active measures to spread consciousness of liberal ideals and of representative government, in a 'common marketized' world society under the aegis of the United Nations institutions. This is the very crusade which inspires the backlash from non-Western civilizations, which see 'the international community' as none other than the West arrayed in the garb of idealism. In this simplified view, the West is aligned against a nascent alliance between the Chinese and Islamic worlds, and the divisions within the 'West' are understated while the cohesion of supranational civilizations is over-exaggerated. Indeed, the weaknesses inherent in liberal internationalism undermine its ability to provide any clear guide to policy in complex situations.

The One Worlders are much more at home with the cosmopolitan mentality. After all, equal access to markets for all is one of their cardinal tenets, and a society of mankind is what both aspire to. For both, the historical divisions of mankind may provide their spiritual home or their political association, but these are transcended by their belonging to a wider fraternity of peoples. Both tend to use the expression 'a borderless world' as a prescription for policies that allow people and goods to circulate with little hindrance. Stripped of their rhetoric, both accept that political communities, organized as states in the modern world, form the essential units of world society. Peoples are represented in the UN through their states, and trade is among the nations. Differences among the peoples have to be negotiated through permanent institutions and formal procedures available to all.

Similarly, the realist view is highly compatible with the 'clash of civilizations'. Both are concerned with differentiation and the conflicts that ensue. Realists differentiate between the rich and powerful, or the poor and weak, while the protagonists of civilizational or racial clashes postulate a world of unremitting warfare. Eventually, as the civilizations reach parity of capabilities, they may be able to live together on principles of mutual recognition. But this is a dream of compromise, which in effect is alien to both positions. The true realist sees no let-up in the permanent struggle for power and wealth between states and peoples. The religious or racial prophet sees the world as a theatre where good and evil, supremacy and slavery, are forever at stake. If realists and civilizational ideologues disagree over the units in conflict, or the purposes for which the struggle is fought, that only underlines the depth of their discord.

Realists, though, may make common cause with cosmopolitans, and some cosmopolitans may prefer them to liberal internationalists. The problem for cosmopolitans in the position of the One Worlders is that they are altogether too naïve: differing interests may not be amenable to negotiation. The issue may have to be settled by encouraging one side to comply with the preferences of the other. Encouragement in a realist world can come only from the more powerful offering inducements or punishments to the weaker, which the weaker are ready to acknowledge. The only state with such powers is the US. As long as the US considers that a world society of traders is in its interest, it will sustain open markets. But if the US considers that others are bending the world markets in their favour, or are making cumulative gains at the US's expense, then the US as a realist will end its opportunistic association with the cosmopolitan mentality.

Conclusion

The pairs of compatible and incompatible views are illustrated in Figure 2.2. One Worlders and cosmopolitans are wedded in mutual comprehension, and realists are wedded in conflict with the 'clash of civilizations'. One Worlders and the 'clash of civilizations' are incompatible, while realists and cosmopolitans are only circumstantial allies. The states may be pictured as located in the centre, reluctant to move in any direction, and fearful of adapting to any one of the choices they confront. In Figure 2.2, they face four options:

1 *'One bed, two dreams'*: They can move into the inhospitable terrain, such as the Middle East, where liberal internationalism and 'the

clash of civilizations' conflict. Partisans to the many conflicts in the region, from the Kurdish or Palestinian demands for national self-determination, to the Iranian theocracy's labelling of the US as 'the Great Satan', may cite any number of One World criteria in advancement of their cause, according to circumstances. The right to self-defence, for instance, can be invoked by Palestinians or Israelis, while Iran's leaders may condemn the US for intervening in its internal affairs. Non-intervention in domestic affairs is the lead principle of diplomacy for the states of East Asia, which borrow this Western principle metaphorically to flay Western powers.

Figure 2.2
CLASHES OR COMPATIBILITIES BETWEEN CONTEMPORARY VISIONS

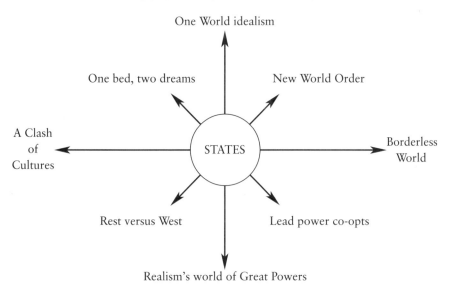

2 'The Rest versus the West': They can move into the inhospitable terrain where Realpolitik and the 'clash of civilizations' meet, as in the case of US trade relations with East Asia. All countries in the region depend to some degree for security and prosperity on the openness of US markets, the flow of US investments, the international role of the dollar or the US armed presence. This is particularly true of Japan. And it is one of the main structural factors which restrain trade tensions

between the US and Japan. Japan may be tempted to assert its distinctive interests in Iraq, but it nonetheless contributed towards the cost of Operation Desert Storm in February 1991.

3 *'The New World Order'*: The states can be drawn into global markets and be supportive of liberal international principles. But that assumes that their populations will be ready to accept both the benefits and the costs associated with the international division of labour, and that they will accept the extension of such rules and regulations. France, for instance, is a champion of such rules and regulations under the EU, but instinctively rejects globalization. Britain, on the other hand, embraces globalization but instinctively rejects the EU.

4 *'Lead Power Co-opts'*: The world trading system can fall prey to conflicts between the leading economic powers. This may lead in two directions. It may encourage the leading power to forge ahead in the development of 'soft power', or the policy instruments that enable it to co-opt challengers into a series of regimes whose parameters it has largely shaped.[18] The US, for instance, shaped the global financial system, and others adapted. Or the challengers may force a 'head-to-head' confrontation with the US,[19] to which the US will have to adapt. Either way, the dynamics and operations of world markets will be affected by the policies of the major powers.

If most states are reluctant to move from their present position, what are the prevailing forces at work in the post-Cold War world that will force them from their perch of non-choice – the preference of those who have not already been forced to choose by the forces unleashed in the world political economy because of the dramatic events of the past decade? Let us explore this in the next chapter.

Notes

1 See J. Dunning, 'Changes in the Level and Structure of International Production: The Last One Hundred Years', in M. Casson (ed), *The Growth of International Business*, London, Allen and Unwin, 1984.

2 A. G. Kenwood and A. G. Lougheed, *The Growth of the International Economy, 1820–1990*, London, Routledge, 1992.

3 Quoted in Michael Howard (ed), *War and the Liberal Conscience*, New Brunswick, NJ, Rutgers University Press, 1994.

4 Henry Nau, *The Myth of America's Decline, Leading the World Economy into the 1990s*, New York, Oxford University Press, 1992.

5 Francis Fukuyama, 'The End of History', *The National Interest*, Summer, 1989.

6 John J. Mearsheimer, 'Disorder Restored', in Graham Allison and Gregory F. Treverton (eds), *Rethinking America's Security: Beyond Cold War to New World Order*, New York, W. W. Norton and Company, 1992.

7 This was a central tenet of Marxist-Leninist practice, and is presented in its most erudite form in E. H. Carr, *The Twenty Years' Crisis, 1919-1939: An Introduction to the Study of International Relations*, London, Macmillan, 1939. Carr, the historian of the Bolshevik Revolution, became a standard textbook in US universities.

8 Samuel P. Huntington, 'The Clash of Civilizations', *Foreign Affairs*, Summer, 1993.

9 Huntington, op. cit.

10 Kishore Mahbubani, 'The Pacific Impulse', *Survival*, Vol. 37, No. 1, 1995.

11 Theodore Levitt, 'The Globalization of Markets', *Harvard Business Review*, May–June 1983.

12 Susan Strange, *The Retreat of the State: The Diffusion of Power in the World Economy*, Cambridge University Press, 1997.

13 Cited in Shadia B. Drury, *Leo Strauss and the American Right*, New York, St. Martin's Press, 1997.

14 David Ricardo, *Principles of Political Economy and Taxation*, Harmondsworth, Pelican, 1971.

15 Strange, op. cit. note 12, p. 65.

16 Kenichi Ohmae, *The End of the Nation State: The Rise of Regional Economies. How new engines of prosperity are reshaping global markets*, London, HarperCollins, 1995.

17 For a recent discussion of multiculturalism in the US, see Denis Lacorne, *La Crise de l'Identité Américaine, Du Melting-Pot au Multiculturalisme*, Paris, Fayard, 1997.

18 Joseph S. Nye, *Bound to Lead: The Changing Nature of American Power*, New York, Basic Books, 1987, p. 267, fn. 11.

19 Lester Thurow, *Head to Head: The Coming Economic Battle Among Japan, Europe, and America*, New York, William Morrow, 1992.

Chapter 3

THE MARKET UNBOUND[1]

The prevailing force at work in the 1990s is the global economy. The freeing of short-term capital flows and German unity in the pivotal year 1990 proclaimed the end of the government-centred design for the world economy that had been created at Bretton Woods. In this chapter we first recall the extraordinary successes recorded by this US-dominated system, and then chart the creation of a world labour market, the rapid shift of financial and corporate investment flows to the 'emerging markets', and the explosion of the integrated, round-the-clock global financial market. With such factors at work, there appears to be little reason to doubt that the post-Cold War economy is launched on the path to globalization. One World cosmopolitans see a radiant future for economic convergence as the poor countries grow wealthier, the world is 'common marketized' and 'market democracy' spreads.

Fifty years on

The freeing of short-term capital flows in Europe in 1990 delivered the final blow to the Bretton Woods accords of 1944, when the US and British negotiators in effect drew up the blueprint for the development of a world economy predicated on the central role of governments in supervising and regulating markets. Governments were responsible for providing high levels of employment and rising living standards for all. If one country began to run permanent surpluses or deficits on trade, the rate of exchange of its currency relative to others would be negotiated in the IMF and among governments. Optimally, the visionaries of the postwar world economy looked forward to enlightened governance of peoples by officials of international organizations rather than by the well-heeled denizens of world financial markets. Short-term capital movements were to be kept, figuratively, under lock and key, and currencies were to be fixed based on a gold price of $35 an ounce.

Another crucial ingredient of postwar policies for the world economy was import substitution, championed by Raul Prebisch,[2] one of the central figures in the UN's Economic Commission for Latin America and the Caribbean. The intellectual roots of import substitution could be traced to the 1850s, when the German economist Friedrich List and the American Henry C. Carey called for restrictions on trade in order to promote local industries.[3] Such ideas were applied in part to agriculture, textiles and steel in the 1880s, but international trade was driven by demand for raw materials and between 1900 and 1913 export volumes rose by 4.3 per cent per annum for thirty-two countries representing four-fifths of world output, population and exports.[4] These ideas came into their own in the particular conditions of the 1930s. States should promote industrialization and reduce dependence on volatile raw material markets by protecting national markets, channelling credit and planning social development.

This postwar government-centred design for the world economy, inspired by the ideals of liberal internationalism but implemented within the bounds of the Western containment policy, proved an unprecedented success. Fifty years on, the rising tide of wealth had lifted most boats. The highest period of growth for all countries with a degree of stability was recorded during the 'Golden Age' of the 1950s and 1960s. In the 1970s and 1980s, rich countries' growth halved to an annual average of just over 2 per cent, while East and South Asia growth rates rose to 8 and 6 per cent respectively. Latin America and Africa recorded growth rates well below those of the rich countries. In the early 1990s the rich countries slowed further. Africa stagnated, and the communist party-state economies of Central and Eastern Europe collapsed. Recovery began in the second half of the decade, while Latin America joined East and South Asia in expansion.

Continuous expansion brought extraordinary improvement in living conditions for literally billions of people. Out of a world population of 3.3 billion in 1960, about 18 per cent enjoyed relatively high per capita incomes and had life expectancies ranging from 50–70 years. About 10 per cent had median incomes and life expectancies. Over 70 per cent lived in poverty, with life expectancies in the range of 30–40 years, and hardly any access to basic education and health care.[5] By 1994 the world population had expanded to 5.6 billion: of these 1.3 billion had nearly quadrupled their income, had life expectancies of between 70 and 80 years, and had adult literacy rates ranging from 75–99 per cent. A further 2.6 billion were in a medium category with a life expectancy averaging 67 years, a literacy rate of nearly 80 per cent, and per capita incomes also up four times over 1960. The poorest numbered 1.8 billion people, whose per capita incomes had barely risen by one half, whose life expectancies were in the 30–40-year range and with adult literacy of just under half of their number.

The decades of world economic expansion saw living standards rise for between 3 and 4 billion people as child death rates tumbled, along with malnutrition and illiteracy. During this period, there were some startling success stories, especially from southern Europe, the Gulf states and East Asia. At the same time, the gap in income between the richest 20 per cent and poorest 20 per cent of countries widened from a factor of 30:1 in 1960 to 60:1 in the 1990s, with the gap between the richest 20 per cent of the world population and the poorest 20 per cent widening to a factor of 150:1, in terms of the three broad categories mentioned in the previous paragraph. This meant that the rich 1.3 billion were fed by markets roughly 26 times the value of markets serving the poorest 1.8 billion people on earth.

This concentration of wealth in the markets serving the rich world was particularly visible in the trading system. During the Cold War years, growth in merchandise trade regularly grew faster than the world economy. At the heart of this expansion was the growth in manufacturing exports, fostered by regular rounds of trade liberalization talks among governments in the context of the General Agreement on Tariffs and Trade (GATT). Agricultural trade remained outside the scope of multilateral negotiations until the late 1980s, and financial services continued to be considered as vital instruments of state policy in managing the economy. Hence, trade growth essentially occurred in natural resources and manufactures. As producers of consumer and capital goods had to defray the costs of design, production and sales of their products, they were driven to sell into high disposable income markets.

Rich country producers therefore internalized trade among the industrialized nations, where the purchasing power was situated. As Table 3.1 shows, trade by the 1990s was concentrated heavily among the rich countries: the US and Canada were prime trade partners and had major markets in Western Europe and Asia – especially Japan, America's single largest export market. Europeans traded mostly among themselves, but were also a major market for Russia (CIS), Africa and the oil-producing states. Asian countries traded increasingly among themselves, and continued to win an ever larger world market share in exporting to the rich markets of North America and Europe. The same could not be said of Latin America, Russia, Africa and the states of the Middle East and Gulf, not to speak of India. These regions had barely 13 per cent of world market share but accounted for about 45 per cent of the world population.

Table 3.1
Network of world merchandise exports by region: 1995 (%)

	North America	Latin America	Western Europe	CEE/CIS	Africa	Middle East	Asia	World (%)	World ($b)
North America	36.0	12.9	19.0	0.8	1.4	2.4	27.2	100	776
Latin America	48.0	20.8	17.6	0.8	1.4	1.1	9.9	100	225
Western Europe	7.4	2.4	68.9	4.4	2.8	2.7	9.6	100	2190
CEE/CIS	4.8	2.2	57.3	18.9	1.4	2.2	12.8	100	150
Africa	14.2	1.7	54.6	1.4	10.0	1.6	13.5	100	105
Middle East	11.7	2.1	22.9	1.0	3.2	8.0	47.6	100	140
Asia	23.8	2.2	16.4	1.0	1.4	2.4	50.9	100	1300
World '95	15.9	4.6	44.8	3.1	2.1	2.9	26.6	100	4890
World '85	16.0	5.6	40.1	8.1	4.1	5.3	20.8	100	

Source: WTO, Annual Report 1996, Vol II.

The world's leading corporations had been hesitant to incur the costs of investing in a foreign market, only to see local governments nationalize their assets. Following the wave of decolonization in the 1950s and early 1960s, many governments of newly independent states considered that public ownership of mines, factories and financial institutions was essential. Public control of key resources within a national market protected from Western suppliers was widely considered as a sure route to national development. In these conditions, the name of the game for multinational corporations was to befriend local governments, and set up local production and distribution behind tariff walls. 'Tariff-hopping' yielded a reasonably secure stream of income, given that the corporations in effect negotiated their entry to a local oligopoly, where prices were secured from foreign competition, and profits were merely a matter of keeping costs below those of local rival-partners.

This pattern of corporate investment in developing countries began to be modified in the 1970s, as US and European investors sought to counter competition from Japanese corporations in home markets by shifting production offshore. The whole process was given a mighty boost by the yen's sharp revaluation against the dollar in 1985, and the fall in world mineral prices in early 1986. Japanese corporations, facing high costs at home and continuing wage rises in South Korea and in Taiwan, turned to new low-cost locations in Malaysia, Indonesia or Thailand. Their governments figuratively rolled out the red carpet. Japanese foreign direct investment in South-East Asia rose fourfold, as corporations moved to integrate their production processes in the region. The Japanese government was eager to export its own experience as part of a broader regional expansion policy.[6] East Asia's trade surplus with the US grew, as did pressures in Congress for a tougher stance on market opening. By 1995 East Asia had 30 per cent of world exports in manufacturing, and, minus Japan, accounted for 12 per cent of world manufacturing output, compared to Latin America's meagre 3 per cent and the former Soviet economies' 2.3 per cent.

The arrival of the world labour market

German unity acted as a catalyst for the creation of a world labour market. Its most immediate effect was to precipitate upwards of 3 billion people on to the world labour market, from the former Soviet Union, Central and Eastern Europe, China, and India. In addition, the resolu-

tion of the 1980s debt crisis under a plan advanced by US Treasury Secretary Brady enabled mid-income debtor countries to restructure their
debt to commercial banks through officially supported debt-reduction
programmes tied to broad policies of liberalization, stabilization and privatization. Brady's debt-relief plan spurred Mexico to negotiate the
NAFTA accords with the US and Canada, while Brazil and Argentina
formed the MERCOSUR customs union with Uruguay and Paraguay.
Given demographic trends, that 3 billion would become 6 billion by
2025. By comparison, the 'world market' of the Cold War had expanded
its total workforce by about 270 million, as Japan, Spain, Turkey, Korea
and the South-East Asian countries moved to industrialize.

The Soviet collapse also ended the separation of world labour markets between the advanced industrial countries, the communist party-
states and the developing countries sheltering behind high tariff
barriers. Indeed, Cold War segregation was comparable to the system
of apartheid in South Africa, where the state ensured that there was a
labour market for each class or race of
worker. And as with apartheid's end,
and the creation of a single labour market throughout South Africa, so the end
of the Cold War created one world
labour market. In other words, whereas
one unit of capital in the 1980s had at its disposal, say, ten units of
labour, after the end of the Cold War, one unit of capital had, say, 100
units of labour at its disposal. The average cost of labour around the
world has fallen correspondingly. The implication for high wage countries is that their relative wage is bid down at home as immigration
rises, or as companies dis-invest and move to cheaper wage locations.

Between 1995 and 2025, 95 per cent of children born into the world would be born in poorer countries.

Labour-rich poor countries faced formidable challenges in the
decades ahead. Between 1995 and 2025, 95 per cent of children born
into the world would be born in poorer countries. This simple figure
encapsulated six key features of the coming years:

1 The richer world – particularly Japan and Continental Europe –
was ageing fast: whereas the average age in developing country populations in 1995 was under 20, in Germany and Japan the figure was
closer to 40.

2 Poorer countries held a growing supply of cheap labour – India and China, for instance, each had 20 million new labour market entrants per annum. Trying to stimulate the business environment to provide jobs represented an all-absorbing priority.

3 The steady rise in the world's population implied a continuing stream of people leaving the land, as farmers sought to reduce their costs of production in order to provide food for expanding urban populations.

4 This rural exodus led to the growth of mega-cities, particularly in Latin America and in Asia, and the creation of an urban proletariat, dependent on city employment.

5 Urban populations faced the prospect of scratching a bare existence like the impoverished masses of Kinshasha, or of raising their living standards through value-added activities in manufacturing and in construction.

6 Bringing value-added activities to urban populations in turn meant the importance for them, and for the organizations where they worked, of ready access to world markets. Only by earning hard currencies in the developed markets could the poorer populations of the world hope to improve their lot.

Fortunately, merchandise trade in the 1990s grew twice as fast as national economies, notably in manufacturing. Commercial services, such as travel, transport or communications, expanded even more rapidly. The trend was furthered by widespread movement in developing countries to liberalize trade and payments in relations with the rich countries and in exchanges among themselves. Industrial countries opened their markets further in the course of the Uruguay Round of trade negotiations. Markets were in any event becoming more contestable on account of the secular fall in transport costs, and revolution in information technologies (IT), driven by the convergence of telecommunications and microelectronics. Lower transport costs extended the reach of corporate production to labour-intensive production, while IT facilitated the reorganization of production processes on a global basis. Companies more than ever were in a position to exploit comparative cost differentials.

Post-Cold War governments around the world were only too eager to play host to corporate investors. As Tony Blair, Britain's future prime minister, stated when wooing Rupert Murdoch, the US-Aus-tralian-British satellite TV mogul, for his support in the forthcoming UK elections, the role of government in this unforgiving world is 'to create a competitive base of physical infrastructure and human skills to attract the capital that will produce the wages for workers and the profits for investors'.[7] It is a statement which General Pinochet, the architect of free market policies in Chile, would have little difficulty in supporting.

A crucial feature of corporate calculations was that labour was now worldwide an abundant resource, and in some cases both highly skilled and low cost. This did not mean that rich-country corporations would inevitably be drawn to 'cheap labour' in the poor countries, creating – in Ross Perot's memorable words – a loud 'sucking sound' as jobs were cleaned out of the US and dispatched southwards across the Rio Grande into Mexico. Roughly 80–90 per cent of much manufacturing added value of a product lay in its brand name, merchandising or research and development. But the availability of highly skilled and low-cost labour did mean that corporations from the industrialized countries would become sensitive to wage cost differentials if they were large, and if the differentials could not easily be bridged by major differences in pro-ductivity between workforces in the rich and the poor countries. In many areas of business activity, both conditions held in the 1990s.

The end of the Cold War and the death of import-substitution as a viable development strategy opened up steep cost gradients between the US, the EU and Japan, and their immediate neighbourhoods. Wage differentials from the highest costs in Germany to the lowest in East or South Asia ranged between 200:1. Skilled workforces were available. The Swedish-Swiss power generator giant, ABB, for instance, bought an asset in Poland as soon as communism collapsed, turned the opera-tion around and within three years recorded the highest productivity rates in the ABB family in Europe, but with wage levels fifteen times below the Continental level. Firms' ability to break down production processes into stages enabled them to out-source to different countries according to comparative advantage. This was particularly noticeable in components in machinery and transport – the sector which accounts for 50 per cent of world trade in manufactures.

Productivity differentials between rich and poor countries in the 1990s could be bridged to the extent that some poor countries had also invested heavily in education and training. Not all had done so, but there could be no doubt that if there was one message which circulated the globe and reached into every nook and cranny of our planet, it was that investment in human capital yields the surest returns. Mao had tried to reverse the trend during the Cultural Revolution of 1966–70, when students left their studies to tend pigs as a way of coming closer to nature: the result in the 1990s was that China's prime weakness as a host for foreign investors was the lack of skilled labour.

In international assessments of educational progress, Chinese, Korean and Taiwanese thirteen-year-olds headed the proficiency test scores.

By contrast, Korea invested heavily in education, following in the tracks of Japan and Taiwan. Indeed, in international assessments of educational progress, Chinese, Korean and Taiwanese thirteen-year-olds headed the proficiency test scores, ahead of Switzerland, Russia and France, and well ahead of the UK and the US.

Another indication of the narrowing educational lead of rich country workforces over those from poorer countries was the position of women. On average, women's literacy in developing countries in 1995 was nearly 60 to a benchmark 100 for women living in rich countries, compared to an overall adult literacy rate in 1970 of 43 per cent.[8] This upward trend covered extremes of around 20 per cent of female literacy in many countries of Africa, to well under 40 per cent in India and Pakistan, and around 50 per cent in the Middle East and North Africa. Women enjoyed literacy most in East Asia, Latin America and the Caribbean, while women in the countries of Central and Eastern Europe were probably better educated than their sisters in Western Europe. The figures pointed to two conclusions: the number of women capable of helping their children in their schooling would continue to rise; those parts of the world which excluded their women from participating in the modern world of literacy and numeracy would continue to lag.

This huge world workforce was now accessible to corporations, which could organize the movement of capital equipment to any locations where conditions were judged suited to production in the value-added chain. Local labour could be hired with its mixture of skills and cost in order to produce for international trade. Total final costs of output in a poor country could exceed those in a rich country, if productivity was far below that in the more developed country. But the gap was bridgeable by:

- the dissemination of sound management skills, enabling the poorer country workforce to learn on the job;
- the use by management of up-to date information about the market, helping the poor country workforce to respond more flexibly to changing patterns of demand;
- a continued effort by management to lower the costs of logistics, with regard to inputs, storage and distribution; and
- the continued upgrading of the capital goods deployed for production, ensuring that products could be manufactured to quality standards and sold anywhere at a competitive price.

Regional protection against 'unfair' competition from low-wage countries was the answer sought by interested lobbies in the US and the EU. Very high rates of unemployment in the EU gave the argument some resonance, and merged into intra-EU negotiations on monetary union designed to prevent 'competitive devaluations', i.e. where governments had their currencies devalued in order to grab market share by undercutting product prices on the markets of more virtuous countries. In the US much more flexible labour markets, and consistently growth-oriented macro-economic policies, ensured that jobs galore were created. But strong competition among producers servicing the domestic market from home or abroad kept average wages from rising rapidly. A sense of stagnating incomes was all too easily blamed on low-wage countries. Both the US and the EU favoured having labour standards discussed in future world trade negotiations.

Corporations go global

From the early 1990s, the flow of world capital recorded a marked shift in direction, from concentration on the markets of the advanced industrialized countries to a renewed interest in developing countries.

In part, this reflects the longer-term expansion of trade, investment and capital to meet the unsatisfied demands of the world's growing population. But it also attests to a qualitative change in the global economy from being essentially a playground for the wealthier countries' producers and consumers to becoming more truly inclusive.

For at least two decades, international exchanges had been growing faster than the world economy. The result in the 1990s was much greater interdependence of markets, accompanied by a contradictory sense of the huge opportunities, the daunting tasks and the greater vulnerability of local societies and cultures to events around the globe. There was also a more purposeful adoption of liberal market policies, following US Treasury Secretary Brady's arrangement to swap debt for equity participations in Latin American assets. This enabled one Latin American government after another to embark on policies of trade liberalization and privatization, combined with domestic institutional reforms and the introduction of more welcoming FDI regimes. The set of principles equated with such policy shifts came to constitute the new model of economic development, loosely referred to as the 'Washington consensus'.

- Governments the world over had been revisiting the policies inherited from mid-century, when national economies were more closed. More or less reluctantly, they agreed to remove obstacles to cross-border flows.
- Greater openness of markets enabled corporations to increase trade between their subsidiaries in different jurisdictions, and allowed for a sharp rise in manufactured exports from the newly industrializing countries of the Asia-Pacific.
- Local producers previously on the sidelines of the world economy jostled to claim a stake in the chains of production under construction around the globe, by joining elaborate networks of intra-firm alliances and arrangements of all shapes and sizes.
- International institutions and non-governmental organizations negotiated new regimes with governments, business associations and trade unions in efforts to establish common norms governing labour, environmental or patent protection standards.

'Globalization' is the word most frequently used to describe the process of transformation on which the world embarked following the collapse of the Soviet Union and the end of import-substitution as a viable strategy for development in India or across Latin America. Like similar all-purpose words, its popularity is a function of its utility. In its simplest expression, it describes the availability on the European early morning markets of cut flowers flown in overnight from Colombia or from Kenya, or the fresh salmon available to New Yorkers from suppliers in Chile. At its loftiest, it suggests a programme for action to create common institutions, laws, rights or duties and equal access for all to markets in what is fast becoming a global village.

One pointer to 'globalization' in the early 1990s was the sharp rise in capital flows to developing countries. Capital flows include four different categories of international transactions: foreign direct investment by firms from home to host countries; commercial bank loans to governments or businesses; bond purchases or sales by governments or corporations; and the acquisition of equities or shares in companies listed on world stock exchanges.[9] They grew fourfold between 1990 and 1993, stabilizing for a while at about $170 billion, and then soared to $245 billion in 1996, when they represented in value about 4 per cent of the combined economies of all developing countries. Developing countries opened their stock markets to overseas investors, so that 'emerging markets' came to represent 10 per cent of the total global capitalization. Four-fifths of the flows represented private capital, in contrast to earlier decades when commercial banks loaned to governments and the foreign aid budgets of the industrialized nations were more generously provided.

Capital flows grew fourfold between 1990 and 1993 and soared to $245 billion in 1996.

These capital flows reflected a number of more fundamental trends at work around the world. One was the expanding role of portfolio investors from the United States, Japan, the UK and the Netherlands, as well as from Singapore and Hong Kong. These institutions looked for high returns in order to satisfy their clients' demands for a secure source of income on retirement. And because the populations of the industrialized countries were ageing, the magnitude of the funds at their disposal continued to grow. Financial market reforms and free capital movements immensely widened the range of opportunities available to them. They could choose between buying a long-term stake in a company, sit tight, take the dividends and wait for capital growth; or they could opt for a fast buck, sell before the investment climate turned sour, and move on to sunnier climes elsewhere around the globe.

A key component of capital flows in the 1990s to developing countries was foreign direct investment (FDI), reflecting the expansion of cross-border production by multinational corporations, their affiliates or their subcontractors and partners. Western corporations discovered that the world was their metaphorical oyster, and accelerated the adoption of global strategies, i.e. integrated production and marketing strategies intended to reconcile the contradictory exigencies of competition in world markets, and the need to be responsive to local conditions. Whereas in the late 1980s investment flowing to developing countries had been 15–18 per cent of the total recorded, in the 1990s flows to developing countries leapt to 30–40 per cent. The overwhelming majority of FDI went to the countries of the Asia-Pacific, and notably to China (see Figure 3.1). New technologies facilitated the process as corporations learned to integrate their component manufacturing processes, and flexible manufacturing enabled distinct markets to be serviced at low cost.

Five home countries accounted for the bulk of the outward stock of FDI. The US was still by far the largest home country, followed at a distance by the United Kingdom and Japan, which in turn were followed by Germany and France. Corporations from the small European home countries of the Netherlands, Switzerland and Sweden had a disproportionate percentage of their assets held abroad, in view of their small home base and the direct urgency of access to wider markets. A number of 'threshold' countries, such as Mexico, the Republic of Korea, Brazil and Venezuela, joined the ranks of home countries to the 40,000-odd parent firms, with their 270,000 affiliates. Sales by all foreign affiliates were reported[10] as exceeding the total of world exports of goods and services. These figures did not include partner firms linked to the global network through non-equity arrangements, such as technology transfer accords or alliances.

Figure 3.1
FDI INFLOWS BY HOST REGION, 1975–1996: $ MILLIONS
CONTEMPORARY VISIONS

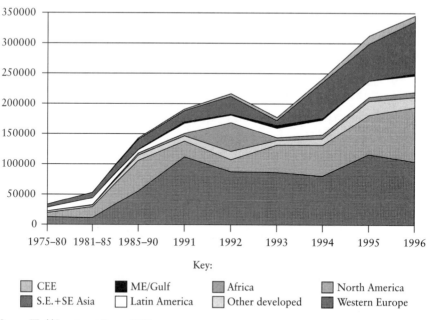

Key:

☐ CEE	■ ME/Gulf	▨ Africa	▨ North America
■ S.E.+SE Asia	☐ Latin America	▨ Other developed	▨ Western Europe

Source: World Investment Report 1997

The direction of FDI has not always been towards the Asia-Pacific. Latin America had lost its attractions in the wake of the debt crisis in 1982 when Argentina, Brazil and Mexico had to suspend interest payments on their borrowings from Western commercial banks. Over the following four years, Latin America's net transfer of resources to creditors amounted to 4 per cent of the continent's GDP, precipitating a sharp decline in living standards. But by the early 1990s Latin America was once again a target for FDI, though in changed conditions. Motives for inward investment varied: expansion of the automobile industry in Mexico and Brazil, natural resources in Chile and privatization in Peru and Argentina. The main investors came from the US, Germany and, notably, Spain, whose state-owned Telefonica and Iberia bought up nearly all the region's public sales in the fields of telecommunications and air transport.

If the 1980s are remembered as Latin America's 'lost decade', they will no doubt be recorded in Africa as the years of the locust. Africa's positive growth rates in the 1960s had been sustained in the 1970s by public loans from the EU, by high prices for natural resources and by a steady inflow of FDI. Even in the 1990s the stock of FDI in Africa – at $50 billion – far exceeded that in Russia, and represented about 10

If the 1980s are remembered as Latin America's 'lost decade', they will no doubt be recorded in Africa as the years of the locust.

per cent of the continent's GDP. In general, though, political turbulence, armed conflict, the struggle to end apartheid in southern Africa, massive mismanagement of public resources in Nigeria and restricted local markets kept investors away, as incomes fell to the levels of the early 1970s.

Conditions were not uniformly bleak: Botswana demonstrated that good government, sensible investment in human capital and rapid growth rates were not the preserve of East Asia; Mauritius developed its strategy to expand as a service centre for the region; Morocco, as well as Tunisia, pursued market-friendly policies, aiming to supply markets in the EU. The year 1994 marked the election of Nelson Mandela to the Presidency of a new South Africa, and the stirrings of renewed interest by foreign investors in African prospects.

Not least, the collapse of the Soviet Union and the end of India's soft currency trading relations with the communist party-states opened new vistas that had been almost forgotten since the first decade of the century, when India was part of the British Empire and Russia was a fast-growing 'emerging market' for French investors. Hungary and the Czech lands were initial recipients, but it was only in 1994, when Poland resolved its outstanding debt problems with its Western creditors along Brady lines, that the world's corporations looked more closely at the prospect of integrating their operations on a pan-European scale. Whereas in 1991 the broad region of Central and Eastern Europe (CEE), including Russia and its European successor states, attracted 1 per cent of total FDI, by 1995 the region accounted for 5 per cent. Even so, the estimated stock of FDI in the CEE amounted that year to $46 billion, equivalent to one year's inflow to China.

A further novelty of FDI in the 1990s was the pattern across the four sectors of primary products, manufacturing, infrastructure and services.

- Investment in agriculture and mining attracted about 20 per cent of total flows, in contrast to the first half of the century when most FDI was to primary producing countries. Predominant home countries were the United States and the United Kingdom. German, Japanese, French and Italian oil and mining companies then entered the markets to ensure home supplies, and were joined by corporations promoted by host country governments, determined to appropriate the profits for their own purposes. Geographical location and political sensitivities about foreign ownership and depletion policies would remain central considerations governing FDI in the primary sector.

- The key change since the early decades of the century was the rise of manufacturing to account for 47 per cent of total FDI. The heart of these investments were, first, the US investments in Western Europe and Japan in the 1950s and 1960s, followed by the reverse inward flow of European and Japanese investments to the US in the 1970s and especially the 1980s. Meanwhile, the inward investment of manufacturing capabilities in the newly industrializing economies of East Asia grew at an annual rate of 16 per cent between 1975 and 1990. As these countries worked their way up the value-added chain of activities, their firms integrated into the networks of 'strategic accords' between corporations, seeking to share the costs and know-how required to supply markets driven by fast-changing technologies and consumer demands.

- Investment in services and infrastructure represented about a third of the total and, like the other broad areas, had been restricted by national government sensitivities. Relatively stable technologies in telecommunications, power generation and transport had facilitated national control or ownership of what economists call 'natural monopolies' – areas of business activity which tend towards the generation of monopoly profits. Prevailing doctrine asserted that governments should appropriate the profits in the public interest. In the 1980s this doctrine came under attack from a combination of free market ideas, new technologies and the urgent requirements of financially strapped governments. In the 1990s, infrastructure investments grew rapidly.

The world financial markets

The rapid expansion in the scope of world business was also underpinned by an integrated, round-the-clock global financial market, allocating world savings to end uses on a truly international scale. The old equation underlying postwar national economics where local savings equalled local investment no longer bore much relation to reality. True, households, companies and governments in a national economy did most of their saving and investing at home, but a growing fraction filtered on to the international markets as national financial systems became more porous, with the growth of international trade, investment and capital flows.[11] The density of local interests and cultures sustaining local arrangements ensured that they evolved at a snail's pace in comparison to the speed of change in the global system.

This transformation in world financial markets undermined the assumption informing the Bretton Woods accords, that governments should manage their national economies because unregulated markets were not to be trusted. In fact, states had adopted very different and often incompatible financial arrangements. Many states centralized control over financial flows in their finance ministries. Others created distinct public and private markets. The UK and the US in particular fostered shareholding, and allowed markets for corporate control to develop. Elsewhere, states hitched national financial systems to their policies of growth and market conquest. National corporations and financial institutions owned one another's shares, and were represented on one another's boards, with a view to restricting local bankruptcies and maximizing sales abroad. Germany and Japan proved to be champions at this mercantilist game, running huge trade surpluses which had to be recycled on to the world financial markets.

Another force for change was the breakdown of public finances in the world's democracies. The architects of Bretton Woods had assumed that governments would reign over markets in the public's interest, and for the first two decades after 1945 most governments used their discretionary powers cautiously. This reserve gave way in the 1960s, as one Western government after another moved its budget to deficit. In the recession of the mid-1970s, France, Spain, Japan and

India joined the profligate majority. Elected politicians learned that re-election was best secured by having governments issue 'securities' to cover expenditures rather than raise taxes. As governments sold a growing volume of their paper, financial institutions discovered the virtues of trading paper in a liquid world market. The share of the world financial market which was liquid and tradable grew at the expense of the market under governments' control, i.e. the domestic money supply. Bretton Woods was undermined by fiscal excess.

As long as the dollar provided a stable reference price to other currencies and monetary systems, the US's central role in international financial affairs went unchallenged. But dollar and sterling balances began to build up abroad, and in 1965 General de Gaulle attacked the whole monetary system as highly inflationary. The US and the UK, he suggested, should return to payments discipline based on agreed rules. Both the US and the UK considered that international imbalances were due to trade discrimination in the EU and Japan,

Global daily trade in foreign exchange markets shot up from $15 billion in 1973 to $1,300 billion by the mid-1990s.

and that continued growth in the world economy required easy money and expansionary public finances. In August 1971 President Nixon announced the end of the dollar's convertibility into gold, thereby terminating the US economy's role as anchor of the world financial system. Within two years the major currencies had abandoned fixed exchange rates. Global daily trade in foreign exchange markets shot up from $15 billion in 1973 to $1,300 billion by the mid-1990s, or 60 to 100 times the average turnover of trade in physical goods.[12]

The years 1973 to 1979 were marked by two surges in world oil prices, both driven forward by Iran, and by the ensuing recycling of funds which could not be consumed by oil-producing states on to the world dollar markets, located in London and New York. Commercial banks lent dollars to oil-importing states, and especially to Central and Eastern Europe, Africa and Latin America. Interest rates on the international markets stayed around zero, so borrowers flocked there and banks fell over one another to lend. But the mood in the US and Europe turned in favour of price stability, and in October 1979 the Federal Reserve engineered a worldwide rise in interest rates. Debtors were figuratively strangled by the high interest rates, and in 1982 the markets responded to the debt crises in Latin America by 'securitization' of commercial bank debts. Between 1982 and 1990 the region sustained a negative resource transfer, as mentioned, precipitating a sharp decline in living standards.

The 1982 switch to securities marked the prolonged boom on world capital markets. Bank debts were converted to bonds. The exponential development of wholesale capital markets was driven by the growth of government and corporate bond markets, as the US and European states vied for world savings, and the world's corporations raised capital by the issue of shares. New York and Chicago set the pace in breaking down the inherited barriers to efficient financial markets, and were followed by London, Paris and Amsterdam, with Frankfurt and Tokyo in the rear. Poorer indebted countries were squeezed until, as it were, their pips squeaked.

Not surprisingly, for the rest of the decade multinational companies invested overwhelmingly in the markets of the developed world, according to the '80 per cent principle'. The principle operated as a rule-of-thumb, to the effect that 20 per cent of the world population in the developed countries of the OECD enjoyed 80 per cent of world income, output, trade, savings and investment. It also recorded the fact that investments in the United States, the EU and Japan were infinitely more secure from government takeover than investments in, say, Iran, where German corporations had invested heavily prior to the collapse of the Shah's regime in late 1978. The one exception to the rule was France, where President Mitterrand's election in 1981 was followed by an extensive programme of expropriation, leaving the government in control of over a third of French industry and nearly all the financial sector. But Mitterrand soon discovered that his nationalized banks would not lend to his nationalized corporations: the remainder of his two presidencies was spent shuffling the assets around from public pillar to private post.

Global financial markets grew by leaps and bounds as all countries were pulled into their vortex in the course of the 1980s and 1990s. The ranks of net suppliers of funds to the markets widened from the initial list of the US and UK, to oil-producing states, and to Germany and Japan as chronic trade surplus countries. Central banks, financial institutions and corporations, all in varying form protected from bankruptcy, placed their surpluses and took their bets in the world casino. The rich from Latin America and Africa, and party bosses from the communist states, joined the party. By the 1990s, the main sources of net savings were in the Asia-Pacific, and the net borrowers were the EU and the US. Flows to Africa and Latin America were once again positive, but the structures of world finance had been transformed; world foreign exchange, government and corporate bonds and equities formed a seamless web to span the whole risk and return spectrum.

Developing countries were eager to tap global capital markets, in order to finance the balance of payments or to accelerate the build-up of their productive capacity. This entailed reforming their financial systems in order to meet investors' demands for liquidity, or for transparent information about local opportunities. Whether or not they were far advanced in reform, the markets would form a favourable view of their declared intentions and rush to buy assets in the local currency. The frequent result was a local boom fuelled by cheap credit, a surge in real estate prices, an appreciation of the exchange rate and a widening deficit on external accounts. Fleet-footed financial institutions were fast to sell out and move into alternative investments. But in Mexico in December 1994, and again in East Asia in 1997–8, they left behind them devalued currencies and governments in disrepute, facing bankruptcies and rising unemployment.

The world financial markets had, in effect, become judge and jury of the world economy. Nothing escaped their attention. National economic performance was judged in the foreign exchange markets. Government policies were assessed through the bond markets. Corporate returns were measured through the world's integrated corporate bond and equity markets. Their verdict was recorded in the risk-assessment agencies of the major financial capitals, which assigned credit ratings to currencies, bonds and shares. A rise in the credit ratings of, say, Moody's or Standard and Poor's would lower the cost of capital, while a negative verdict would raise the cost of capital – for firms as for governments. Some governments, currencies or firms were treated with more respect than others, for most of the time, but if governments did not respond to the markets' policy prescriptions, the markets' sanction was to withdraw confidence. They could not impose policies on sovereigns who refused to comply, but they could make the cost of non-compliance very high.

The EU's bid to create an integrated financial area and monetary union represented an ambitious attempt to throw off the dominance of international financial markets. By the 1980s Germany was Europe's prime industrial, exporting and financial power. France resented this, and feared that a united Germany would consolidate a prior alliance with the US, consolidating the DM–$ axis. The axis would perpetuate the offshore financial markets in London which had prospered on the back of allied imbalances in trade and public finances.

The main argument in favour of European monetary union was that governments could not simultaneously manage a stable exchange rate regime, retain control over domestic economic policy, and free short-term capital movements. They could do two, but not all three together. They could control domestic economic policy and free short-term capital movements, but any deviation in inflation or interest rates among the member states would lead to movements of short-term capital. Large movements of short-term capital across the exchanges greatly reduced the ability of governments to stick to stable exchange rates. As both Germany and Britain had liberalized, in 1961 and 1979 respectively, both backed free capital movements for the EU's internal market. But Chancellor Kohl also favoured monetary union by 1999 in a closely knit EU. France, Italy and Spain made the final move to liberalize capital flows during the negotiations.

Monetary union would introduce a Euro capital market, the size of the US capital market. Success in this crucial experiment for the world economy would create a counterbalance to the dollar. It would complete the transition from the Cold War structure to a bipolar world, centred around relations between the US and the EU.

Conclusion

There can be no doubt that the dominant trend of the 1990s has been globalization. The freeing of short-term capital flows and German unity marked the end of the Cold War structure which had simultaneously contained both communism and capitalism. The novelty was US primacy in an integrating world market characterised by unprecedented inequalities. This held a number of implications:

- Ways that had worked when Japan and Germany were winning the mercantilist struggle for market share in industrial exports from compact national bases in the years 1949 to 1991 were no longer viable. That was the lesson of the East Asian financial crisis of late 1997.
- The world financial markets were no longer under lock and key, they had emerged and been transformed into judge and jury. Furthermore, they had achieved their eminence thanks to incontinent governments pissing deficits for decades on end.

World financial markets had achieved their eminence thanks to incontinent governments pissing deficits for decades on end.

- There was one labour market, in a multi-civilizational world, with unprecedented gaps in wages and shrinking gaps in education and mobile technology. Another Achilles heel of the world economy was therefore rich country mobilization against 'unfair wages'.
- Multinational corporations had graduated from being the targets of nationalization and of radical Marxist rhetoric to being the allies of development in a world which seemed to be on the path to 'common marketization'.

Where would all this end? One World cosmopolitans saw a radiant future of 'convergence'. The world economy was at long last launched upon a voyage to integration. The opening up of markets previously closed to trade and capital flows allowed a levelling of living standards around the world and – in the discernible future – for the creation of a world civilization. The engine of change driving convergence was the pool of world savings in search of returns, and that could now be allocated through the world financial markets. Lower returns on investments in the richer and saturated markets of the industrialized world appeared less attractive than the higher returns attached to business operations in poorer countries. The mobility of capital, notably via FDI, would accelerate world economic growth and much higher rates of accumulation than was the norm in the industrialized world.

Realists disputed the thesis that more liberal flows in trade and capital were moving the world along the road to a convergence of living standards on a higher norm. They cited evidence to the effect that just twelve developing countries attracted between 70 and 80 per cent of the FDI going to poorer countries. The near-hundred other developing countries received a tiny fraction of resources, and faced an accelerated relative deterioration in living conditions as they accounted for an increasingly small share of world markets. The realists' main contention was that world markets were imperfect, and that the imperfections derived from the depredations of history and of past civilizational clashes. Higher returns accruing to business operations in developing countries represented a return to the excess profits denounced by revolutionaries in the past; capital mobility fatally weakened the ability of governments to manage their economies in the interest of their citizens.

In both views, states were seen as vital partners for business in an integrating world economy. That has meant extensive changes for public policy and corporate governance in advanced industrial states, and an unprecedented wave of 'market democratization' among poorer countries. These are the subject of the next two chapters.

Notes

1 The title is that of an excellent book by Lowell Bryan and Diana Farrell, *The Market Unbound: Unleashing Global Capitalism*, New York, John Wiley, 1996.
2 Raul Prebisch, *Economic Development of Latin America and its Principal Problems*, New York, United Nations, 1950.
3 Friedrich List, *National System of Political Economy*, New York, Longmans, 1904; Henry C. Carey, *Principles of Social Science*, Philadelphia, Lippincott, 1859.
4 A. Maddison, *Monitoring the World Economy*, Paris, OECD, 1995.
5 Figures from UN Development Programme, *Human Development Reports*, (annual) 1990–97.
6 D. Unger, 'Japan's Capital Exports: Moulding East Asia', in D. Unger and P. Blackburn (eds), *Japan's Emerging Global Role*, Boulder, Colorado, Lynne Rienner, 1993.
7 *Financial Times*, 21 July 1995.
8 Figures from UN Development Programme, *Human Development Reports* (annual) 1990–97.
9 World Bank, *Global Development Finance*, 1997.
10 UNCTAD, *World Investment Report*, various years.
11 M. Baxter and M. Crucini, 'Explaining Savings-Investment Correlation', *The American Economic Review*, Vol. 83, No. 3, 1989.
12 Bank for International Settlements, 1995.

Chapter 4

STATES, BUSINESS AND MARKETS

S tates are the pillars of the international system, but they are not the
sole authorities in the world. They exist alongside one another as
units in a system from which they cannot escape, and they coexist with
other organizations, notably business enterprises which compete and
prosper in a world market. What common conditions they face is the
question prior to the observation that states differ, and that the capitalisms which they help to create are also significantly varied. This
chapter focuses very much on states, and the competitive context for
business which they shape, in contrast to Chapter 2 which presented
the state as an abstraction in an empty circle, as though states were
amoebas forever taking their tone from the world around them. First,
this chapter examines the expansion of state activities and the changing context of ideas; second, it presents a framework for analyzing the
process of state policy; third, it contrasts the very different national
financial and corporate systems which developed over time in
advanced industrial states, as a prelude to discussing the political and
economic transitions under way in most developing countries.

The state and public policy

A central feature of the outgoing twentieth century has been an
unprecedented expansion of state activities. Debate about public policy
had long centred on the best means of achieving national wealth. Liberals, taking their lead from Adam Smith, urged that the individual decisions of millions were best co-ordinated through the 'invisible hand' of
the market; government tasks should be limited to ensuring external
security, law and order, and public investment projects. Collectivists, by
contrast, advocated non-market mechanisms as the best means to co-

ordinate economic life. Experience of what state-directed economies could accomplish under conditions of wartime mobilization strengthened their appeal to socialists eager to cure the injustices of capitalism, or to nationalists who sought to accelerate industrialization.

Collectivists gained the upper hand in the turbulent years following the end of the First World War. The old liberal idea of a self-regulating market, with minimalist government, proved vulnerable when market imperfections were everywhere evident in the form of cartels, and millions were out of work. Confidence in the ability of government to put wrongs to right was widespread. Communist parties propounded the abolition of the market, and a monopoly of political power for themselves. Fascism and national socialism borrowed from wartime experience and created centralized organized interests, with monopoly functions to promote production at the service of national aggrandisement.

How, in these circumstances, could political liberties and market freedoms be reconciled? John Maynard Keynes's genius was to make the market, rather than the bureaucracy, the instrument for an indirect system of planning. The problem in the depression of the 1930s was not, as socialists or capitalists argued, the inevitable conflict of the classes. Unemployment, he urged, was the result of under-consumption and too much abstinence.[1] Government's task was to tickle savings into investment through control over taxation and financial policy instruments. Otherwise, markets were to be left as the main co-ordinating mechanisms for the creation and distribution of wealth.

Postwar reconstruction policies in Europe and Japan broadly followed similar minimalist paths. Social democrats sought to keep the extended postwar state accountable through parliamentary democracy. Conservative parties in Japan, Germany, France and Italy adopted the politics of productivity through the dissemination of management principles, and hitched national financial institutions in various ways to the urgent task of reconstruction. But in the late 1950s the Western democracies were seized by panic, when the boom from reconstruction petered out, and fears surfaced of a return to the depression conditions of the 1930s.

Panic was compounded when the Soviet leader, Khrushchev, boasted that the West would be 'buried' within a decade by a communist cornucopia of consumer goods. A more attractive image than death through a surfeit of consumption gained currency in the form of the railway theory of international economic relations. It depicted states running on parallel tracks, where the US feared being 'overtaken' by the USSR, the British by the Germans and French, and the developing countries sought to 'catch up' with the West. Japan's government launched its 'doubling income' programme, in compensation to nationalists for continued US use of the Okinawa base.

Growth economics envisaged states as manufacturing plants. Working the economy at full compared to actual capacity could be achieved by a more efficient use of resources, and by state promotion of investment, saving and demand. Civil servants were envisaged as 'steering the economy', much as managers were supposed to steer corporate activities. The formula enjoyed a wide appeal. Managers, whether from the public or private sector, based their prestige on positive growth records; free marketeers appreciated the drive for efficiency; nationalists studied the growth league tables; socialists saw the chance for friction-free redistribution of resources from one group in society to another.

The ideology of political pluralism, too, provided an explanation of 'who gets what' in the scramble for resources. Public policy, political scientists proclaimed, was a temporary product in the lasting struggle among competing interests operating in a political system. The system was fed by inputs in the form of demands by private interests, political parties or public agencies. Political authorities in the black box labelled 'policy process' discarded, selected and implemented proposals in a never-ending cycle of 'policy-making'. Their outputs came in the form of symbolic gestures, regulation or implementation of policies. The whole was sustained by a continued capacity to extract resources from the system's environment.[2]

With such encouragement from the halls of academe, and political parties competing for swing voters, activist public policy operated as if the sky was the limit. Government spending in rich countries jumped from an average among advanced industrialized countries of about 28 per cent of GDP in 1960 to 43 per cent in 1980. Ten years later, spending was up to an average 45 per cent, and the upward creep continued in the 1990s. The main source of the spending boom was an explosion in public transfers and subsidies, in good times as in bad. Government clientele fastened themselves like barnacles to the hull of the ship of state. Authorities and functions of all sorts mushroomed, yielding a cornucopia of public policies.

With similar growth trends, institutional diversity among industrialized states remained effectively disguised during the heyday of the Cold War. All adopted the formalized idiom of Keynesian economics to explain their policies. But their very different reactions to the oil crises of the 1970s revealed the peculiarities of their domestic structures.[3] The opposite ends of the spectrum in policy were allotted to the United States as a paragon of liberal markets, and to Japan as the successful practitioner of a mercantilist strategy characterized by extensive intervention by state institutions in the market. France, Germany and Italy were somewhere in between, with the UK tilting the US way.

Authorities and functions of all sorts mushroomed, yielding a cornucopia of public policies.

This more jaundiced view of Western economic policies pointed to differences in internal structures as the source of conflicts in international relations between states. Japan and Germany were both running massive trade surpluses, and politicians of the left were campaigning on populist platforms of extensive nationalizations and worker participation in corporate decisions. The crusade to roll back the state, and slay the dragon of socialism, was launched in the 1980s by President Reagan and Prime Minister Thatcher. The two leaders set Western diplomacy the task of strengthening markets as the main co-ordinating device for Western societies. Doing things 'my way' (as the late Frank Sinatra sang) was no longer an excuse for national protection.

The pluralist politics of expansionary government meanwhile prompted countervailing strategies. Firms responded to restrictive labour market legislation by introducing more flexible production systems, and farmed out tasks to part-time employees; slower growth and fiercer international competition stimulated technological innovations and revived price wars; with bond holders asking a return on their investments, governments made halting efforts to control government expenditures, accompanied by sales of loss-making state-owned enterprises. Not least, the inclusion of financial services in the liberalization programmes of the EU and the GATT threatened the states' leverage over their own financial systems.

With the implosion of the Soviet Union, the triumph of 'capitalism' over 'communism', and democracy over autocracy, seemed secure. But which capitalism among those on display among the rich countries of Western Europe, North America and Japan would win out in the post-Cold War world? There are a number of responses:

- Free marketeers maintain that Friedrich von Hayek, Keynes's free market opponent in the 1930s, has won a posthumous victory. States everywhere are embracing free markets. The market, this view holds, is a self-regulating system, which co-ordinates the activities of millions and serves as an exploratory device for new needs and technologies.[4] The driving force behind this self-regulating system is the entrepreneur, not government. Entrepreneurs require predictable conditions in order to fulfil their vital functions. These can be assured only when governments are constrained by binding rules, and policy is farmed out to independent expert institutions, such as central banks and competition authorities.

- Institutionalists concur on the central importance of markets, but add that 'the polity specifies and enforces the property rights of the economic marketplace, and the characteristics of the political market are the essential key to understanding the imperfections of the market'.[5] In other words, there are many capitalisms, and not a one-fit-for-all.[6] Societies have more than the two choices implied in the dichotomy of production as either centralized under a hierarchy composed of very large organizations and a few powerful managers, or a decentralized system of production where production and managerial powers are widely dispersed.[7]

- Culturalists argue that cultural values lie at the root of different national economies, and 'we never escape from the culture that trained us'.[8] These different national economies, they are saying, have been brought into competition with one another, and have become more or less compatible over time. One common theme is the struggle which culturalists maintain has broken out after the end

of the Cold War between the 'Anglo-Saxons', with their individualist and cosmopolitan ideologies, and the communitarians, in Germany, France and Japan.[9]

● Structuralists point out that states create competitive advantages,
which enable sustained rises in productivity to be achieved.[10] States
upgrade infrastructure and skills; influence demand for products by
setting technical standards or by procurement; encourage interna-
tionally competitive supplier industries; and ensure favourable conditions for competition among national firms and for their
organization and management. Japan and Germany, with their
tightly integrated societies and their massive trade surpluses, were
clearly the states that structuralists most admired.

The state as policy process

Before expanding on the theme of rival capitalist models in the post-
Cold War world, let us examine more closely the idea of the state as a
policy process. An adequate definition of the state would hold that,
within their territorial boundaries, states are represented through a
configuration of coercive, administrative and legal organizations which
are distinguished from organizations in civil society by their monopoly
over the legitimate use of violence. Externally, they conduct relations
with other states in order to ensure security and prosperity for people
within their boundaries. Within, they promote some sense of common
citizenship in order to ensure compliance with binding rules. Citizens
in democracies enjoy a wide discretion, and their civil society of
churches, political parties, clubs and sundry other associations exists
autonomously but always in some relation of intimacy with the state.

In advanced industrial states, the permanent activity of public policy
has been described as having three features:[11]

1 Government constitutes the central actor in public policy, but oper-
ates in the context of its domestic civil society and of the society or
system of states of which it is a part.

2 Public policy is a set of actions, and also of non-actions. Even a symbolic gesture is an action with implicit content, while a decision not

to act is a policy statement just as powerful as, if not more so than, a decision to act.

3 The process of public policy and the content form two sides of the same coin. This may be illustrated in the form of a feedback loop, when first a problem is identified; then solutions are formulated; subsequently, decisions are taken and the programme is implemented; finally, the action is evaluated, altering the assessment of subsequent flows of policy.

> *A decision not to act is a policy statement just as powerful as, if not more so than, a decision to act.*

This unceasing flow of public policies through the institutions of advanced industrialized states is illustrated in Figure 4.1, and responds to the four key questions: Who participates in public policy? Why do they act as they do – in other words, what are the rationales for their policies and preferences? How do they seek to achieve their goals, through which policy instruments? What are the results and performances which they achieve as a direct or indirect result of their

Figure 4.1
POLICY FLOWS AND PROCESSES

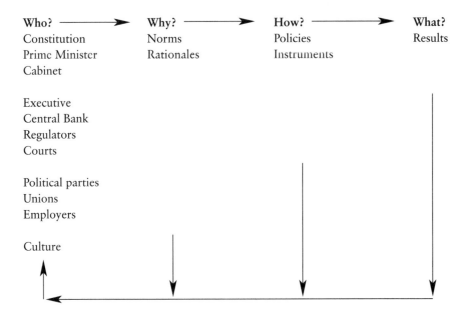

Who?	Why?	How?	What?
Constitution	Norms	Policies	Results
Prime Minister	Rationales	Instruments	
Cabinet			
Executive			
Central Bank			
Regulators			
Courts			
Political parties			
Unions			
Employers			
Culture			

policies? The elements in the chain are interactive, and the flow of influences and events is in the form of a feedback, so that past policies condition the present situation and future options.

Who?

Who? means which public offices and organizations are key political players in the arena of public policy that business people must be aware of. Every state has its particular design of government institutions, its own peculiar mix of bureaucracy, law and markets, its special structure for corporate or union representation, its own tradition of political parties and electoral system, and its political culture. How a state handles the flow of business thus requires a mental map of the state's institutions and of key players in civil society. In Germany, for instance, the federal design of the constitution displaces the implementation of industrial policies from the federation to the states. National policy changes take an inordinate amount of time, because so many interests clamour for consideration before a consensus emerges.

But the state alone does not exercise control over outcomes, and politics is not an activity restricted only to politicians. As Bertrand de Jouvenel has pointed out, whenever two or more people gather together to plan some enterprise they are engaging in politics.[12] Alone, the entrepreneur cannot accomplish his or her objective; he has to have the support of other wills. Political science, de Jouvenel writes, is 'the study of political life – the capacity to bring into being a stream of wills: to canalize the stream and regularize and institutionalize the resulting co-operation'. It is 'the study of the way in which aggregates are formed'. Hence, the Who? must be extended to include all enterprises, official or civilian, where politics is made.

Why?

Why do they act as they do? requires an understanding of the formal and informal norms which suffuse politics and inform the rationale for state or other policies. These norms precede 'strategy' – a word which is over-abundantly used to refer to the reasons for and methods of deploying resources to particular ends. They define the revealed intent of the organization – revealed because they may only be understood *ex-post*, and intent because they define the motivations for actions and strategies in the future.

The Why? of policy is revealed in the use political entrepreneurs make of deeply held beliefs or ambitions to give meaning to their project. Language and myths provide the bedrock of identity among separate wills and the invisible hand which guides common action. They imbue a political project with roots in a created past, and project its realization forward into the future. Intent here is the father of ambition. The appeal is to the collective identity provided, say, by nationalism, which in the twentieth century answers to 'the need for collective immortality and dignity'.[13] The same goes for corporations. They serve markets well to the extent that they stimulate a voluntary commitment beyond remuneration. The best-known example, perhaps, is that of Konosuke Matsushita, who announced on 5 May 1932 – the fourteenth anniversary of the founding of the company – his business philosophy and a 250-year plan for the company, broken down into ten 25-year segments.[14]

European monetary union in France, for instance, is not presented to the public as contributing to greater market efficiency in the EU. Anybody seeking to advance such arguments risks being tarred and feathered as an 'Anglo-Saxon'. A surer rationale, sung in the salons of Paris, is that monetary union is a vital step towards achieving the 'construction of Europe', a euphemism for a French-centred alliance to contain the threat of a renascent Germany. Even this appeal to the court of history does not win unanimous consent: 'The basic reason [for EMU] is the will to power of the French politico-administrative class,' writes Jean-Jacques Rosa, 'which reconciles gaullism and socialism in pursuit of the dream of subordinating German power in the service of its own grandeur, which is the true reason for this policy.'[15]

How?

How? answers the question of the methods used by policy entrepreneurs to achieve their goals, and through which policy instruments. One approach is to list the variety of policy instruments at the state's disposal, and the 'policy community' of players clustering around them. Each state has its own particular pattern of policy communities, which have achieved prominence or been relegated to insignificance for one reason or another. The industrial relations nexus includes trade unions, corporations and their human resource management teams, the courts, various ministries and local government departments, and trade associations with delegated powers to negotiate with unions on behalf of members. Financial policy communities include the finance ministry and central bank, capital and money market participants, financial institutions, newspaper editors and sundry academic commentators as well as depositors and borrowers. Other policy nexuses, with rather different policy communities, would be clustered around health, education or transport policy.

Distinctive patterns of policy communities in states are one feature determining business performances far above or below the average: the technical versatility of German machine tool workers derives from Germany's excellent apprenticeship system, funded by trade associations and local government, and is reflected in the prominence of German machine tools on world markets; the US lead in higher education, space, agricultural innovations and communications technologies reflects the heavy commitment of the US federal government in all of those areas; the UK's position as a location for international finance results from consistent policies by all governments since the end of the war in 1945 to reconstitute London as an international financial centre. France has become a major provider of farm products on world markets, reflecting the weight of the farm lobby in a country which still identifies itself in terms of its rural past, and as a high-point of cuisine in the world.

What?

What results? may be answered in general terms of macro-economic performances, or it may be answered by looking at the impact of public policies on firms, on education or on crime prevention. If performances do not meet expectations, the conclusion may be that the public policy was wrongly formulated, or even that the institutional context through which it was filtered requires alteration. This line of reasoning has fed a fascination with foreign 'models', or institutional designs, which appear to produce better results measured in almost phallic terms of comparative growth league tables and the size of trade surpluses. French fascination with 'the German model', for instance, feeds also on envy at the size of German trade surpluses, while US anxiety waxed over the trade successes of Japan, South Korea and Taiwan in responding to 'the international competitive challenge'.

What results? in effect yields two categories of answers, one from free traders and one from mercantilists. Both derive from differing intents, or hymns that 'a community sings to justify and make legitimate what it is doing'.[16] The first is individualist, where property rights provide the backbone of individual freedoms, which are best secured under limited government, com-

By this token, trade deficits are a sign of expanding national wealth and trade surpluses of national impoverishment.

petitive markets and pluralist politics. The second is communitarian, where relations between individuals are governed by consensus, a hierarchy is preserved and equality of result is sought.

Free traders have always argued that the reason for international trade in the first place is that countries differ in their natural endowments, their organization and their cultures. Relative prices of goods in one country before trade will differ from relative prices in another. Even when one country has an absolute advantage in the production of all goods for sale to another, it will benefit if it specializes and opens its markets to the exports from the other. In the last resort, the objective of international trade must be to import, since a country which imports also supplements its own deficiencies and enables its producers to specialize, thereby using their scarce resources more economically. By this token, trade deficits are a sign of expanding national wealth and trade surpluses of national impoverishment. This was the accusation levelled by Indian nationalists against the British Raj: India was running a trade surplus, and India's impoverishment was the result.

Mercantilists argue the reverse. The reason for international trade is for the national community to win preferential access to world markets, while keeping its own markets as closed as possible. As David Hume, the Scottish philosopher, argued, 'strong jealousy' prevails among nations 'with regard to the balance of trade and a fear that gold and silver may be leaving them'. Mercantilists accordingly measure success in terms of the build-up of reserves in corporate or national coffers, which may be used to buy markets abroad or as insurance against adverse international conditions. At home, their programme fosters a communitarian ideology, rooted in an ethno-history of the race and implemented through multiple public policies for procurement, standard-setting, taxation or labour markets which all give expression to a 'Buy National First' creed. So mercantilists and free traders agree that trade exists because countries differ, but mercantilists add that some are better than others, as measured in terms of results: trade surpluses in the last resort are a measure of superiority in organization, or even in race.

Public policies, financial systems and the adjustment process

Let us turn, then, to the variety of capitalist models on display after the end of the Cold War, ones developing countries are invited to learn from. The starting point must be the implicit Western model of an ideal state which informs much of the activities of the Bretton Woods institutions. It is very different from the practice of Western managerial capitalism, and leagues apart from Soviet communism. Whereas both Western managerial capitalism and Soviet communism are predicated on the practice of managerial authority in large organizations, the Bretton Woods institutions prescribe a limited domain for public policy coupled with free trade. According to this implicit model, minimum government is a vital complement to an open economy composed of small, family farms and firms which compete sharply on price. Their survival depends on specialization and on predictable business conditions. These are best secured by effective government policing of their local markets to prevent abuses, and by international free trade. Free trade binds the whole world in a web of trade relations, and requires close co-operation among governments to ensure that none cheats.

Even if this implicit Western model is more prescriptive than descriptive, it serves a purpose as setting world standards for government–business relations. Free trade and limited government are indispensable standards against which the actual behaviour of states and national economies may be measured. Invariably they fall short of the ideal, but without such a world standard governments and national economies would have to operate in a world which functioned according to their own self-centred norms. The rhetoric of limited government and free trade is the compliment that vice pays to virtue in order to maintain the benefits of an open world economy.

In effect, very different national financial and corporate systems have developed over time in advanced industrial states. As institutionalist economists point out, how the markets are structured, what values are embedded in the prevailing rules and which organizations develop within the range of prevailing incentives makes all the difference to outcomes. Economic policy within and between states is thus about different conceptions of politics, and distinct patterns of policy process.

This is particularly so of financial markets, which bond public authorities such as central banks, finance ministries and market regulators to financial institutions and the broad public of depositors and borrowers. A stable monetary regime is a prerequisite to an orderly and prosperous society, and the flow of funds through the markets is the most immediate form through which citizens transact with one another.

One prominent feature of financial markets is the way that large corporations, which provide up to four-fifths of value added and exports in advanced industrial countries, fund their activities. Corporate strategy is understood here as the link between the external capital market, populated by shareholders and financial institutions, and the internal process of corporations through which the organization's resources are allocated.[17] The corporate population of different states may therefore be structured along two dimensions, as illustrated in Figure 4.2: one dimension is the concentration of ownership, whether dispersed among a wide public or concentrated in the hands of a few institutions; the other is the degree of corporate concentration in terms of assets, sales and numbers employed.

The resulting matrix provides four models – the implicit model of the Bretton Woods institutions, and three distinct types: the Anglo-American shareholder system; the German or Japanese system of cross-shareholding; and the French statist model, which has many variants around the world.[18] We shall use Figure 4.2 here to portray different corporate governance and financial market systems, and revisit the matrix later when we look more closely at the link between national structures and corporate strategies.

Figure 4.2
MARKET COMPETITION, CORPORATE STRATEGY AND NATIONAL STRUCTURES

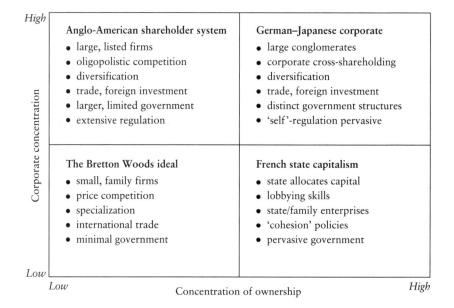

The Anglo-American shareholder system

Though both the US and Britain adopted their own specific responses to the depression of the 1930s, both followed similar lines of development, despite the 'socialist' rhetoric of postwar Britain and the 'capitalist' megaphone of the US. Managerial hierarchies ran large, publicly quoted and diversified corporations and predominated over shareholder interests until the sweeping changes in the tightly linked financial markets of New York, Chicago and London in the 1970s and 1980s. The revival of shareholder capitalism in both countries drew on common roots of political culture, favourable to co-ordination of preferences through markets and essentially individualist in inspiration. Just as the soul has a direct relation to God in the Protestant religion, so the individual is best equipped to calculate his or her own utility in the affairs of this world. Hierarchies must be reduced through legislation and market competition. Companies are a private entity, set up by investors for their own benefit. As principals, they hire managers as their agents to conduct the business with the interests of the shareholders permanently in mind. This means that managers should keep constant track of input costs, such as labour, raw materials or capital, and seek the most efficient use of state-of-the-art technologies or organizational practices to produce goods or services that provide value for the consumer at attractive prices.

Corporate financing is provided by short-term funds from commercial banks, but the major source of external funds for firms is the capital market. In the capital markets, shares of corporations are held by the public, either directly or through institutional vehicles, like funds managed by insurance companies, mutual funds and pension funds, and are actively traded. Corporate restructuring, involving the shrinking of the firm's assets or their shifting to alternative uses or locations,[19] is triggered by exploitation of a control premium between the existing market capitalization of a firm and that which an unaffiliated acquirer (whether an industrial company or an active financial investor) perceives and acts upon by initiating a takeover effort designed to unlock shareholder value through management changes. There is a high level of transparency and reliance on public information provided by auditors, with systemic surveillance by equity investors and research analysts. Concerns about unwanted takeover efforts prompt management to act in the interests of shareholders, many of whom tend to view their shares as put options, options to sell. The control structure of this essentially outsider-based system is confined mainly to arm's length financing, including takeovers and internal corporate restructuring, although investment banks may be active in giving strategic and financial advice and sometimes taking equity positions in (and occasionally control of) firms for their own accord.[20]

This Anglo-American system gives priority to the shareholder in the payment of dividends even when profits are down, and compensates him or her in the event of bankruptcy after other stakeholders have been paid. Its supporters rest their claim to the system's legitimacy on its providing the most efficient set of incentives for all participants in the market to maximize wealth. Hence, both the US and UK governments have sought to widen the shareholding public. A shareholder-driven corporate economy, underpinned by a shareholder democracy, ensures maximum participation by the voting public in the performance of corporations and in the material rewards in the form of distributed dividends.

Supporters also argue that free markets are the most compatible with political democracy as a system of limited government. If, for instance, financial markets are free to allocate savings to the most efficient rather than the most politically influential users of capital, then the returns for the savers will be higher than if some of them use their vote to extract rents from less remunerative, but politically determined investments. Labour market legislation in particular has to be supportive, so that labour forces may be shrunk or shifted in task or location with the minimum of friction. The model also assumes that the government will not prove a light touch for corporate lobbies seeking to avoid restructuring or takeover through access to the public purse, as a less demanding source of funds. Government's major tasks are to provide the regulatory and legal structure within which open capital markets may function and to supply a safety net for the unemployed, the infirm or the old. Not least, this Anglo-American approach assumes that the two rulers of the corporate roost are shareholders and customers: if other types of financial systems in world markets have different priorities, benefiting other interests, they will eventually be forced to adapt or to lose market share to rivals focusing firmly on consumer and shareholder interests. Managers and workers, in short, must sweat to earn their keep.

Publicly listed corporations in Anglo-American conditions are constantly under pressure to deliver satisfactory results to shareholders and customers. They have to achieve a competitive advantage in markets which are deliberately kept open to foreign competitors and to inward investors. Markets are deliberately kept open because government policy is predicated less on giving political advantage to national producers than on satisfying the demands of national shareholders and consumers. Other states tend to give much more support to national producers, giving an additional incentive for Anglo-American corporations to invest

The Anglo-American approach assumes that the two rulers of the corporate roost are shareholders and customers.

abroad. Foreign investment in the Anglo-American system is driven by the need to challenge competitors on their home turf, and to diversify the corporation's portfolio of assets away from over-dependence on the home market. In that way, shareholder value can be maximized, consumer needs met and managers can stay in business. Both US and UK corporations have worldwide reach.

The German–Japanese cross-shareholding system

The German and Japanese cross-shareholding systems hold significant institutional differences, but also a few important similarities. Both countries were late industrializers and promoted universal banks taking deposits and investing shares in order to accelerate industrial growth. Both fostered the development of large corporate conglomerates in private hands, and sought to reduce trade and financial dependence on foreign sources. Much of the foundation legislation of Germany's postwar financial system was laid in the 1930s, just as Japan's Ministry of Trade and Industry grew to prominence as a central force in Japan's state-corporate promotion of war industries. After 1945 both were initially fashioned by US policies in the Cold War. Anti-monopoly policies were put on hold, and growth was promoted in order to win over reluctant populations. The US imposed a separation of commercial and investment banking on Japan, while German universal banks were reconstituted alongside savings and communal banks serving local communities.

Managers were placed in the driving seat of corporate Germany and Japan, though family-run companies were able to flourish. Fears that unaccountable managers would abuse their powers were dealt with by appealing to the spirit of corporate or national loyalties, or through mechanisms to promote worker participation. The three pillars of Japan's managerial style have been listed as the granting of lifetime job security for employees in the major corporations, the promise of promotion by seniority and the organization of enterprise unions.[21] In Germany the internal relations of German firms were nationally regulated, notably through the obligatory membership of firms in trade associations which supplied them in return with services, and through detailed legislation with regard to participation of worker representations in works councils and on the boards of companies.[22] Corporate hierarchies managed markets, along with bureaucracies, political parties and, in Germany's case, trade unions. Labour was a fixed cost for managers, and capital markets were designed as a means to achieve a cohesive national polity, and to overcome the wounds of the wars, rather than as a means to create an efficient economy. The battle field for firms resided in product markets, which remained highly competitive, particularly in Germany, whose economy was smaller and much more open to competition from foreign suppliers than was Japan's.

Financial markets in both economies are highly regulated in order to ensure monetary stability and to protect depositors from bank failure. For much of the postwar period, companies relied on borrowing as the prime source of external financing alongside internally generated funds, and the cost of capital for firms was low. Germany in particular benefited from the expansion and prosperity of highly specialized medium-sized firms, run by their owner-managers. Savings were high, consumption was kept down and export surpluses mounted. In both Germany and Japan, large, diversified corporations also protected themselves against takeover threats in the share markets by dispersing shares among one another and among financial institutions. Shareholders thereby enjoy institutional representation on the boards of the companies whose shares they hold, and whose boards they share. In Germany employees are also represented, and act as additional allies with roots in the labour markets against hostile takeovers.

In both the German and Japanese financial systems of corporate control, it is the internal market to allocate resources within corporations that takes precedence over the demands of the external capital market. The shareholding public is invited by corporate managers to be patient and to hold shares in return for capital gains and collateral business in the long run as the firm expands, rather than to higher dividends now that could deprive management of the financial resources needed to invest in the firm. Financial disclosure tends to be relatively low as accounts are drawn up essentially to meet tax and reporting obligations rather than to inform a shareholding public. The portion of shares which float freely on the market is small, so that stock markets may be thin and volatile as investors (including foreigners) move in and out of shares. Thus, many of the market disciplinary functions performed by impersonal capital markets on companies must be generated by the insider elites of corporations – the managers.

Obviously, under such a system, managers prefer to deal with one another rather than be pestered by intrusive questions from the shareholders who advance them the funding for their operations in the first place. They seek out stable shareholders who are sufficiently patient to enable managers to recoup investments in the development of products and processes, and in their stable labour force. As banks are suspected of wanting even a modest flow of income from their lending exposures as market processes start to alter the financial system, the best condition for corporations with high fixed costs is to achieve self-financing by building market share. If bank/industrial cross-holdings are pervasive, banks in any event are most comfortable when the corporations in which they hold stakes rely mainly on their own resources.

The bank/industrial cross-holding system complements close domestically based supplier–customer relationships, with dependability and co-operation often dominating price as business criteria. The financial system as a whole must be prepared to deal with the consequences of large trade surpluses, which flow from joint corporate interest in market shares. Domestic inflationary pressures have to be kept down through rapid recycling of funds earned from exports. This entails building up portfolio investments in other markets around the world. Revaluations of the currency from exports and investment income abroad may be delayed by further external portfolio investments, as well as by corporate direct investments abroad, as domestic production costs continue to rise relative to other locations around the world. The other motivation for foreign direct investment is to challenge competitors on their home turf.

The central paradox of such a bank/industrial cross-holding system is that it seeks to restrict foreign market access and ownership, while requiring open markets for exports and for corporate assets in other countries. In the 1950s Japan insisted on excluding US or European investors from production within the national market – in stark contrast to Germany, which was a major target for investment by US corporations. Instead, US and European companies licensed technologies to Japanese corporations, for which they earned royalty payments. But in the 1970s Japan's corporations, exporting from their home base, challenged US and European corporations on world markets. We shall return to this crucial development in Chapter 7. But both Germany and Japan have received by far the smallest proportion of inward direct investment of major industrialized countries in the 1980s and 1990s. Not least, corporations become detached from banks as their external sources of funds on world markets grow, while regulatory segmentation within the financial system breaks down as financial institutions compete across boundaries for new clients. They become world corporate citizens, like their Anglo-American brethren.

The state-led financial market system

France is the reference-point for the model of top–down development through a state-led financial market system.[23] In terms of precedence, though, the title should arguably be awarded to Italy or to Turkey. Typically, the state-led model of industrialization appealed to countries whose agriculture was backward, where small business enterprises predominated and larger corporations were few and far between. Often, as in Spain or Latin America, they were foreign owned. It was Mussolini's state corporatist arrangements that Vargas sought to duplicate in his New State in Brazil, while Ataturk imported Italy's criminal justice system to Turkey, and instituted a state capitalism centred on the creation of government-run manufacturing enterprises.

Turkey's first five-year industrialization plan (1934–8) provided for the establishment of a series of industrial plants, designed to reduce Turkey's needs for imported consumer and intermediate goods, using domestic raw materials. State agencies were to be responsible for financing, constructing and managing these plants. To finance and control the expanding state industrial sector, two new development banks were established. By the 1940s, through its ministries, independent agencies and subsidiaries of its wholly owned banks, the government had become the nation's major industrial producer, largest employer and leading exporter.[24] Vargas pursued a similar path of import-substitution industrialization (ISI). Incentives were created to establish domestic industries that would substitute for imports. The state's power to guide the country's industrialization was extended through the nationalization of key sectors and natural resources.

France, like India, sought to find some 'third way' after the war between US capitalism and the Soviet system. Both sought to transform a backward, peasant economy; both extended the state's regulatory reach over private enterprises; both created planning commissions to co-ordinate public sector investment programmes through five-year plans;[25] both focused their plans on basic inputs, such as steel and fuel, much along the lines of the Soviet Union. Both hitched their financial systems to their goals of industrialization. In France the Ministry of Finance became the dominant focus for savers and borrowers as it regulated the capital market directly. Deposit-taking institutions with surplus funds placed them in the capital markets, and they were taken up by public-sector institutions which lent them to specific industries, such as housing, agriculture and nuclear energy, or used them for regional investment. Both lending and borrowing institutions fell under the tutelage of the Ministry of Finance, which formally drew up investment priorities through elaborate consultations with trade associations recorded in 'The Plan', through negotiations with the Ministry of Industry or in response to requests filtered through the political parties. Public officials in the Finance Ministry enjoyed prestige conveyed by their position in the state hierarchy, and because of the value of their contacts across the extensive state corporate sector to those seeking access to it.

Over time, the French state-led financial system ran into difficulties. It promoted larger corporations along with inflationary growth, which were compensated by regular devaluations of the franc. As resources of personnel and time in the Finance Ministry were scarce, such a state-centred administrative mechanism at the heart of the financial system promoted a queue. Organizations with close contacts and claims on the loyalties of public officials, such as state-controlled economic enterprises or large private firms, were served first. Small and medium-sized firms were squeezed aside, so their representatives joined one or another of the political armies contending for privileged access to the state's resources through elections. The regular cycle of local, regional and national elections thus also became a series of contests between competing producer coalitions for a silver key to public finance. This political process of distributing credit to specific end-users ran against the government's proclaimed objectives in the 1970s to 'disinflate' the economy to match German price stability. The whole edifice ground to a near halt when, in 1981, the new Mitterrand administration extended the public sector just as the external debt exploded and domestic savings shrank. France's financial market reforms of 1984–8 were introduced in order to promote Paris as an international centre, and above all to lower the cost of government financing.

The whole edifice ground to a near halt when, in 1981, the new Mitterrand administration extended the public sector just as the external debt exploded.

A state-led financial system features other characteristics as well. Financial resources are not alone in flowing through the hands of public officials. Patronage flows too, in the form of appointments to the management and boards of state enterprises or to large private enterprises in receipt of various state benefits. Public officials enter into competition among themselves, through their own organizations and to a lesser extent through their proclamations of party political fealty. Their legitimacy derives from a claim to act in the public interest, expressed in the extension of rights for employees within the public domain. Institutions whose resources they deploy directly or indirectly expand their stakes in business enterprises, extending further the field open to public patronage in the pursuit of private promotion. Corporate cross-shareholdings centre around state financial institutions.

Indeed, a cynic could argue that such a state-led system has a vested interest in nationalizing private enterprise in order to expand the reach of public officials, and then privatizing the assets in exchange for comfortable positions in the management or on the boards of companies.

Ownership of these corporations is less significant than the fact that they remain on the career circuit, and that they stay within the bounds of what is in effect a political market for economic control. Such a political market extends throughout the multiple levels of government, as local mayors become businessmen and bankers for their local communities through resources obtained through the political process. Ultimately, the state can lose its status as acting in the public interest, and merges into the surrounding maze of non-transparent political markets. The stench of corruption creeps under the doors and floats through the windows of the most exquisitely perfumed salons, and the ruling oligarchy's legitimacy becomes more, not less, difficult to defend.

Because the state-led financial system is prone to public deficit, inflation and devaluations, it cannot do without inward direct investment by corporations hailing from other countries. Foreign inward investment provides jobs, new technologies and products, as well as much needed export revenues. But it also moderates the state's ability to 'plan' the allocation of resources, though the state is not entirely powerless. France, Brazil and India have all negotiated the terms of access of foreign corporations to their nuclear or military industrial sectors. A more significant consideration is that national corporations are challenged by foreign competitors on their own home market, and therefore have to take moves to challenge them on their home markets. But they can become viable partners or investors abroad only if they distance themselves from their state tutor, and begin issuing shares to a national or an international public. In the longer term they too join their foreign corporate brothers and sisters as world citizens on the world market stage.

Contrast and conclusion

Advanced industrial states tend to be inward-oriented in their policy processes, but incorporated into an integrated world political and market system. Internal differences between states have become more evident particularly as they affect the operations of business. Admirers of Germany and Japan point to the extraordinary success in reconstruction after the wars, their social cohesion, the priority given to investment and saving over consumption and imports, their corporate structures which allow for the development of products and processes, and their world market shares measured in the size of their trade surpluses. In the early 1990s institutionalists, culturalists and structuralists were confident in arguing the superiority of the nationally rooted German and Japanese systems over the individualism and cosmopolitanism of the Anglo-American model. France was keen to adopt its own very peculiar version of what its elites considered to be 'the German model'.

At the end of the decade, the academic *Begleitmusik* was less confident. Both Germany and Japan are mired in difficulties. Their populations are ageing fast. Government finances are in disarray. Unemployment rates are disturbingly high. Institutional shareholders have failed to play their allotted role as monitors of business performances. Political institutions have failed to provide policies adequate to the task of sustaining national cohesion and economic efficiency. Major German and Japanese corporations have managed to detach themselves from their national roots, and are becoming citizens of the world polity and markets. Furthermore, the permanent improvements in technologies, and their diffusion to lower wage countries, threaten to reduce their previous advantages in product quality, in innovations and above all in creating polyvalent workforces.

By contrast, admirers of the Anglo-American financial systems of corporate control were down at heel in the early 1990s and riding on a crest of optimism bordering on arrogance in the late 1990s. Share ownership continues to widen, facilitating political deals in Washington DC or London on the importance of keeping low marginal tax rates, and flexible labour, financial, and – in the US case – housing markets. Financial institutions manage the shares of millions, and quickly relocate them if corporate performances are below expectations. The system has generated continuous growth rates in productivity, along with new jobs – many of them in technology-intensive service sectors. Both countries enjoy a high proportion of their total manufacturing exports in high-technology goods. An open market for corporate assets has enabled conglomerates, built up in previous merger booms, to be unwound, reducing the number of layers in corporate hierarchies, and allowing companies to sharpen the focus of their activities.

But there are also shadows. Managers reward themselves bonuses and stock options to compensate for the risks of being responsible for corporations whose share prices may fall, making them an easy target for a corporate raider. They thereby join the ranks of shareholders, and are in a privileged position to extract dividends as a priority from profits. Non-shareholding wage earners see their total yearly earnings stagnate, as world competition keeps a lid on wage rises. Hence, the gap between wages and productivity rises is redistributed more than ever in the form of dividends. Flamboyant life-styles of managers on ego trips associated with very large pay packets and bonuses reinforce public prejudices that capitalism serves primarily the interests of 'fat cats'. Giving priority to the dividend makes managers risk-averse, prone to cut research budgets, and prefer to seek growth primarily through acquisition rather than organically.

Flamboyant life-styles of managers on ego trips reinforce public prejudices that capitalism serves primarily the interests of 'fat cats'.

The French state-centred system occupies a halfway house between the two, and is much closer in many respects to less wealthy countries, which have started to move away from the model of import substitution. The exit path from communist party-states is a different and unprecedented story, but has some features analogous to all three types. French financial reforms in the mid-1980s were modelled on those of the US, as indeed was the case in the UK and still is in many developing countries which are seeking to strengthen their regulatory agencies. But privatization of state corporations has been informed by an aspiration to create cross-shareholding groups on the German or Japanese model. The result, as in many developed countries, has been to create major industrial–banking–insurance power centres, more loosely tied to the state and more open to some of, but not all, the exigencies of global financial investors.

Like France, countries exiting from party-state planning or import-substitution economies occupy this unstable halfway house between nationally embedded capitalisms and a more footloose, global capitalism. In the post-1945 world the many newly independent states could choose between various models of state 'capitalism' and 'communism', or their own version of the Third Way between the two – a modern version of the knightly quest for the Holy Grail.

In the post-1990 world the choice is between two forms of capitalism, one predicated on national managerial privilege, associated with Germany and Japan, and the other justified by ultimate shareholder control over 'fat cats', which denigrators and proponents alike identify with the UK and the US. Let us now broach this central question for the future of developing countries in the next chapter.

Notes

1 Robert Skidelsky, 'The Decline of Keynesian Politics', in Colin Crouch (ed), *State and Economy in Contemporary Capitalism*, London, Croom Helm, 1979, p. 60.

2 G. Almond and G. Powell, *Comparative Politics: A Developmental Approach*, Boston, Little Brown, 1966.

3 See Peter Katzenstein (ed), *Between Power and Plenty: Foreign Economic Policies of Advanced International States*, Madison, WI, University of Wisconsin Press, 1978.

4 Sam Brittan, *Capitalism with a Human Face*, Cheltenham, Edward Elgar, 1995.

5 Douglas C. North, *Institutions, Institutional Change and Economic Performance, Political Economy of Institutions and Decisions*, Cambridge University Press, 1991, p. 109.

6 Colin Crouch and Wolfgang Streeck, *Political Economy of Modern Capitalism. Mapping Convergence and Diversity*, London, Sage, 1997.

7 Oliver E. Williamson, *Markets and Hierarchies: Analysis and Anti-trust Implications*, New York, Free Press, 1975.

8 Charles Hampden-Turner and Fons Trompenaar, *The Seven Cultures of Capitalism*, London, Piatkus, 1995.

9 See Michel Albert, *Capitalisme Contre Capitalisme*, Paris, Seuil, 1991; Hans-Peter Martin and Harald Schumann, *Die Globalisierungsfalle: Der Angriff auf Demokratie und Wohlstand*, Hamburg, Rowohlt, 1996; Y. Suzuki, *The Rapid Advance of the Japanese Economy*, Tokyo, NTT, 1991. Also, Lester Thurow, *Head to Head: The Coming Economic Battle Among Japan, Europe, and America*, New York, William Morrow, 1992.

10 Michael Porter, *The Competitive Advantage of Nations*, London, Macmillan, 1990.

11 Yves Mény and Jean-Claude Thoenig, *Politiques Publiques*, Paris, Presses Universitaires de France, 1989, pp. 129–58.

12 Bertrand de Jouvenel, *Sovereignty: An Inquiry into the Political Good*, Chicago; University of Chicago Press, 1957.

13 Anthony Smith, *National Identity*, Middlesex, Penguin, 1991.

14 Christopher A. Bartlett and Sumantra Ghoshal, *Managing Across Frontiers: The Transnational Solution*, Boston, Harvard Business School, 1989.

15 Jean-Jacques Rosa, *L'Erreur Européenne*, Paris, Grasset, 1998.

16 George Lodge and Ezra Vogel, *Ideology and Competitiveness: An Analysis of Nine Countries*, Boston, Harvard Business School, 1987.

17 See Michael Porter, 'Capital Disadvantage: America's Failing Capital Investment System', *Harvard Business Review*, September–October 1992.

18 See Jonathan Story and Ingo Walter, *Political Economy of Financial Integration in Europe: The Battle of the Systems*, Manchester University Press/MIT, 1998.

19 See Henry Ergas, 'Does Technology Matter?', Centre for European Policy Studies, Brussels, 1986.

20 T. N. Rybczynski, 'Corporate Restructuring', *National Westminster Bank Review*, August 1989.

21 James C. Abegglen and George Stalk, *Kaisha, the Japanese Corporation*, New York, Basic Books, 1985.

22 Wolfgang Streeck, 'German Capitalism: Does it Exist? Can it Survive?', in Crouch and Streeck, op. cit. note 6.

23 John Zysman, *Governments, Markets and Growth: Financial Systems and Policies of Industrial Change*, Oxford, Martin Robertson, 1983.

24 William Hale, *The Political and Economic Development of Modern Turkey*, London, Croom Helm, 1981.

25 Fancine R. Frankel, *India's Political Economy, 1947–1977*, Princeton University Press, 1978.

Chapter 5

TRANSITIONS AND THE DRIVERS OF CHANGE

In the 1990s, market democracy reigns supreme, with no challenger in sight, and that it will enlarge its geographical area of influence seems self-evident. Does this mean, as the One Worlders and market cosmopolitans contend, that the future of the world is 'common marketization'? The Zeitgeist – the dominant world view – definitely suggests so. In this chapter let us first look closer at how changes in political regimes occur. That is where the problems begin. Such changes never occur in isolation. We can unravel the complexity inherent in regime changes by applying an analytical framework for the global business environment. Whereas market factors point to the spread of Western formulas of governance, diplomacy, geopolitics and, in particular, the juxtaposition in time of cultures which have developed along different trajectories provide a less monochrome picture of the world's future. Ancestral voices find the tools of modernity particularly congenial to broadcasting their particularistic messages of salvation and vengeance.

The Zeitgeist of the century's end

The last decades of the twentieth century have not been kind to dictators.[1] In 1975, 68 per cent of the 140 states in the world were dictatorships of one kind or another. Twenty years later only 28 per cent of the 190 states in the world were so governed. The turn away from strong-arm rule around the world is generally held to date from 1974–5, when the regimes in Portugal and Greece were overthrown and General Franco finally expired from old age. King Juan Carlos began immediately with the sophisticated political manoeuvring which made Spain the model on managing transition out of dictatorship to constitutional governance, the rule of law rather than of men, and democratic multi-party elections. The contagion of transition spread to Latin America, to the Asia-Pacific, then into the party-states of Europe and to Africa. Democratization was accompanied by a general shift from state-led growthmanship to more market-oriented policies, as dictators left behind them economies wracked by inflation, debt, pollution and poverty.[2]

There are no Western contestants left to challenge constitutional democracy, unlike the 1930s when a number of alternative regime formulas were on offer. Fascism and national socialism succumbed to defeat, and communism by Brezhnev's time was clinically dead. The Catholic Church has lined up with the Protestant churches in support of democratization:[3] since his election in 1979, Pope John Paul II has carried the crusade for freedom first to Poland, and then to Latin America, the Philippines and Korea. Military regimes around the world have helped inoculate the left against dictatorships. In Africa strong men and one-party states have been a disaster. Yugoslavia's experiment in worker management unravelled under pressure from demands of Western creditors into a wrangle between party leaders to retain their political jurisdictions, and then deteriorated into ethnic massacre when the party-states disintegrated.[4]

Nor is there any challenger for the three Western but competing variants of 'market democracy', in stark contrast to seventy years before, when the financial disaster of 1929–31 undermined the legitimacy of capitalism, leading to a general sidelining of securities markets in the name of market failure. But decades of government failures in public policy followed. As the Indian economist Deepak Lal wrote in the 1980s, 'many developing countries are closer in their official workings to the rapacious and inefficient nation-states of the seventeenth or eighteenth century Europe, governed as much for the personal aggrandizement of their rulers as for the welfare of the ruled'.[5] The conclusion is that the necessary, but not sufficient, institutional arrangement to generate the efficient allocation of resources is competitive markets. Accountability of regulators and transparency of markets are credible only under democratically elected governments.

Neither theocracies nor Asian developmental authoritarianism are likely candidates for a world role. Theocracies claim to substitute the law of God for the law of man. In fact, men interpret the law of God according to their own lights, and erect arbitrary rule in His name. Pakistan, the first Islamic republic, has swung from parliamentary government to military *coups d'état*, martial law and long periods of states of emergency. Three constitutions have come and gone, as the armed forces, *ulemas* and political parties swing in and out of the corridors of power. Ayatollah Khomeini's Iran failed to deliver a new Islamic man, untempted by Western ways, and now faces a long journey down the road to compromise and disillusion. Nearly two decades after deposing the Shah, the mullahs live under the shadow of Lord Acton's dictum that 'power corrupts, and absolute power corrupts absolutely'.

Khomeini's Iran failed to deliver a new Islamic man and now faces a long journey down the road to compromise and disillusion.

The Asian developmental state, exemplified in Taiwan, attracts wider acclaim as having a demonstrated ability to drag populations out of poverty in the space of a generation.[6] But the virtues required of its leaders are those of an elite, chosen through a rigorous process of selection. They are not servants of the electorate's whims, in the manner of a pluralist democracy, so much as masters of the markets. They subordinate their private passions to the public interest. Honour rather than riches is their reward. They distribute agricultural land in order to ensure an equal dispersion of wealth. They direct the flow of funds, and subordinate financial capital to the requirements of industrial capital. They foster foreign competition in the domestic economy through the reward of scarce foreign exchange to importers who re-export. They promote a national capacity to absorb and develop technologies, and emphasize capital accumulation as the principal engine for growth. Such elites are rare.

Why the trend to market democracy?

Prevalent ideas about modernization are more mundane. They assume that greed and self-interest, not service in some higher cause, motivate people. Integration of states into the world economy, it is claimed, brings democratization in the wake of economic development.[7] The more 'well-to-do' a nation is, the more democratic it is likely to be.[8] The assertion is a heady mixture of description, prediction and pre-scription. It describes the fact that most wealthy states have democra-tic forms of government. It predicts that a growing 'middle class', higher levels of education and greater access to communications create a predisposition around the world to embrace Western ways and val-ues. And it prescribes policy to win over 'distant lands' to Western ways of governance. In essence, it states that societies develop political insti-tutions which correspond to their particular level of social and eco-nomic progress. The world, in this vision, is conceived as a pilgrimage from vice (tradition) to virtue (Western modernity).

Political change, this line of thinking continues, is driven by eco-nomics. Development out of agriculture to an industry-based economy dilutes the political clout of landowners and fosters organized business and urban working classes. New political values evolve as the classes mobilize in political organizations and coalitions, and bring a new type of demand to bear on the political system. But it does not follow that there is only one passage to modernity, and only one (Western) desti-nation. The passage to modernization, Marxists have argued, is con-tingent on the particular relations between classes – peasantry, landowners, urban bourgeoisie – and the state, and may end in democ-racy, fascism or communism.[9] Put another way, rapid economic growth is not a stabilizing factor but a sure-fire prescription for political insta-bility.[10] Too rapid social and economic changes erode traditional soli-darities, widen wealth gaps, multiply sources of dissatisfaction and promote political decay.[11]

The assertion that economics drives political change is weakened by the lack of an evident link between economic conditions and the moti-vations of masses of people. Enter group psychology. 'Why men rebel', Ted Gurr argues,[12] is because they are angry, and ready to use political violence. They are angry because economic development fosters expectations which cannot be met under the present political dispen-sation. Frustrations intensify and people organize collectively to nar-row the gap between what they experience and what they have been led to expect. The flaw here is that group psychology does not explain how collective anger is channelled to effective political purpose. *A prerequisite to rebellion is that rebel leaders mobilize the discontented into a collective, organized force able to take advantage of the political opportunities on offer.* In short, it is opposition elites who organize discontent rather than discontents that mobilize people.

The economics-drives-politics argument thus transmutes into an observation of the primacy of politics. Economic development triggers the action of competing elites and stimulates expectations for a better life.[13] What matters is perceptions of the politics of economic policy and the public's judgement about the performance of the political economy: it is not the economy itself. Governing elites may differ about appropriate policy, while significant sections of the population judge performance of the political economy in the light of their beliefs about the legitimacy of the regime. Legitimacy refers to the state of mind of citizens with respect to the exercise of authority by public officials in the name of the state. It answers to the question asked of governors: 'By what right do you rule?' Some respond, 'I govern by consent', and others state: 'I govern by coercion.' Most governors mix the two, and seek to strengthen consent by delivering on performance.

Promising rapid growth to buy consent of populations is a well-tested recipe. The problem is that the economy is cyclical, as bad times follow good. Good economic times generate support for regimes, but bad times generate contending factions inside and outside the regime. Some groups withdraw their support; rural and urban classes mobilize, and the ruling coalition divides over how to deal with the resulting distributive conflicts.[14] This prompts heated debates about what to do: who should take responsibility, why should they do what they do, what objectives to pursue in which order of priority, which policy instruments to use and who is to be advantaged or disadvantaged. Interests which have gained from past policies will be well placed through their contacts in the regime to plead their case; potential beneficiaries from policy change are uncertain what the future holds.

How institutions help to process these conflicts has much to do with the regime's ability to survive. As Douglas North has written, 'the polity specifies and enforces the property rights of the economic marketplace, and the characteristics of the political market are the essen-

The electorate has the prospect of voting the present rascals out of power and substituting another dispensable bunch of rascals.

tial key to understanding the imperfections of the market'.[15] Different polities, it follows, will specify different property rights, some leaning to inequality in their distribution and others to greater equality. Dictatorships, by definition, are rule of the few, exclusive of the many, so tend to foster inequalities. The many excluded from policy may be satisfied as long as a rising tide of prosperity lifts everyone. Politicians in democracies are also eager to be associated with prosperity, but if a balance of payments crisis strikes or inflation runs out of control the electorate has the prospect of voting the present rascals out of power and substituting another dispensable bunch of rascals. The political regime endures.

In dictatorships downturns in economic performance strike at the substance of the regime. They promise growth but they deliver penury, is the cry. Opponents organize somehow, and economic policy becomes a stake in a wider political struggle between governing and opposition elites, both in competition for the loyalty of the indifferent many as to who has the most credible economic programme. If the belief takes hold in the public that alternative policies are available that promise to narrow the gap between public expectations and performance, calculations about the political economy of legitimacy and consent or coercion change dramatically.[16] Problems which seem without solution in the existing regime appear eminently soluble in a different regime.

The interactions between elites in search of legitimacy and an opposition mobilized in the name of an alternative programme to meet the gap between expectations and performance are illustrated in Figure 5.1. The economy has been launched on a path of development; this changes the social structure and the 'mode of production' as well as yielding a more educated public. Public expectations change about what constitutes good governance, and the belief takes hold in the public that alternative policies to those supplied by the regime are available. Rumours of public discontent and fears about the activities of agitators penetrate the inner citadels of power, where governing elites are locked in discussions about which alternative policies to pursue. Discussions may or may not split the regime over the policy initiatives to take. This depends on the degree of popular mobilization and the governing elites' perceptions of the threat to their continuing in power.[17]

Figure 5.1 presents three pairs of stylized situations involving relations between the governing elite and the leaders of a mobilized public. The first may end in blood, the second in bargains and the third in barter.

Figure 5.1
RELATIONS BETWEEN STATE ELITE AND LEADERS OF A
MOBILIZED PUBLIC

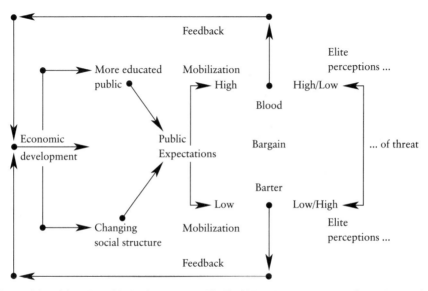

Source: Adapted from Samuel P. Huntington (1991) *The Third Wave: Democratization in the Late Twentieth Century*, University of Oklahoma Press.

1 The most confrontational situation is where the population is highly mobilized and the governing elites share the perception that the threat to their governance is high. This is what occurred in China, when the party-state cracked down on the students demonstrating for political freedoms in Tiananmen Square in May–June 1989. By this show of strength, the party-state illustrated its determination not to follow Gorbachev's example. As Deng Xiaoping repeatedly stated, economic reforms required for China's modernization could be implemented only by maintaining the party-state as the guarantor of China's unity.

2 The combination of high popular mobilization, and a low threat perception by elites is more likely to occur when governing elites share many of the concerns and objectives of the opposition leaders. The conservative groups who ushered Hitler and the National Socialists into office in January 1933 shared many National Socialist views about the deficiencies of the Weimar Republic and the communist threat. Similarly, business interests in Brazil, which had backed the military dictatorship, came round in the late 1970s and 1980s to back opposition demands for democracy as likely to ensure more competent economic governance. Hungarian regime and opposition elites negotiated the transition in the years 1987–90 on the same grounds.

3 Bargains are likely to be struck by a divided governing elite, with generally moderate views about the threat posed by the leaders of the mobilized public, who also have low expectations and are divided. This describes the situation in Brazil, Spain, Chile and Korea in their transitions to democracy in the 1970s and 1980s, when core constituencies in the regime came to consider that the authoritarian regime had outlived its usefulness, and that they could do better in a democracy. In all cases, key business interests came round to the view that the dictatorship was no longer indispensable.

4 Bargains are also likely to be struck when governing elite perceptions are divided but moderate about the threat, as in 3 above, and the opposition is well organized and has high expectations. This in effect turned out to describe the transition in South Africa: the escalating costs of administering the policies of apartheid were aggravated by the Western trade and investment embargoes introduced in 1986. Afrikaner and South African business leaders opened negotiations in Dakar with the African National Congress, and in 1989 Prime Minister de Klerk announced vaguely defined plans to 'create a new South Africa within the next five years'.[18]

5 A public which has low mobilization and is poorly organized should not scare a confident governing elite. Rather, a confident governing elite takes action to buy back the support of a significant portion of the public through modest concessions, attractive kickbacks, or through co-option of leaders. The Franco regime, for instance, was sufficiently well entrenched in the early 1960s to ride out the recession fol-

lowing the introduction of a stabilization plan under the aegis of the Bretton Woods institutions. Controls on the press were eased, elections to the state syndicates were opened to militants with known communist party orientations, and business was kept sweet on a promised diet of growth and stability. The Chilean and Korean dictatorships were able to ride out the deep recessions of the early 1980s in similar fashion.

6 A governing elite with low confidence may take fright at the mobilization of opposition, however low its expectations and its organization. Policy failure is deadly for governing elites who are unsure of their bases of support. Defeat unhinged the Spanish monarchy in the 1898 war with the United States, dethroned the Hohenzollern and Hapsburg monarchies in 1918, and brought Mussolini's fascist regime to a bloody end in 1945. Military failures hastened the demise of the dictatorships in Portugal in April 1974, in Argentina in 1982, and in the Soviet Union in 1989. Equally, dictatorships are particularly vulnerable to economic failure. From 1945 to 1988, the probability that a non-democratic regime would survive three consecutive years of negative growth was 33 per cent, whereas the probability that a democratic regime would survive the three years was 73 per cent.[19]

The novelty in the 1980s was not that dictatorships fell when economic performance deteriorated, so much as the wave of new democracies in Latin America and then in Central and Eastern Europe survived deep recessions. This could not be ascribed just to the learning process under military dictatorships of erstwhile radicals or the failures of dictatorships *Political transitions in one country are never a purely domestic affair.* to deliver on their promises of law, order and prosperity. It was also to do with the profound changes in the world economy, the end of the Cold War, and the removal by the Great Powers of their political vetoes over the domestic politics of former dependent states. The end of the Cold War was heralded by a move away from state-led inward-oriented development to an emphasis on the market, on privatization and greater openness to trade and foreign investment. Political transitions in one country are never a purely domestic affair.

An analytical framework for business in world markets

Regime changes or revolutions are complex events. They are complex because they occur in states, and they have many causes and multiple dimensions, as illustrated in Figure 5.2. The four categories of causes – economic structures and transactions, driven by the constant stream of technological innovations; cultural values and ideas; diplomatic relations between states; geopolitical structures and relations of dependency – are material representations of the four ideas presented in Chapter 2. The multiple dimensions are those of global markets and politics, the state's policy process, industrial competition and the firm. Juxtaposition of the four categories and four dimensions provides a framework for analyzing the environment of international business, in all circumstances.

The four categories are at work in all dimensions. For instance, economic structure and transactions between the relevant units may be analyzed in terms of global markets and politics, as well as within the territory of the state, or in the context of the industrial sector. The firm is influenced by all three dimensions. Furthermore, developments within any of the dimensions or categories interact across the whole web of relationships. Not least, Figure 5.2 shows the arrows from the four categories pointing both ways, signifying that the four dimensions continually interact, and that discretion may be exercised by players on all dimensions. State or corporate policies are devised by human beings, with their own resources and capabilities to shape in part the world that they live in. Corporations are placed centre stage, and will be dealt with in Chapters 7 and 8. Here, we shall review the categories as they affect the policy process of states caught up in changes of regime.

Economic structures and transactions

International economic relations between one state and world markets may be traced through flows of goods and services, investments and capital movements. Governments seek to macro- and micro-manage their economies through their array of policy instruments, public policies and related policy communities. The key medium is the financial system, which may be deployed to channel savings to investment through gov-

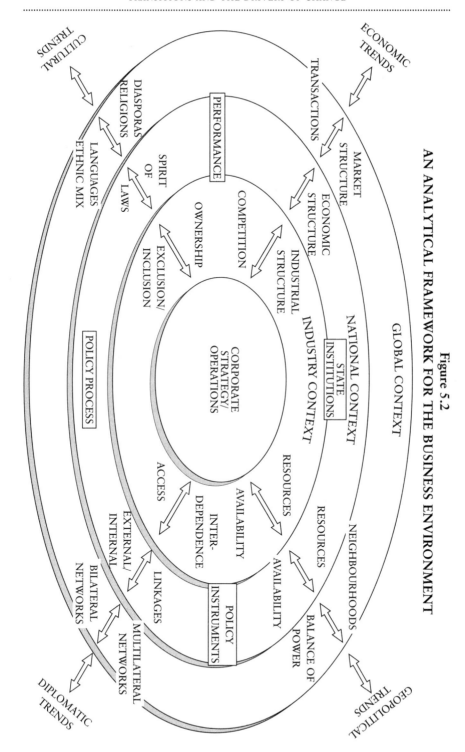

Figure 5.2
AN ANALYTICAL FRAMEWORK FOR THE BUSINESS ENVIRONMENT

ernment fiat, via market mechanisms of supply and demand, or through a combination of both. Government taxation and spending policies influence the level of demand, interest rates and capital outlays in the economy as a whole. Relative prices for goods and services within the national economy relate to relative prices on world markets through the balance of payments, and the foreign exchange rate of the national currency with regard to other currencies trading on world markets.

International economic relations also involve relations between states, corporations and markets, and may be presented in triangular form:[20]

1 They may be affected by state–state relations, which condition access to markets through political negotiations, and exert a significant impact on business conditions. Here, relational power refers to a situation where country A seeks to make country B do what it would not otherwise do. The US Treasury, for instance, organized the $40 billion bail-out for Mexico in early 1995, after the peso's collapse, and in essence dictated the terms of Mexico's adjustment programme.

2 Technological changes in production systems and markets that straddle political frontiers will affect business conditions elsewhere. Developments in the market of one state may have a direct bearing on corporate operations in the markets of other states. The break-up of AT&T in 1984 challenged governments around the world to transform their own infrastructure, or be left behind in the race to convert their territory into an attractive production platform by the world's corporations. It prompted a surge of new technologies and underpinned the development of world financial markets.

3 Initiatives by states in the public policies of their own markets may alter conditions of market access for corporations, and thereby for business in the markets of other states. Western pharmaceutical companies facing cash-strapped government health services and more competition across frontiers react through accelerating research and development programmes in the rush to bring new products to market worldwide.

Typically, the starting point for governments in Turkey, Brazil or India in moving to outward-oriented export policies has been to be a 'megaforce'[21] in the markets, originally to reduce dependency on foreign suppliers, to build up local productive capabilities or to develop a national technological base. They controlled financial flows, issued licences, deployed procurement, promoted labour 'aristocracies', kept high tariffs or quotas, and regulated foreign exchange. They supervised competition in domestic markets among state enterprises, large private businesses, local firms and multinationals. The informal business sector developed alongside. Governments controlled barriers to market entry, sought to promote product substitutes, and distributed benefits from supplier or buyer bargaining power this way or that. But the more such political markets developed, the greater was the volume of political transactions. The state became a centre for redistributing wealth to insiders.

Operating in such markets is time consuming, and not always rewarding. Managers of the world's major corporations, with the structural power to decide what is produced, by whom, how and in what conditions, turned away in the 1980s from markets in the Middle East and in Latin America to invest in the US and the EU. Japanese corporations proved a partial exception in that the yen's sharp revaluation against the dollar in 1985 prompted them to redeploy their lower value-added activities away from their high-cost home base to Thailand, Indonesia or Malaysia. But even they placed the bulk of their overseas investments in the main rich-country markets. In the early 1990s Cold War restrictions on technology flows were lifted, and Western countries' restrictions on capital flows ended. In the following six years, as many foreign direct investments were undertaken on a yearly basis as in the four years prior to the end of the Cold War.

This shift to invest in 'emerging markets' coincided with new-found enthusiasm among developing countries to get a slice of the value added chain in the activities of the world's leading corporations. Inward investment had demonstrably fostered the fortunes of Malaysia and Indonesia, both of whose governments rolled out the red carpet for foreign investors after the collapse in oil and raw material prices in the mid-1980s. East Asian shares in world manufacturing exports shot up, along with growth rates and living standards. Not surprisingly, the East Asian 'growth model' attracted widespread interest around the world in the 1990s among the many countries exiting from import substitution.

As the World Bank argued (with some support from the Development Bank of Japan):

> the body of East Asian evidence points to the dominant contribution of stable and competitive economic policies to the unleashing of private entrepreneurship. More often than not, the key to the policymaking process was the positive role of government in charting a development course, creating a longer-term vision shared among key participants, and fashioning an institutional framework for nonideological and effective policy implementation.[22]

In the 1990s developing countries too were eager to attract capital to boost their capital markets and to finance their external deficits. This meant reforming their financial systems in order to meet investors' demands for liquidity, or for transparent information about local opportunities. Whether or not they were far advanced in reform, the markets often formed a favourable view of their declared intentions and rushed to buy assets in the local currency. The frequent result was a local boom fuelled by cheap credit, a surge in real estate prices, an appreciation of the exchange rate and a widening deficit on external accounts. It took little urging, as Mexico discovered in the winter of 1994, and Thailand and Indonesia experienced in 1997–8, for fleet-footed institutions to sell out and move into alternative investments. But they left behind them a devalued currency, and a government in disrepute, facing bankruptcies and rising unemployment.

The exponential development of wholesale capital markets, under indirect management of the Western powers, held far-reaching implications for states which ran into financial difficulties and had to turn to the Bretton Woods institutions, or to the treasuries and finance ministries of the major powers. Debt relief always came with conditions attached:[23]

- 'No funds without regime change' was one slogan. Following the precedent set in the Germany-led credit to Portugal in 1975, and the US Treasury nod in favour of the 1976 Kingdom of Spain $1 billion credit, financial institutions attached *de facto* human rights and democracy conditions to their lending practices in Poland, South Africa and the Philippines.
- 'No funds without structural adjustment' was the other slogan. Fol-

lowing the tightening of interest rates by the Federal Reserve in October 1979, bank lending to Eastern Europe, Turkey, Africa and Latin American states dried up. IMF and World Bank teams duly circumvented the globe in the 1980s dispensing blueprint reform projects, which entailed financial liberalization, the freeing of domestic prices, stabilization, privatization and export promotion.

International diplomacy and geopolitics

Inevitably such external demands were the price of debt relief overtures, and they inevitably affected relations between governing and opposition elites in developing countries. This was all the more so as One World idealism revived in the last decades of the Cold War. Conflict resolution between states would be reduced not just by recognition of different interests, and the deployment of diplomatic skills to negotiate compromises, but because states would share the same values, as Kant envisaged in his vision of a perpetual peace among 'republican' governments, i.e. constitutional democracies. The reference point is the UN Charter, as the source of international law and of international norms of conduct in the world society of states. Therein states may not 'interfere' in the affairs of other states, but they are beholden to respect collective and individual rights and duties, and to ensure mutual access to markets.

One World idealism revived, in fact, as a sub-plot in the Cold War. The temporary relaxation of tensions between the Western powers and the Soviet Union in the early 1970s led to the lifting of Western vetoes on the activities of Western communist parties and allies, and the acceptance by the party-states of responsibilities with regard to human rights, the free flow of information, minority rights, freedom of travel and reunion of families. The result in Western Europe was accentuated by party and trade union competition on the left of national political spectrums, prompting a surge in welfare outlays and labour market concessions as incumbent governments bid to retain the centre ground of politics. The result of subscribing to the human rights commitments laid down in the Helsinki Final Act in August 1975 proved more lethal for the party-states. The Western powers now added human rights advocacy to their diplomatic baggage, and thereby gave voice to dissidents around the world.

Human rights advocacy did not win uniform and immediate support in Western democracies. The German and Japanese publics proved reluctant to criticize abuses in their party-state neighbours, and only in June 1982 did the Reagan administration come to terms with the US

Human rights advocacy did not win uniform and immediate support in Western democracies.

Congress on adding human rights amendments to foreign aid and trade deals. Human rights was also a two-edged diplomatic sword, which governments with local skeletons to conceal were reluctant to deploy. But human rights issues were too powerful in their resonance at home and abroad not to turn against the party-states, while churches and human rights organizations were only too prepared to mobilize support against dictatorships. As Samuel Huntington writes, Cardinal Sin of the Philippines probably did more to overthrow Marcos than any prelate had done to change political leadership since the seventeenth century.[24]

South Africa's apartheid regime also fell to the new diplomacy of human rights.[25] In June 1985 both the Republican-dominated US Senate Foreign Relations Committee and the House of Representatives approved economic sanctions. Chase Manhattan then stopped rolling over South African loans and froze unused lines of credit. Other banks followed. The rand fell and foreign currency reserves drained away, forcing South Africa to declare a six-month moratorium on debt repayment and to reintroduce restrictions on capital outflows. South Africa became a bankers' pariah. Trade sanctions by the Western powers and forty-nine Commonwealth countries began to bite. By the end of 1986 a large number of major US and European firms had pulled out of South Africa, many citing anti-apartheid pressures at home. Negotiations between the ANC and the Afrikaner government began that October, resulting in Nelson Mandela's release from prison in early 1990.

The Cold War's end lent multilateral diplomacy a new impetus. Because prestige counts, and they do not like being talked about when they are not present, states seek membership in international clubs, such as the United Nations, its ancillary organizations, and regional arrangements. Japan, for instance, as the world's second largest economy, seemed an obvious candidate for permanent membership of the

UN Security Council. But the post-Cold War world proved much less amenable to Japan's old success formula of security dependence on the US combined with one-way-street cross-shareholding mercantilism. Japan's reaffirmation of the 1960 Japan–US security treaty in April 1996 alienated a China ever vigilant about Japanese support for Taiwan, while Japan's 'financial mess',[26] aggravated by the Asian crash of 1997–8, kindled US concerns that Japan would once again seek to export its economy out of recession. As permanent members of the UN Security Council, both China and the US wield the right of veto over new members.

Diplomacy is also about resolving conflicts between states through negotiation – as realists emphasize. Each state lies at the centre of its web of bilateral relations, but each state tends to have a key bilateral relationship. France, for instance, has a worldwide diplomatic reach, but its prime relationship is with Germany, while Germany's prime relationship is, or has been, with the United States. This Franco-German imbalance in preferences, added to the inequality in capabilities between them, has been moderated through their being embedded in the two key multilateral institutions of NATO and the EU. If one seeks to impose its preferences on the other, countervailing alliances and offsetting deals are struck in one or other of the multilateral clubs. Member states are thereby encouraged to moderate their parochialism, and to act more as citizens of the world than as local bullies on the bloc.

Asian affairs have no such mechanism to moderate the propensity of states to parochialism. Bilateral relations prevail, and states' interests clash. This is particularly so in the battle between the US and Japan over financial arrangements throughout East Asia. Japan's cross-shareholding mercantilism fails the test of transparency and of accountability. Its corporate reports provide limited information to investors. Public confidence in financial institutions is further undermined by serial reports of corrupt officials, and securities houses in cahoots with crime syndicates. Lax Finance Ministry controls over bank lending left Japan's banks at the end of 1997 with bad debts equivalent to at least 16 per cent of GDP, plus estimated exposures of $24 billion to South Korea, $37 billion to Thailand and $15 billion to Indonesia. Unable or unwilling to reform at home, Japan has failed to back IMF proposals for US-type financial market reforms in Indonesia, Thailand and South Korea.

The 1990s have been the US's decade in dimensions of the world power structure other than finance. In the security domain the US-led coalition in the Gulf war of early 1991 used the recent NATO military doctrine, whereby communications and control allow war plans on land to duplicate the movements of war at sea, to smash the Iraqi armed forces, deployed according to Soviet military doctrine and equipped with Soviet military equipment. In the domain of production, Japanese corporations developed operational effectiveness in the 1980s, suffering persistently lower profits as operational lessons spread, and then lagged in the 1990s when corporations shifted to emphasize the uniqueness of products and services brought to market.[27] In the knowledge structure, the main communications groups, dispensing news, information and popular culture worldwide, are Anglo-American giants such as CNN, Time Warner, Walt Disney-ABC, Murdoch, the BBC, Reuters and Associated Press.

There is no disguising Realpolitik in the garb of One World idealism in the domain of geopolitics. An objective, but insufficient, measure of the global balance of power is the distribution of capabilities between the units in the system – that is, the states. A list of capabilities may include demography, natural resources, value added in industry, the military potential of the state and its technological resources. Such a list is incomplete because it fails to account for disparities in organizational capabilities between states, and for the propensity of weaker states to mitigate dependency on stronger states by hook or by crook. China, for instance, is a near-solitary survivor of the defunct communist system, and confronts a world whose major powers promote market democracy as a prescription for the world's ills. Its strategy of opening to the world without surrendering the party-state's control lies at the heart of China's policy of co-operative resistance towards the United States.

A comparative list of capabilities between states is also inadequate because subjective assessments of a state's position in the world hierarchy play a crucial role in determining how it is treated by others, and how it views itself. China's rapid growth presages the emergence of a world power within decades – a prospect which colours world perceptions of China, and provides a major challenge to Chinese diplomacy on how to deal with international perceptions which risk an overestimation of China's present capabilities. Similarly, India – as the world's largest democracy, and by that token a natural ally of the United States – seeks to blast a nuclear way into the inner sanctum of the UN Security Council in defiance of the permanent members, because Indian nationalism craves prestige, which relative failures in economic policy have not provided. Pakistan chooses to 'go nuclear' because it either values its security above offers of Western aid or calculates that Western aid and trade may be gained through doing so. Many poorer states can be counted on to follow the international community's policies towards Pakistan with vigilant interest.

A simple key to understanding the principle which animates the policy of a state is to ask about its neighbourhood. As neighbours tend to fall out, so states tend to make reverse alliances with their neighbours' neighbours.

The spread of market democracy does not, and cannot, bring peace and tranquillity to the world as it is.

It is the disposition of states and peoples towards one another, nurtured in history, that is most indicative of a state's propensity to make the types of choice which it does in international affairs. Vietnam remains a communist-party state and therefore has a certain affinity with Beijing, but the country's proximity to China has been an ever-present Vietnamese preoccupation. Geographical location also weighs heavier in the balance of Greek relations with Turkey than their common membership of NATO and the Council of Europe. Greece, it may safely be said, is mesmerized by Turkey, with which trade is minimal and hostility permanent. Both Turkey and Vietnam tend to look to the United States as a counterweight to the EU and to China.

Diplomacy and geopolitics, then, are not necessarily favourable to the spread of market democracy and, even if the formula is spread among more states than before, the enlargement of its area does not mean that states do not continue to have serious differences over their domestic arrangements or international aspirations. The spread of market democracy does not, and cannot, bring peace and tranquillity to the world as it is.

The battle of cultures in world time and local time

The main reason sharp limits are set to the enlargement of market democracy is not the clash of cultures between the West and the Rest, or a possible alliance between Sinic and Muslim cultures against the overbearing might of the industrial powers, but the universal tension between world and local time. World time is instantaneous.[28] It is conveyed by the trinity of communications, prices and products. It is ahistorical as the past is interesting only in so far as it provides clues to the future. It substitutes memory for choice and trade-offs. It embraces all populations of the world in the moment. It provides titillation to the many, and great wealth to the few. It offers to satisfy desires for reward and retribution that have lain dormant in the dreams of individuals or, even more, of civilizations. It is imperial in that it is impatient of any other source of rationality, and distributes wealth in its moods of generosity only to dispense punishment in vengeful typhoons of vindictiveness.

Local time stretches far beyond the life of individuals into mythologized pasts which populate the many mental landscapes of the world's peoples, with holy places, ruins and legends. It is conditioned by long-dead technologies and its distances are measurable in the hours, days, weeks or months which journeys took by foot or horseback. It is bound by history and geography. It is rooted in the malleable memories of communities, in their habits and languages. Its rationality is exclusive of choice, of trade-offs and of aliens. Its appeal is to the inner well-springs of loyalties on which it draws. Local time cultivates trust and tribalism, as two sides of the same coin. It is patient and particularist. Its expressions are secretive and its reflexes are coded. But it also lives in and is seduced by world time. Local times seek to realize their ambitions and wreak their unconsummated vengeance through the deliverance from limits which the instant provides.

This juxtaposition of the two categories of time is the well-spring of the world's turmoil. It is not the 'Great Satan', as Khomeini categorized the United States in his attempt to locate and personify the source of evil. Nor is it 'the roving, predatory money'[29] which President Mitterrand referred to in his bid to saddle the 'Anglo-Saxons' with the blame for his own financial manipulations. Rather, the turmoil of world politics and therefore of world markets is endemic to the cacophony of local aspirations which are radiated around the world through the mechanisms of modernity. A relatively post-religious Europe lives only a few hours' flight from Saudi Arabia, where opponents of the royal family aspire to introduce a true rendering of Koranic law in Islam's Holy Places. Western anti-drug measures seek to deprive Andean Indians of the revenues which promise to deliver them from the four centuries of deprivation they have endured since the arrival of the Spanish conquerors in the early decades of the sixteenth century.

World time incorporates also the preferences of the world's leading corporations, which are attracted to invest in developing countries because that is where potential world demand is located. Per capita growth in East Asia from 1986 to 1997 was double that of rich countries and returns on investments were high in order to compensate for the risks. A crucial determinant of their decision was the quality of policies provided by host governments. Four criteria held pride of place:

1 Governments should promote outward-looking trade and investment policies, which would enable corporations to source inputs to their new location from abroad, service world markets, ease access for expatriate employment and repatriate profits.

2 Governments should invest in the development of local human capital, particularly by raising standards of literacy and numeracy among children attending primary and secondary schools. An abundant supply of people educated to a good secondary school level was more important in terms of the availability of skillable labour than over-investment in university education.

3 Governments should ensure that local markets were open to competition, otherwise foreign investors would be buying into local oligopolies, local companies would fall asleep at the switch, and political markets for influence would replace competition between producers for the benefit of consumers.

4 Not least, governments should run tight fiscal ships, give equal treatment to foreign and local companies, and develop open and trans-

parent financial markets. In order to provide infrastructure to world standards, cash-strapped governments should turn to private capital by privatization, or by such project finance techniques as build-operate-transfer or build-own-transfer.

The decade saw an explosion of bilateral and multilateral treaties to protect and promote such investment, both in order to secure access and because local communities insisted on setting their own conditions. In this, they received intellectual support from the new institutional economics which argues that inefficiencies in developing country markets result from higher transaction costs. These are recognizable through the prevalence of non-market relations or, in vulgar parlance, of cronies and personal ties in government–business relations. The one condition is that these local arrangements be adaptable to changing conditions, compatible with 'adaptive efficiency'.[30] Activist state policies and private cartels, in short, are justified under certain conditions,[31] and will tend as those conditions mature to produce different incentives for organizations, and shape the kind of economic activity that will be viable and profitable.

But these are the arguments of economists, battling among themselves for space on Western airwaves. They are not the rationales of local time. Most states in the world are composed of many peoples, none more so than India where the number of different tongues and dialects spoken runs to more than 1,000. India's population is 80 per cent Hindu, and its society is riddled with caste distinctions which cover every aspect of life. The government has had to come to terms with the phenomenon in its labour market policies of 'affirmative action', opening 10 per cent of government jobs to 'untouchables'. Central power has trickled away towards the states, as the Brahmins of the Congress Party have lost the hegemony they enjoyed in the early years after independence. Regional conflicts and separatist movements in several states have repeatedly wracked the country. And yet India's democracy, with an electorate over 600 million strong, has a proven ability to absorb these vast differences.

Local time also provides its own rationale for the existence of cross-shareholding structures as ensuring that ownership of key corporate assets is distributed along tribal lines. Indeed, cross-shareholdings in many rich countries are tribal arrangements to exclude foreigners, disguised in high-sounding platitudes borrowed from the ample bag of Western economics. These platitudes are widely serviceable around the world, but have come under fire from the discourse of market democracy, and its insistence on transparency – a transparency which, once introduced in the corporate accounts of Mexico, South Korea and Indonesia, facilitates purchase at attractive prices of local crown jewels by rich-country institutions.

Yet these local arrangements of cross-shareholdings replicate local realities which, however unpalatable to flat-earth cosmopolitan One Worlders (they *are* palatable to round-earth cosmopolitan One Worlders), are the stuff of enlightened government retaining balance among peoples. Malaysia, for instance, has long been a multi-racial society, where commercial activity, particularly in finance and industry, was dominated by the Chinese and Indians. Following severe riots in Kuala Lumpur in 1969, resulting in several hundred deaths, the major communities negotiated the New Economic Policy (NEP). The NEP, launched in 1971, aimed to increase the Malays' share of wealth, education and employment, principally through greater ownership of commercial and industrial share capital by Malays and other indigenous groups, known as *bumiputras* (literally meaning 'sons of the soil'). It inspires all aspects of the Malaysian economy, from the spending pattern of the budget, to labour market policy, to the details of privatization in the 1980s and of capital market legislation.

South Africa's political economy is no less structured around relations between its many peoples. The apartheid economy was run under a form of state capitalism, aimed at satisfying the Nationalist Party's constituency of poorer Boers and working-class whites. Substantial public corporations (SOEKOR for oil exploration, ISCOR in steel, SASOL in chemicals) were financed in part by obligatory siphoning of funds from the large, family-owned conglomerates – such as Anglo-American or Anglovaal. These conglomerates dominate the Johannesburg Stock Exchange, and were vulnerable to ANC suggestions to nationalize the bastions of white corporate power. But during the negotiations of 1990–4 over the political transition, the ANC shifted tack in favour of creating black-owned conglomerates, such as New Africa Investments (Nail) and Real Africa Investments (RAI). Mandela supported ANC Secretary-General Cyril Ramaphosa's move to join the management team at Nail.

In local time, ownership by nationals of major corporate assets is crucial to establishing the legitimacy of the market economy. In Poland, for instance, the political parties took until July 1995 to agree on a new privatization law that resulted in almost all adult citizens acquiring share certificates. Fear of losing jobs from the closure of redundant operations mingled with anxiety at key assets being absorbed into German ownership. As one official told the author, 'we welcome foreign investors from other Western European countries and from the US, but we are worried at the prospect of an overpowering German corporate presence'. The rationale for Korea creating its own *chaebols* (conglomerates) and protecting the domestic market is inspired by similar sentiments towards its powerful neighbour, and former colonizer, Japan.

Local time takes a different colouring in Russia, where Western rhetoric about the benefits of democracy and capitalism contrasts with the experience of the Russian people. The economy stagnates at half the level of output in 1989. Corporate tax payments have shrunk. Pensioners have seen their miserable pittances reduced to near-zero. The armed forces have collapsed. When President Yeltsin's popularity level shrank to a bare 3 per cent in 1995, he struck a deal with seven leading bankers to swap loans for equity in return for their backing in the presidential elections of June 1996. Their media swung into action, helping Yeltsin to victory against the odds. The seven bankers went ahead to create a corporate oligarchy, accounting for up to 50 per cent of the Russian economy. As George Soros, the Hungarian-born billionaire philanthropist, said: 'The assets of the state were stolen, and then when the state itself became valuable as a source of legitimacy, it too was stolen.'[32]

Concluding remarks

Where does this leave market democracy? In its one-fit-for-all guise, it does not provide a guide to the world of the 1990s and beyond. Too many other factors muddy its waters. Markets are of course an indispensable social arrangement, without which the preferences of hundreds of millions of people could never be met. But the peculiarities of how those social arrangements for markets are constituted are as varied as the peoples of this earth. So are the authorities which rule them: some of them are states, with their own histories, myths, peoples and neighbourhoods; others are the Bretton Woods institutions or the Western powers; and still others are the corporations of the Western world, or the webs of ethnic ties which bind diasporas together and to their real or imagined land of origin. The power structure in the world is not state-centred – as Susan Strange has often argued – but is heterogeneous and pluralist.

World time incorporates all these forces, but exists in its own right. Being instantaneous and ahistorical it unites the world now, but also provides a permanent moment when all aspirations – ancient and modern – meet and exchange. It does not move according to the standards of market democracy, of accountability and transparency, but according to the multiple and contradictory measures and standards, some religious, others ethnic and yet others economic,

It is only the conceit of the rich to claim that they are 'rational', and the less rich are less so.

which populate it. Hence, its propensity to mete out reward or punishment by visiting on its victims a cornucopia of generosity or a typhoon of vengeance. The ancestral voices, which it relays so effectively along with world prices, the *Larry King Live* show, and the latest technologies, are universal. It is only the conceit of the rich to claim that they are 'rational', and the less rich are less so.

World time first flattered President Gorbachev as the champion of reform, and then ditched him in ignominy in 1991; honoured Saddam Hussein as the sword of modernism against the barbarism of religious zealotry, then had his forces annihilated in February 1991 by the UN coalition of states, whose wealthier members had previously armed him to the teeth; it elevated Chancellor of the Exchequer Norman Lamont as the champion of sound finance and then defenestrated the Chancellor from office and sterling from the European Exchange Rate Mechanism in August 1992; it praised Mexico for the liberal market reforms implemented in the late 1980s and for membership of

NAFTA, and then pulled the rug from under the Mexican peso in December 1994; conversely, it dumped the Bill and Hillary show as soon as the presidential couple from Arkansas hit Washington in 1993, and then elevated them to unprecedented heights of popularity in US public opinion, despite or because of Bill's hassles over his zipper problem; not least, it elevated President Suharto as an architect of Indonesia's remarkable transformation from dire poverty to the threshold of prosperity, and then catapulted him to disgrace in spring 1998, and Indonesia back to deprivation.

Where will world time's typhoon strike next? Trying to predict the future is a major concern of foreign investors. To this we shall now turn.

Notes

1 Samuel P. Huntington, *The Third Wave: Democratization in the Late Twentieth Century*, Norman, University of Oklahoma Press, 1991.
2 José Maria Maravall, *Regimes, Politics and Markets: Democratization and Economic Change in Southern and Eastern Europe*, Oxford, Oxford University Press, 1997.
3 George Weigel, 'Catholicism and Democracy: The Other Twentieth-Century Revolution', in Brad Roberts (ed), *The New Democracies: Global Change and U.S. Policy*, Cambridge, MIT Press, 1990.
4 Susan L. Woodward, *Balkan Tragedy: Chaos and Dissolution after the Cold War*, Harrisonburg, R. R. Donnelly, 1993.
5 Quoted in Robert Wade, *Governing the Market: Economic Theory and the Role of Government in East Asian Industrialisation*, Princeton, Princeton University Press, 1990.
6 See Wade, ibid.
7 Walt Rustow, *The Stages of Economic Growth: A Non-Communist Manifesto*, London, Cambridge University Press, 1960.
8 Seymour Martin Lipset, *Political Man*, London, Heinemann, 1960.
9 Barrington Moore, Jr, *Social Origins of Dictatorship and Democracy: Lord and Peasant in the Making of the Modern World*, Boston, Beacon Press, 1972.
10 Mancur Olson, Jr, 'Growth as a Destabilizing Force', *Journal of Economic History*, Vol. XXIII, December 1963.
11 Samuel P. Huntington, *Political Order in Changing Societies*, New Haven, Yale University Press, 1968.
12 Ted Gurr, *Why Men Rebel*, Princeton, Princeton University Press, 1970.
13 Juan Linz and Alfred Stepan, *Problems of Democratic Transition and Consolidation: Southern Europe, South America and Post-Communist Europe*, Baltimore/London, The Johns Hopkins University Press, 1996.

14 Stephen Haggard and Robert Kaufmann, *The Political Economy of Democratic Transitions*, Princeton, Princeton University Press, 1995.

15 Douglas C. North, *Institutions, Institutional Change and Economic Performance*, Cambridge University Press, 1990.

16 Linz and Stepan, op. cit. note 13.

17 See David Collier (ed), *The New Authoritarianism in Latin America*, Princeton, Princeton University Press, 1979.

18 *Financial Times*, 8 September 1989.

19 Fernando Limongi and Adam Przeworski, 'Democracy and Development in South America, 1945–1988', unpublished paper, Chicago University, dated October 1993, cited in Linz and Stepan, op. cit. note 13.

20 John Stopford and Susan Strange, *Rival States, Rival Firms. Competition for World Market Shares*, Cambridge, Cambridge University Press, 1991.

21 James E. Austin, *Managing in Developing Countries: Strategic Analysis and Operating Techniques*, New York, Free Press, 1990.

22 Danny M. Leipziger, Vinod Thomas, *The Lessons of East Asia: An Overview of Country Experience*, Washington DC, The World Bank, 1993.

23 Laurence Whitehead, *The International Dimensions of Democratization, Europe and the Americas*, Oxford, Oxford University Press, 1996.

24 Huntington, op. cit. note 1.

25 See Martin Holland, *The European Community and South Africa: European Political Co-operation under Strain*, London, Pinter, 1988.

26 Edward J. Lincoln, 'Japan's Financial Mess', *Foreign Affairs*, May–June 1998.

27 Michael E. Porter, 'What is Strategy?', *Harvard Business Review*, November–December 1996.

28 For a discussion on world and local time, see Zaki Laïdi, *Un Monde privé de sens*, Paris, Fayard, 1994.

29 'Taste for Regulation Revived', *Financial Times*, 2 November 1989.

30 Douglas C. North, op. cit. note 15.

31 See Wade, op. cit. note 5.

32 Cited by Grigory Yavlinsky, 'Russia's Phony Capitalism', *Foreign Affairs*, May–June 1998.

Chapter 6

MEMORIES OF DIFFERENT FUTURES

Managers have to think about the future because that is where expected costs and rewards are located. Yet the history of foreign investment is a graveyard of shattered expectations as the promised El Dorado has proved time and again to be built on sand. Foreign investors flooded into the Gulf states and Latin America, but the attraction waned when Khomeini came to power in Iran in 1979, and again in 1982 when Argentina, Brazil and Mexico suspended interest payments on their loans from Western commercial banks. After the yen's rise in *The history of foreign investment is a graveyard of shattered expectations.* 1985, investors poured into East Asian markets until the sudden withdrawal of confidence in June 1997. On each occasion, managements failed to anticipate events and to take timely action. This chapter discusses ways of thinking about the future that can serve as tools of corporate strategy; introduces the key components of scenario-building; and presents the assumptions underlying different types of scenario. In the next chapter we discuss corporations as key players and participants in the world political economy, whose dynamics they must understand in order to anticipate future trends.

Thinking about the future

People have always been interested in the future. As Cicero wrote in *De Divinatione*, 'what is doubtless true is that there is no nation in the world, however polite and knowledgeable it may be, nor so barbarous and little cultivated that does not believe in future signs, and in those who know and predict it'. Let us examine the Roman's statement more closely. Concern about the future, he is saying, is universal, like life and death, and lies beyond the particular fortunes of peoples. If the future is uncertain, our concern is a certainty as we all share a common fear that the future may deliver more pain, or a lesser degree of pleasure. We worry whether the future is continuous or discontinuous. We ask what the future holds for us, just as we ask what the prophet's intent may be. If he is a charlatan, we need not heed him. If he is a preacher, we may want to mend the error of our ways before we are damned. Or a more secular prophet may want to alter the future by influencing the decisions we take.

What are the ways that people in the past have thought about the future and how can we evaluate them? One ancient way is to consult the gods, read the signs and decipher presages in order to *deduce* the implications for life in this world. The Oracle at Delphi delivered famously ambiguous statements, not in order to provide a cover against events turning out differently from what was said, so much as to indicate to mortals how the gods could be propitiated. The interpretations of the Oracle's words were left to the listeners, and to their understanding of what may assuage the gods. But it was up to the gods to decide whether or not to take heed. There were thus many alternative outcomes buried in the Oracle's statement, and that ranged from some satisfactory result to misinterpretation by the listener, a faulty choice of gift, or to the sheer cussedness of the gods who had other activities to pursue rather than spending their time worrying about mortals. The future is inevitable, but its possible content is multiform.

With Christianity, time becomes teleological, tending to a specific future where Christ rises anew from the dead, and wakes the faithful from their sleep. The novelty is that this future is in the power of people to shape, in that they follow in the footsteps of the Shepherd and obey His Gospel. Those who do not, carouse their way to hell as illustrated on the portals of the cathedral at Chartres, or fall into the Devil's jaws, as depicted on the murals of the cathedral of Bologna. Of this, the wicked can be sure. The faithful, on the other hand, traverse this life in the uncertainty of God's judgement at the second coming, when a final link is established between secular time and eternity. Not surprisingly, such a momentous event is not readily predictable, indeed is only conceivable in the medieval imagination as preceded by calamitous events that serve as a warning for sinners to repent before it is too late. The future is thus composed of certainties and of uncertainties.

Intuition is another source of information about the future. Its practitioners claim an insight to the inner workings of destiny that amounts to an unprovable hypothesis until the sell-by date of the prophecy expires. By definition, astrology therefore places itself beyond the bounds of science. If a forecast event actually occurs – as in the case of Nostradamus's reputed prediction of the flight of Louis XVI from Varennes on 21 June 1791[1] – it would take a robust sceptic to refute the method used to come by the prediction. The further into the future that the event is predicted, the longer the reputation of the soothsayer is assured. Alternatively, the closer that the prediction lies to the present, the greater is the likelihood that its veracity may be tested after the fact. The test is to compare prophecies which use the same set of assumptions. If all astrologers make the same prediction, then collusion, chance or intuition are at work. We choose what to believe.

Calling on the imagination to anticipate the future is yet a further method. Our futurist consults experts in science and technology about what is in the pipeline of research, and produces a list of insights, such as those offered by Mr John Watkins, writing in the *Ladies' Home Journal* of December 1900. In the next century, he assured his readers, mosquitoes will disappear, the life expectancy of Americans will rise from thirty-five years to fifty, air vessels will constitute no competition for ships, and automobiles will substitute for horses in pulling hearses at funerals. Alternatively, we anticipate some imaginary solution to a recurrent problem, such as André Robida's vision that political alternance in France in the twentieth century[2] will be solved by institutionalizing revolution once a decade through a simulated *coup d'état* and street fighting that end in the staged arrival in power of the new ruling group. A credible picture of the future has to establish some link between cause and consequence.

A model of structured relationships facilitates forecasts. From the summer of 1987, I argued to executives attending INSEAD courses that Germany was heading to unity around the winter of 1989. My model incorporated the US-centred system of alliances, coupled with the Western world's massive superiority in resources, pitted against a third-world challenger in the form of the USSR, with its allies or clients in Africa, the Middle East, the sub-continent and in Indochina. Gorbachev's evident recognition of the USSR's weaknesses was prompting seismic shifts in the post-1945 settlement. Germany was the focus of competing policy proposals by France (EU integration), the US (unity in NATO), and the USSR (unity via 'neutrality'). The timetables of these proposals merged around December 1989. One chief executive said 'So what?' and another suggested that I be sacked. To no avail. Like the cat's grin in *Alice in Wonderland*, a model's predictive powers disappear with the situation that it captures.

Scenarios present different narratives of possible futures, and are the most relevant to corporate needs. Developed by the US airforce in the Second World War, the technique was applied to business by Herman

Like the cat's grin in Alice in Wonderland, a model's predictive powers disappear with the situation that it captures.

Kahn in the Hudson Institute during the 1960s, and then adapted by Shell to anticipate the oil price rises of the early 1970s.[3] As a technique, scenario building calls on all the insights already mentioned, such as the multiform content of the future, the distinction between certainties and uncertainties, the warning about believing what we want to, the requirement to establish some credible link between cause and consequence, and the regular obsolescence of models as they are superseded by circumstances. It requires us to take imaginative leaps into possible futures while remaining rigorously aware of the assumptions we make. We ask what the key decisions are facing the company, and the time horizon in which those concerns are framed. Scenarios are a vital ingredient of corporate strategy.

Scenarios serve a number of corporate purposes. Most importantly, they facilitate institutional learning throughout the organization.[4] Individuals are constantly thinking about the conditions they face in the future, based on the information they carry with them from the past, and what actions they should take as a consequence. A sum of individual 'memories of the future' makes for conflict. Elaborating scenarios together helps to create a common discourse throughout the organization, and to clarify the assumptions on which mental models of the future are based. An organization introducing a process of common reflection must be patient initially, but once the process is entrenched the time between listening, digesting and action may be accelerated. Ericsson, the Swedish telecommunications giant, involves over 500 experts and managers in its 'Ericsson 2005 process', the aim of which is 'to share knowledge as a means to facilitate creative and constructive dialogue'.

Scenarios represent a sketch of the future based on today's facts, and on assumptions of what can be extracted from the trends which we are able to identify in the present. They are descriptions of possible futures and are not forecasts. Ericsson's Lars Ramqvist explains:

> Our aim is to understand trends and uncertainties. This makes us better prepared to act quickly and correctly in response to change better and faster than any competitors. Of course we don't have the ability to predict what will happen in this fast moving business up until the year 2005 – history proves this impossible. But we can ensure that whatever happens in the future, it will not take us by complete surprise.

Ericsson, he adds, has gained a 'great pool of knowledge and insights' through the scenario process. It has served to hone skills to identify 'risks and opportunities, new markets, new players and moves by our competitors', and it enables Ericsson to face the future 'with confidence and determination'.

Scenarios also serve to challenge conventional thinking. Managers are busy people, and spend much of their time on routine. Hence their general propensity is to extrapolate past experience and to assume the future as a continuation of the present. That is why the first scenario in a package should be surprise-free, one that is instantly recognizable and conforms with managers' implicit view of the future. If the package contains only scenarios that break with past experience, they are likely to lack credibility in the minds of participants. They can feel threatened and reject the whole process. So much effort must go into filling the scenario with the necessary mixture of quantitative data, as well as credible evaluations of the interests and motivations of the major players in the drama. But this is only a start. The central objective in narrating scenarios is to expose the dangers of assuming that the future will be a simple continuation of present trends.

Driving forces, predetermined elements and critical uncertainties

To draw up scenarios, three questions must be asked: what are the driving forces? What are the predetermined elements and what are the critical uncertainties?

Driving forces

'Driving forces' are the factors that move the plot of the story, the inner motor that propels the human drama forward. They are sourced in human beings, and not in the gods or some extra-terrestrial elements. A crucial assumption thus is that we people are responsible for the world that we live in, and that what happens is either traceable to human actions or is amenable to human treatment. The major categories are:

- population growth;
- technology;
- the natural environment;
- the market mechanism;
- politics; and
- ideology.

Population growth

Population growth is arguably the key driving force of the twentieth century. In 1900 the world population was 1.7 billion, rising to 2.5 billion in 1950 and 5.3 billion in 1990. One major transformation is the steady shrinkage of the populations of North America, Europe and the ex-USSR from 30 per cent of the total in 1900 to 20 per cent in 1990, and a similar trend in China (see Figure 6.1). Higher population growth rates are recorded in Latin America, India and the rest of Asia. The major growth of population is in Africa from 7 to 12 per cent, rising on known trends to nearly 25 per cent of the total by 2060 – assuming that no disasters befall Africa – when the world will hold over 12 billion, and the whole of Asia will account for over 56 per cent. By then North America, Europe and the ex-USSR will make up about 10 per cent of the world's people. What this spells out for the industrialized

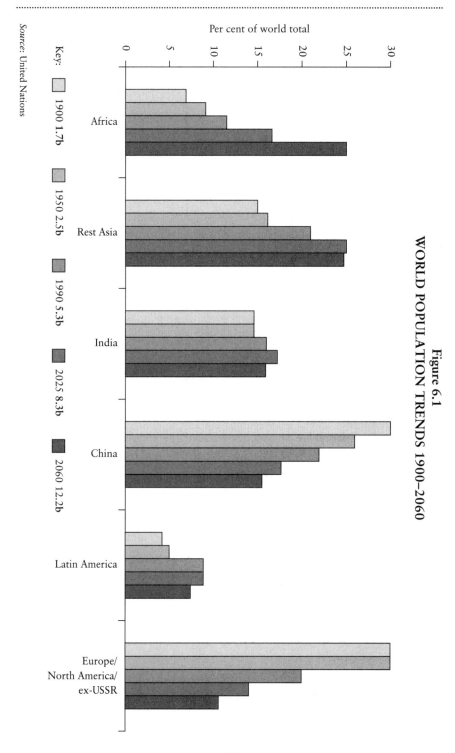

Per cent of world total

Figure 6.1
WORLD POPULATION TRENDS 1900–2060

Key:

1900 1.7b

1950 2.5b

1990 5.3b

2025 8.3b

2060 12.2b

Africa

Rest Asia

India

China

Latin America

Europe/
North America/
ex-USSR

Source: United Nations

nations is an ageing population, a decline in the size of the working-age population, and strains already emerging in the 1990s on pay-as-you-go pension schemes.[5]

Technology

Technology improves at exponential rates, and drives changes in all aspects of human activity. Joseph Schumpeter, the Austrian economist, famously coined the phrase of the gale of creative destruction embedded in competition between industrial corporations for market share. The organization of scientific power has made life the object, in the words of the French author Paul Valéry, 'of an experiment of which we can say only one thing – that it tends to estrange us more and more from what we were, or what we think we are, and that is leading us, we do not know, and can by no means imagine, where'.[6] Techno-optimists profess no such concern and see the world of the 1990s, for instance, sweeping forward over the coming quarter-century to a world of prosperity, freedom and clean environment on five great waves of technology – personal computers, telecommunications, biotechnology, nano-technology and alternative energy.[7]

The natural environment

The natural environment must sustain a rising world population, and extensive exploitation by human beings. It includes the air, water, weather and upper atmosphere, as well as minerals and fuels under the earth and the vegetable and animal life on earth. Environmental concerns are of two types: one is to envisage nature, and hence the economy it sustains, as an infinitely complex totality; the other is to contrast going rates of exploitation with total demand, and to forecast either a rise in prices or catastrophe as exponential growth places an ever greater burden on finite resources. Techno-optimists argue for the diffusion of cleaner technologies to reduce poverty and pollution; environmental pessimists note the world's growth in consumption of fossil fuels, in disposal of hazardous waste, the rise in mega-cities in developing countries, the extension of intensive agriculture, timber and fisheries, and the expanding demands on fresh water resources.

The market mechanism

The market mechanism prices all factors of production – land, labour, capital and technology – through the interplay of supply and demand. Price, von Hayek argued, gathers and diffuses information around the world. A final price for the end consumer incorporates all its components in one number. That is all the purchaser needs to know to decide whether the price for that good should be paid in view of possible alternative uses of his or her budget. The price mechanism also diffuses the relevant information to all participants in the market, in that the prices of goods and services around the world rise or fall according to circumstances. Land is dear in Singapore and cheap in Australia; high wages in the German construction industry attract Polish workers ready to offer their labour at lower rates; capital is priced in terms of interest and exchange rates; and the relative prices of technologies replicate the constant revolution of innovation.

Politics

Politics embraces all undertakings where the wills of two or more people are harnessed to a particular task. This extensive definition enables us to avoid the trap of state-centrism, a prevalent doctrine which claims that the only and ultimate political players are the states, their domestic political processes, the relations between them and whatever goes on in international

Ideology embraces a torrent of conflicting and overlapping beliefs.

organizations. As we discussed in earlier chapters, the definition allows us to populate the political arena with a whole zoo of players, especially firms and corporations of all shapes, sizes and competences. Indeed, it roots corporations in the soil of their cultural and ethnic identities, converts them to prime political players on the world stage, and multiplies the number of competing and overlapping authorities on world markets. These authorities evidently embrace the world's varied religions and life philosophies, alongside mafias, drug barons, money launderers and sundry other criminals.

Ideology

Ideology embraces a torrent of conflicting and overlapping beliefs, whose prophets assert their unique claim to primacy in the hierarchy of human needs. Nationalists demand the self-determination of peoples. Market ideologues proclaim an efficient market economy for the world as a whole as a supreme good. Techno-optimists see universal growth as the source of progress, and environmental pessimists state that exploitation of the world's resources is a sure way to humanity's end. Religious zealots maintain that theirs' is God's only one, narrow path to salvation, while political pluralists argue for a tolerant society where people pick and choose how they live from a *smorgasbord* of options. Free market capitalists praise fat cats, and mercantilists defend managerial prerogatives and tribal cross-shareholdings. Political liberals champion democracy for all, and realists see the future, like the past, as unremitting struggle. The din of ideologies resounds in world time.

Predetermined elements

Having identified the key driving forces, the next step is to isolate the predetermined elements in scenarios. Often, these are so similar to the relevant driving forces as to be barely distinguishable. Their significance lies in a denial of the Epicurean position, whereby all is flux and what happens is chance. We can illustrate this by borrowing the illustration used by Pierre Wack, who presided over Shell's path-breaking scenarios of the early 1970s on world oil markets. A monsoon in the Upper Ganges, Wack reminds us, is known by countless precedents to yield a flood nine days later in Allahabad, and twelve days later in Benares. The floods are certain to occur, they are predetermined as long as human beings have not created dams to divert the waters of the Ganges. For people living along the sacred river's littoral, the phenomenon of floods at regular intervals is a certainty. They are a long-term trend from the past and will recur in the future.

Predetermined elements need not be confined to the relation of weather to geography. They refer to any phenomena which we observe as recurring again and again. The Japanese, for instance, live on an archipelago of volcanic islands, with limited natural resources. The only way for them to prosper is by processing imports and re-exporting them on to world markets. As raw material and fuel prices have tended downwards over the past forty years, and Japanese industries have transformed imported materials into ever higher value-added products, the country has run chronic trade surpluses since the late 1960s. This propensity to run trade surpluses is compounded by high savings rates, reflecting Japanese people's sense of vulnerability to the country's trade dependence on world markets and to the fact that on average every Japanese family must count on having to rebuild its house once in its lifetime. The regularity of earthquakes counsels the Japanese to abstinence.

Predetermined elements may be identified also as any slow-changing trends such as population growth rates, the depletion of fisheries or the upward move in life expectancies. They include any phenomena which are in the pipeline, and that are bound to reach the light of day within a measurable time-frame. The long-term imbalance in German public finances, for instance, is rooted in the 1990 decision to extend West German welfare benefits to East Germany. Ongoing improvements in information technology are likely to yield productivity improvements by 2015, comparable to all productivity improvements since the first industrial revolution.[8] Or the world teenage population by the turn of the century will number upwards of 2 billion, overwhelmingly located in developing countries. For the first time in the history of the world, these teenage masses have access to modern technologies, are integrated into world time and may expect still to be alive in 2050.

Critical uncertainties

The counterparts of predetermined elements are critical uncertainties. Both are crucially linked to each other. As Pierre Wack says, we find our critical uncertainties by questioning our assumptions about predetermined elements. Take, for instance, Japan's trade surpluses and high savings rates. Let's assume that they carry on as usual. We know that this will irritate neighbours and the US Congress. We also know that they will not go on for ever. When will they disappear? We cannot be certain. Nor can we be certain about the detailed circumstances of their disappearance. Or take Ericsson's definition of uncertainties in its 'Ericsson 2005' exercise: 'Who will win "the battle for the consumer"? How fast will wireless access grow? How will telecommunications be de-regulated? How successful will Internet be?' Scenarios are built on inserting these uncertainties into a narrative framed by predetermined elements.

Assumptions about different scenarios

We can relate as many narratives about the future, or indeed about the past, as our imagination encompasses. But the aim of scenarios is not

The aim of scenarios is to escape the tyranny of extrapolation.

to set out a list, select the most probable and then bet the company on it. The aim is to escape the tyranny of extrapolation in order to open people's minds to alternative futures. It is enough for us to elaborate four scenarios for that purpose, and to think through their narratives so that they are internally consistent, credible and relevant to our corporate needs and help us to challenge our own conventional wisdoms. Here, we shall discuss the contrasting rationales informing four possible types of scenario:

- business as usual;
- here we go again;
- discontinuity and choice;
- the forced march.

Business as usual

As its title suggests, this scenario holds no surprises. Tomorrow, it says, is like yesterday. In its most prevalent form, business as usual assumes continuous progress and specifies indefinite incremental changes. Looking back towards the past from the vantage point of the present, the historian recounts events as they happened. One event leads to another in a straight line of causality, so that major historical events may be traced in the manner of a statistical trend from A through B to C, where we now are, to D and E in the future. The future thus acquires a number of known traits: it emerges from the past in an unbroken line of progress; each stage is qualitatively superior to the preceding stage; it is unidirectional, and its driving forces are constant. 'The present', in Leibnitz's words, 'is pregnant with the future.' Or using an architectural analogy, humanity progresses up the great staircase of history.

Such a set of assumptions is particularly useful for corporations, like Ericsson, competing in hi-tech markets. When Ericsson started work on their 2005 exercise, their people saw strong signs of convergence between their industry – telecommunications – and computers and the media industry. The market for a manufacturer like Ericsson was booming in mobile phones; the computer industry was moving to the Internet, and media groups were entering electronic distribution through the Internet and digital satellites. All these developments were, in our parlance, 'in the pipeline' and so 'predetermined certainties': the merger of these three industries would create what Ericsson called 'the Infocom Industry'. The question which had to be answered was: what will this industry look like? Three scenarios were elaborated that built on the continuity of known trends. They were differentiated from one another by different combinations of uncertainties.

But such an assumption of continuous progress is much more dubious when applied to whole societies, as nineteenth-century thinkers tended to do. Consider the father of modern socialism, Karl Marx. His societies ascend the staircase of history through the driving force of the class struggle. New technologies regularly shake the existing edifice of society, and produce new relations of production between owners and workers, yielding social revolutions. Marx has his history of the world begin with the absolutist Asian state, which he depicts as disrupted by exogenous challenges. This in turn is replaced by the societies of antiquity, feudalism and capitalism – each being driven forward by its 'internal contradictions'. Capitalism labours towards its own doom by creating a vast proletariat, which one day organizes, overthrows the bourgeoisie and then rules the means of production. His workers' paradise marks an end to continuous change – a self-fufilling prophecy which well describes Soviet sclerosis under Brezhnev.

The economics-drives-politics school of development barely differs from Marx. This is best illustrated in Walt Rustow's *Stages of Economic Growth*, the subtitle of which was, significantly, 'A Non-Communist Manifesto'.[9] Rustow traces the five stages of growth from traditional agrarian society, through the preconditions for 'take-off' when there is 'some external intrusion by more advanced societies', through take-off, when 'old blocks and resistances to steady growth are finally overcome', to the stage of maturity when modern technology is applied over a wide range of activities, to the age of high consumption, 'which the Soviet Union is technically ready for'. The only hitch in Rustow's determinist construction, other than his significant misjudgement about the USSR, is that 'strategic choices' must be taken by societies as to how their resources are disposed. Obviously, wrong choices are possible, so progress after all becomes a matter of human choice where alternative futures are possible, if not desirable.

The linear view of history knows where it comes from and where it is heading. This is the way that the EU tells its children its own narrative. Before the creation, the heavens were filled with the din of war, and the shrieks of the innocent. Then came peace, and the founding fathers, and they saw coal and steel (stage one). Thereafter was added unto them agriculture, atomic energy and trade (stage two). Whereupon. Ted said, we must join (stage three), and the chosen people crossed the valley of Euro-sclerosis. Then Greece, Spain and Portugal were added unto them (stage four), and they multiplied greatly, increasing their exchanges and negotiating the internal market. A mighty push up the staircase of history was provided by a composite character called François Kohl, and he could see the land of milk and honey stretching out before him (stage five). As they surveyed the promised land, they saw emus, pescs and other strange animals. Brother Jacques was there with his staff, like Moses, pointing the way forward.

A mighty push up the staircase of history was provided by a composite character called François Kohl.

There is a particular difficulty with this staircase view of history. What happens when the energy in the driving force dries up and we reach the final stair? We reach the communist nirvana, says Marx, or enter an age of plenty, argues Rustow: Kohl entones that Union spells the end of war; Brother Jacques envisages a paradise of monetary stability and sound social policies for the Union. For all, the step on that last staircase marks history's end, and the future becomes Cloud Cuckoo Land, where people cease to be people, at least as we have known them.

We can, of course, be propelled forward at an accelerated rate into this new condition beyond history, as the US political philosopher, Henry Adams, maintained.[10] As human knowledge accumulates, the speed of change follows a law of acceleration whereby the length of a historic period is equal to the square root of the number of years of the preceding stage. The first stage lasted 900,000 religion-steeped years. The mechanical stage followed, lasting 300 years. Then came the era of electricity, which lasted seventeen years. Stage four is the era of pure mathematics, and lasts four years. Thereafter, we enter a stationary condition.

Here we go again

The past is forever repeated. This less prevalent version of business as usual holds that human existence is cyclical. A leads to B to C to D to A, and so on indefinitely. This version is in fact very current, and slips into human actions and beliefs in all sorts of ways. It holds, as the Stoics did, that there is nothing new under the sun. Everything is predetermined, like the sun's rise and fall, day after day, as spring follows winter and one year the next. This cyclical view is really pre-industrial because it emphasizes the monotony of repetition and denies the accumulation of scientific know-how. Adapted to the world shaped by human technologies, it lives on in modified form. Technologies change, it says, but human nature remains the same. You and I are born, grow up, mature, age and die, and we take the knowledge that we acquire in our lifetime about what is right and what is wrong to our grave. There is no moral progress in humanity. The French have an expression for it: *plus ça change, plus c'est la même chose*, loosely translated into English as 'here we go again'.

A cyclical view generates beliefs in an eternal return of some great leader, or of a Golden Age which we struggle to re-create in our image. If we wish to have some idea of what people think about the present, we can ask, as a German TV producer did of a Russian peasant in a 1998 documentary, what he thinks about the political class. 'The problem', came the answer, 'lies with the post-communists: once we have swept them away, Russia will start again to prosper.' 'How can this be done?' 'Russia needs a leader with a steel fist', in other words a Stalin who lives on in deep empathy with his people – a Stalin who will strike the evil dead, and leave the righteous to live. Such a belief is only a step away from the mirage of a Golden Age, one of the most dangerous and widespread of illusions in a world of rapid technological change. 'When will you stop killing?' Spain's Prime Minister Felipe González asked of a Basque terrorist, 'When the goats are once again grazing on the streets of San Sebastian.'

What causes this fall from grace, this abasement that afflicts us? The cyclical view readily accounts for decay and renewal. Seneca, the king of Stoics, had human life periodically devastated by some exogenous event, like fire and flood – indeed, Noah's story of taking the animals into the Ark is similar in inspiration. Then the tempest abates, and each period begins with a golden age in which men live simply and in innocence, not because they are wise but because they are ignorant.[11] Learning accumulates, and the arts and science flourish, bringing with them decay, luxury and vice. The gods become angry, and here we go again. The novelty introduced by Vico, the Neapolitan historical philosopher of the early eighteenth century, was to make history the agency of humans. The history of each people, says Vico, starts 'with the origins of society, to follow them in their progress, their period of stabilization, their decadence and their end'.[12]

China is one civilization which has its own cyclical interpretation of history. For nearly four thousand years from 1766 BC to AD 1895, China was ruled by sixteen dynasties which came and went at varying lengths of time. Typically, traditional Chinese historiography has a new dynasty begin with capable rulers carrying out various reforms and extending the boundaries of Chinese administration. These are followed by a golden age of stability, prosperity and cultural achievement. However, as routine sets in so do corruption and decay. Finally, the dynasty falls because of internal rebellion or external invasion, only for a new dynasty to be established in war and violence, and for the pattern to repeat itself. So we may ask: how far along its cycle is the present communist dynasty whose forebears entered the Celestial Palace in 1949? At the beginning of a golden age, or at the stage where corruption and decay set in? The answer to this question illuminates the world of the twenty-first century.

A very different, technology-driven theory of cycles is in effect more of a spiral view than a permanent turn around the wheel of life. The long-term rise and fall of economic activity is recorded in a statistical series developed by Nicolas Kondratieff, the Russian economist who worked for the Soviet government in its early days and was then liquidated by Stalin in the terror of the 1930s. His series started in 1790 and

traced three cycles up to the 1920s, which Schumpeter later inter-
preted as driven by new clusters of technological innovation. According to Schumpeter, these cycles were initiated by the introduction of
steam engines (the first cycle lasting from 1785 to 1851); followed by
the expansion of the railroads, then by electricity and the introduction
of automobiles. In 1926 Kondratieff forecast that the downturn of the
long fourth cycle would take effect in the US in the 1970s, and be
accompanied by a public indifference in the US to world affairs and a
move to social conservatism.[13]

The difficulty with Kondratieff is that he does not spell out the links
between technological innovations, their diffusion, economic policy
and international relations. The task is taken up in part by Michael
Porter,[14] who mixes the staircase with the cyclical view in his attempt
to explain why firms based in particular states achieve international
success. Porter posits four stages of economic progress, where each
stage involves different industries and distinct government roles:

1 In the first stage, technology is imported to complement the local
   factors of production, and the national economy is highly sensitive
   to the world economic cycle.
2 In stage two the economy is investment-driven, with firms using
   technology one generation behind the leaders, and government
   plays a substantial role in channelling resources to key sectors.
3 The third stage is innovation-driven, where consumers and industrial customers are increasingly sophisticated. More emphasis now
   falls on innovation, marketing and service orientation. But the government is still heavily involved in the allocation of capital
   resources, the issuing of licences, the provision of export subsidies
   and protection of the domestic market.
4 Stage four is where Porter slips into a more traditional use of the
   cycle view. This stage, says Porter, is wealth-driven, where position
   maintenance is the dominant strategy. Capital markets expand as the
   pool of capital grows. Industrial activities are downsized, and drift
   and ultimate decline sets in. Here Porter is clearly referring to Britain
   as a warning to the US, and is either preaching to his compatriots to
   mend their ways and/or is seeking to influence decision-making. We

have always to distinguish between the analysis and the motivations of the analyst.

Let us end this section by citing one other contemporary cyclical interpretation of economic performance, which is policy-driven. Why do nations rise and decline, the economist Mancur Olson asks?[15] Distributional coalitions, he says, capture key positions in the state. In the case of developing countries, city-based industries, their owners, managers and trade unions militate for import protection and higher returns for themselves. People in the countryside are poor, badly organized and drift into the cities where they are bought off by food price controls. This lowers returns to the countryside, which in turn militates for subsidies on the budget, as is the case in India where subsidies for fertilizer and energy amount to 10 per cent of GDP. The cycle of impoverishment may be broken only in times of war, or by a powerful government which imposes competitive markets on recalcitrant lobbies interested in the preservation of the status quo, and nestling into the many nooks and crannies of the modern state.

Discontinuity and choice

Humans choose their futures. Images of the future which suppose a change-by-discontinuity are all opposed to the idea of the staircase view of history. The discontinuous approach rejects the idea of unconditional progress, but generally accepts that things are moving in the 'right' direction. The historian rejects the tracing of a path of causality back from results to causes, but moves into the future from situation via choice to results. This entails an explanation of why some options are discarded, and others are chosen, as the participants in the historical process select their way into the future. History becomes a series of discontinuous movements where, *ex ante*, there are possibilities, but during the event these are discarded. Time thus traces a path between a permanent overture and closure of options, of what Bertrand de Jouvenel calls '*les futuribles*'.[16] Discontinuity's route runs from A to B to C to D where C and D need not be on the axis of A to B. Its future is unknown territory.

This scenario is also valuable for corporations because it warns that the future is unlike the past. The future is made by a host of human decisions, which constantly create new threats and opportunities. New technologies are permanently being conceived in a host of laboratories or garages around the world. We can never be sure when they will hit the markets or what their reception will be. In 1985 John Opel, IBM's chairman, assumed business as usual when he announced that sales would double to $100 billion by 1990, and profits would continue to grow exponentially. IBM duly hired more than 100,000 new personnel. But things did not turn out as forecast. Simple extrapolation of market trends failed to account for the fast growth of the personal computer market, the emergence of formidable competitors like Apple, Microsoft and Intel, and the relative decline of IBM's corporate market. Sales of IBM were $72 billion in 1996, and its workforce was halved to 430,000.

One version of progressive change by discontinuous decisions holds that the path embarked upon is modified by key events. The course of history is set for a while during which incremental steps are made, then comes another key event. The task of historians is to study these events, and the cluster of happenings around them. As their path is shaped by a key decision or set of decisions, the historian asks What if? questions.[17] Why were the alternatives not adopted, and what would have happened had they been? What if, for instance, Pontius Pilate had let Christ go free? He could have lived to a ripe old age with his disciples, and his fame would have spread far and wide as a holy man. But his crucifixion, which lies at the very heart of Christianity and where God made man sacrifices Himself for the sins of the world, would not have occurred. What if the Confederates had won at Gettysburg? The war, possibly, may have continued with ultimate victory still going to the Yankees.

The discontinuous view suggests that nothing is written in advance, and that timely reforms are required to make things better. Western liberal society, Keynes argued in the inter-war years, is not bound for the dustbin of history. It is not inexorably crushed between the Marxists' class struggle, and the hammer of fascist will. The source of underemployment is not the worker or the plutocrat but Aunt Jessica, who saves much and spends little. The old dear has to be coaxed by an attractive rate of interest to place her savings in Treasury bonds, which can then be deployed to finance public works. The prime contractors to the public works pay wages to workers who spend and save; they also engage subcontractors who pay wages to workers who spend and save. The spending and saving cascades income through society so that the initial injection of funds is multiplied many times over. More spending generates jobs, and more jobs generate a more contented population.

Discontinuity in policy is advisable when the situation has changed, its advocates maintain. Take, for example, the debate on US policy toward Japan after the Cold War. A commitment by the US to a forward presence in East Asia through to 2015 is anachronistic, the Japan specialist Chalmers Johnson argues.[18] Such a commitment buys China and Japan more time to consolidate their ascendancy before telling the Americans to go home. The policy ignores the shift around the world from military to economic power, and it perpetuates Japan's unhealthy dependence on the US. Japan should be allowed to develop its own defence, while the US should stop thinking that Asian countries prefer 'market democracy' to Asian models of state capitalism. The recommendation is that the US should disengage from its tight security relationship with Japan, thereby encouraging Japan to take more responsibility for its own affairs and allow for the emergence of a multi-polar order in Asia.

The source of underemployment is not the worker or the plutocrat but Aunt Jessica, who saves much and spends little.

Whatever the rights or wrongs of this particular advice, the statesman and the corporate leader have to make up their minds about what is the most judicious policy. They should have a knowledge of history because therein lie the seeds of the present and the future. In other words, they should have a view of time as synchronous.[19] We have, for instance, a vision of the future which serves to pull present and past towards it through policy. This is the heart of the concept of 'core competence' peddled by business strategy gurus. Our future is inherent in the skills and resources that our corporation has inherited, and that exist now, so that rather than focus on the details of the particular products or clusters of products that will emerge in the future, we focus on tending our core competences. The metaphor is one of the tree, where the soil provides the basic nutrients, the roots are the basic technologies, the sap conveys their genetic codes, the branches are the product groups, and the leaves are the products.

Since people are the subject of history, and make their future, radical discontinuities with the past are more than possible; they are highly probable. Brains are equally distributed around a world whose population in the 1990s is well over 5.5 billion people. In twenty or so years that population will number 8 to 9 billion, multiplying the world's brainpower by a factor of six relative to what it was in 1900. As technologies continue to develop exponentially, it is only through intuition allied to imagination that any one of us can anticipate the combinations and novelties which can occur to our fellows.

A radical discontinuity to the political world of the 1990s would be, for instance, a new civil war in the US, due, say, to the accelerated loss of technological leadership on which the self-respect of the US has been built. Another would be the emergence of some great leader in Africa, who welded the world's most populous continent into one powerful unit.

The forced march

The future must and should be a rupture with the past. We are heading in the wrong direction and, unless strenuous corrective action is taken, disaster is our inevitable lot. A wrong turning on our historical path was taken at D, a further mistake was made at E, and now we are going backwards. Here we are verging on prescription and prophecy, an expression of hope that the impending disaster may be reversed by some heroic act of violence and creativity.

We may observe that our call to urgent action is implicitly teleological, or takes its lead from the staircase view of history. We should be pursuing the path of righteousness, its religiously minded advocates hold, or we should be participating in the common ascent of mankind to ever higher levels of prosperity and happiness. Because we are not, vigorous action must be taken to turn things around: the people must be brought back to the paths of righteousness, and the temple purged of false prophets; the 'rigidities' that are holding us back in joining the common ascent must be rooted out for ever; 'Chainsaw Al' Dunlap, the 'Rambo in pinstripes', must be called in to downsize the corporation, and send the share price skywards. This scenario is steeped in high drama.

One cause of decadence is 'structural', and only courageous action suffices to root it out. France's stagnation under the Third Republic led to defeat in 1940, followed by occupation. France fell, the prevalent thinking in the National Council of the Resistance held, because the bourgeoisie were incapable of investing in the long-term prosperity and prestige of their country. These were to be achieved only by state control over the financial system and capital market, so that the financial resources of France would be used for the benefit of the French people. The Fourth Republic's first plan was presented by its author, Jean Monnet, in terms of France facing a choice between 'modernization or decadence'. 'Expansion, production, competition, concentration,' de Gaulle later declared, 'these evidently, are the rules which henceforth the French economy, traditionally circumspect, conservative, protected and dispersed, must impose on itself.'[20]

The reign of money is a favourite target for professional declinists, from the German cultural conservatives of the nineteenth century to Oswald Spengler in his book *Decline of the West*, which appeared in 1918, and Michael Porter of Harvard Business School. Germany's cultural conservatives saw themselves as guardians of an ancient tradition, threatened by modernity, and the radical measures they devised ranged from the ruthless to the utopian.[21] Spengler gloomily extended this vision to the West. The great creators of the past are no more, the West's belief in its own genius is waning, it faces depopulation and is dominated by the 'spirit of money'. But, he adds, the day will come when Caesar will launch the final struggle and smash 'the dictatorship of money and its political arm, democracy'. This struggle, he adds, 'will yield a definitive form of civilisation'. Porter, in less apocalyptic tones, summons his compatriots to abjure the lures of financial wealth, and avoid the way of Britain.

International finance lends itself in particular to advice to undertake a forced march away from disaster. The world financial markets are beyond control, it is said, or, rather, they are in the hands of sinister forces in New York and London. They have precipitated the world into a *'Tsunami* of Transformation' – a tornado of change, driven by impersonal forces which sweep civilization away. 'If this global economy cannot be made to work for working people,' John Sweeney, president of the US trade union movement was reported as saying at the annual jamboree at Davos, Switzerland, for the movers and shakers of this world, 'it will reap a reaction that may make the twentieth century tranquil by comparison'. A best-selling book, by two *Der Spiegel* journalists, has the world financial markets launching their attack on democracy and welfare:[22] Hitler was the result, they argue in a curious re-adaptation of the Führer's own thesis that it was indeed the financial markets which helped bring him to power.

The idea of decadence readily borrows from biology. The body politic is infested with disease, which is the source of decline in inventiveness, the arts and of industry. The task of the statesman-doctor is to diagnose the illness and to prescribe and apply the cure. Note that the analogy invites us to look inwards to the organism, rather than to worry about its environment, although of course an extreme form of political medicine can prescribe isolation from the rest of the world. Mao's prescription for China consisted in part of ensuring that foreign cultural influences, such as Christian churches and Western capitalists, no longer contaminated the country. But the root of his cure was to pluck Confucius, whose teachings taught children to venerate the wisdom of their elders, from the soul of China. China's revolution was to be cultural, or not at all. At the end of his life, he conceded to President Nixon that all he had done was to change a few places in the neighbourhood of Beijing.[23]

The body politic is infested with disease, which is the source of decline in inventiveness, the arts and of industry.

Barbarians at the gate is another analogy for the leader calling followers to a forced march. You sleep while the enemy approaches. Prepare for war in order to ensure the peace. We must act as one in order to survive. We will not tolerate traitors in our midst, and we must rid ourselves of our former easy-going ways. World markets, this line of reasoning holds, are a battlefield on which the producers from the world's nations battle for domination. They say that they seek to satisfy the needs of consumers, but they seek in fact to eliminate rivals. If we do not organize like them, and make our domestic market an impregnable bastion, we will be liquidated. We must organize ourselves like Japan, the US declinists argue, and not assume that Japan's talk of free trade is what they do. We must imitate Germany, say the French champions of importing their 'German model' to France, and run large trade surpluses, subsidize our industries and promote tribal cross-shareholdings.

One variant of the forced march scenario is where there is a voluntary conversion of the masses to a new vision of a world which gives full play to the passions. This world, it says, is falsely rationalist. Descartes's triumph has allowed the bourgeoisie, the authorities – whoever it is that deludes us into obedience to their wishes – to divide the world into thinkers and doers. Those who think, exist, and those who do, execute what they are told. The restraints of civilization are thus a mental prison which we have allowed to be fastened on us to exploit us. Our battle cry should be: 'I feel, therefore I am.' We should drop our tools, and give full reign to our sexual passions. Our slogan is 'Make Love, not War', and our practical advice to working people is to seduce the boss's wife, and then tell him how grateful you are. We work only in so far as it contributes to our leisure: we definitely do not work in order to contribute to 'the GNP' – the modern Moloch to whom only fools sacrifice.

Common to all the forms that the forced march scenario takes is an identification of leader and 'the people', the true as opposed to the renegades. The call to action is in effect a pretender's justification for remaking the world in his own image, and at the extreme to be his own law-maker. What I want is what shall be. It is the plea of pretenders to the title of tyrant.

Conclusion

But let us end this chapter on a high note, and then draw some final points about the value of future-oriented thinking. Our high note is a business as usual scenario, because it would seem to be already present in our minds and our dreams.

'The Long Boom', which we have alluded to, depicts a radiant twenty-five years for the world. We are being propelled forward by a cascade of technological innovations, combined with an unprecedented opening for all on to world markets. For the first time (well, we say, not quite the first time), the regions of the world are interlocking as an ascendant Asia and a reintegrated greater Europe – including a convalescent Russia – join with America in creating a great juggernaut of a world economy which pulls the whole of humanity into prosperity. By 2005 the world economy's productivity levels will have lifted growth to 6 per cent, doubling world wealth within twelve years. By 2020 the great planetary debate will have opened, and the history of the twenty-first century will be one of a civilization of civilizations.

Right, wrong or bold? We cannot know until 2020 whether it is right or wrong. But it is bold, it does illuminate the future context of decisions for companies, and it does lay down a challenge. It is imaginative; it is internally consistent and it holds an essential message. It is plausible, to those who look forward to it as to those who are horrified at the very thought. It is, in short, not *respectable* – the fundamental sin of banality when thinking about the prospects for world business.

To summarize, the major assumptions of the art of thinking about the future hold that the future depends upon our acts, our dreams, our minds and their imagination, their memories and their capacity for reason. It is therefore uncertain, and open-ended, but not necessarily always and in unlimited ways. Thinking about the future requires us to draw on a wide range of information. We have to be ready to use a variety of methods and sources. And because humans make their own history, we focus on individuals, groups, corporations, states and peoples – and their histories. These histories are composed of possible, or probable, futures in constant reformulation.

Notes

1 Quoted in Bernard Cazes, *Histoire des futurs: Les figures de l'avenir de saint Augustin au XXIe siècle*, Paris, Seghers, 1986.
2 André Robida, *Le XXe siècle* (3rd edn), Paris, Editions Montgrédien, 1883.
3 Pierre Wack, 'Scenarios: Uncharted Waters', *Harvard Business Review*, September–October 1985.
4 Arie de Geus, 'Planning as Learning', *Harvard Business Review*, March–April 1988.
5 See Sheetal K. Chand and Albert Jaeger, *Aging Populations and Public Pension Schemes*, IMF Occasional Paper 147, Washington DC, 1996.
6 Quoted in Peter Schwartz, *The Art of the Long View: Planning for the Future in an Uncertain World*, New York, Doubleday, 1991.

7 Peter Schwartz and Peter Leyden, 'The Long Boom: A History of the Future 1980–2020', *Wired*, July 1997.

8 Spiros Makridakis, *Forecasting, Planning and Strategy for the 21ˢᵗ Century*, New York, Free Press, 1990.

9 Walt Rustow, *The Stages of Economic Growth: A Non-Communist Manifesto*, London, Cambridge University Press, 1960.

10 Henry Adams, *The Education of Henry Adams*, ed. Ernest Samuels, New York, Library of America, 1983, p. 1153.

11 See Charles A. Beard, in his 'Introduction' to J. B. Bury, *The Idea of Progress: An Inquiry into its Origin and Growth*, London, Macmillan, 1932.

12 Vico, *Scienza Nuova*, 1725–30, para. 349.

13 Zbig Brzezinski, 'America in a Hostile World', *Foreign Policy*, No. 23, 1976.

14 Michael Porter, *The Competitive Advantage of Nations*, London, Macmillan, 1990.

15 Mancur Olson, *The Rise and Decline of Nations: Economic Growth, Stagflation and Social Rigidities*, Yale University Press, 1982.

16 Bertrand de Jouvenel, *L'art de la Conjecture*, Paris, Sedeis, 1972.

17 Niall Ferguson, *Virtual History: Alternatives and counterfactuals*, London, Papermac, 1998.

18 Chalmers Johnson and E. B. Keehn, 'The Pentagon's Ossified Strategy', *Foreign Affairs*, July–August 1995.

19 See especially the brilliant discussion in Charles Hampden-Turner and Fons Trompenaar, *The Seven Cultures of Capitalism*, New York, Doubleday, 1993, chapter 7.

20 *Mémoires d'Espoir: Le Renouveau, 1958–62*, Paris, Librairie Plan, 1970.

21 Fritz Stern, *The Politics of Cultural Despair: A Study in the Rise of Germanic Ideology*, Berkeley, The University of California Press, 1961.

22 Hans-Peter Martin and Harald Schumann, *Die Globalisierungsfalle: Der Angriff auf Demokratie und Wohlstand*, Hamburg, Rowohlt, 1996.

23 Henry Kissinger, *White House Years*, Boston, Little Brown, 1979.

Chapter 7

CORPORATE TRANSFORMATION AND POLITICAL TRANSITION

Managing far-flung corporations is a task not lightly undertaken. As corporations become global citizens, so they face governments torn between contradictory pressures from global markets and international bodies, and their national constituencies. Managers of corporations with a worldwide spread of assets have therefore to reconcile competitive pressures for efficiency and standardization with the need to tailor corporate activities to local conditions. They operate in a world economy, driven by the dynamics of world and local time. In this chapter we look first at the evolution of different types of corporate strategies, then examine local contexts which serve as home or host to corporate investors, and finally discuss how senior management may conceive of the simultaneous but non-synchronized transformation process of states and corporations.

Corporate strategies and structures

For most of the twentieth century, Big Business and Big Government have reigned supreme. Modern industrial organization dates from 1913, when Henry Ford observed how a whole cow entered a Chicago slaughterhouse at one end and issued forth as sirloin and steak at the other. He determined to invert the process, and assemble parts into a Model-T. Frederick Winslow Taylor had already outlined the Principles of Scientific Management, whereby tasks were divided into discrete forms and executed by specialists, in turn supervised by managers whose job was to control and to motivate. Motivation was ensured through force and fear in the factory, and control over the tiers of managers required to run the organization was maintained through capital budgeting techniques. Lenin was much impressed, and laid the ground for Stalin to turn Russia into a giant factory for tractors and tanks. The mind-numbing experience of life as an industrial worker is immortalized in Charlie Chaplin's *Modern Times*.

New technologies in the 1920s enabled corporations to diversify production into new markets by linking economies of scale to a wider scope of products. Banks arranged for loans to customers on hire-purchase, and provided the likes of General Motors, General Electric and International Harvester with unprecedented market growth. Boom turned to bust in 1929, leading to Roosevelt's New Deal and the closer association of Big Labour with Big Business. Big Government came in the 1940s, when the captains of US industry and finance in effect took over the running of the US war effort. Allied victory paved the way for the dominance of US corporations in European markets, and for the spread of US business practice and experience around the world.

Running large organizations required senior management to elaborate broad strategies to guide policy over the longer term, and to adapt the organization to changing conditions and to new opportunities. The typical US corporation had developed initially along functional lines, but this created major problems of co-ordination between the purchasing, production, finance and marketing departments as the number of products sold multiplied. Some decided like GM to centralize authority, risking 'analysis paralysis' among a senior management far removed from the humbler but vital tasks of production and sales, while others like 3M managed to delegate authority and initiative down the organizational hierarchy. To facilitate assessment of the profitability of operations, the trend set in to split the organization into product divisions, with their own functional sub-units. To this was added an international division as markets developed abroad.

John Stopford and Louis Wells recorded the problems inherent in such an impermanent arrangement.[1] The usual international division held a mandate to run business within a geographic area, and competed for home attention with the foreign desks of product divisions. This led to endless bureaucratic efforts to 'co-ordinate' activities, prompting corporations to take one of two options. Those firms which sold few products and were still organized along functional lines tended to opt for worldwide and regional area structures. Regional structures duplicated the functions back home, and to a degree were able to respond to local conditions. Multi-product firms took the other tack, and tended to expand the responsibilities of their product divisions worldwide. Their strengths played to the demand by consumers for quality and price competitiveness. Marrying local responsiveness with price competitiveness could be achieved by having local managers report to two chiefs in a matrix organization, run on joint regional and product lines.

That was in 1972. Then came the oil shock, and the Japanese *tsunami*, or whirlwind, of competition across a swathe of industries, notably automobiles and consumer electronics. Nixon's recent visit to China, and then Washington's pressure on US oil multinationals to heed US interests first before their commercial instincts, delivered Japan's political and business elites a double shock. The impressive response was to tighten up on consumption, and to make a concerted drive for efficiency in Japan's major export industries. Recent research has shown that Japan's corporations were the first to reverse the general trend among developed country corporations

Japanese corporations rode to victory in market after market in the course of the 1970s and 1980s.

to an ever slower turnover in stocks,[2] and to take the lead in 'lean production'. The method was made famous in the best-selling book, *The Machine That Changed the World*,[3] which recorded how Toyota learned to combine US lessons on mass production with a skilled workforce, who were given responsibility for quality control throughout the manufacturing process. Japanese corporations rode to victory in market after market in the course of the 1970s and 1980s, as Western corporations made desperate efforts to chase down their cost and experience curves.

The corporate strategy fraternity, headquartered in Harvard Business School, took on the challenge by plunging into the study of all things Japanese. Two broad schools of thinking emerged over time, one being championed by Michael Porter, and his studies on corporate and national competitiveness, which we met in earlier chapters. Porter introduced neo-classical micro-economics and industrial organization theory into the analysis of business strategy and performance. In essence, he presents firms as competing among themselves to make profits by selling products that consumers value at the going price. Firms raise profits either by adding value to the product to enable them to charge a premium price, or by lowering production costs.

He thereby proposes two broad categories of corporate strategy:[4] one category emphasizes product differentiation through superior design, quality or functionality. The implication is that the corporation should invest in its employees, their ideas and the knowledge that they accumulate. The other is to lower costs by achieving economies of scale, which refers to reducing the cost of each unit through volume production. The more experience that firms have in making a product, the more cheaply they learn to make it.[5] The implication here is that firms are permanently on the look-out for ways to cut costs while preserving know-how in the organization.

The second school of business strategy thinking took a more political view of the corporation. Corporations were analyzed as social constructs, rooted in their home and host country contexts, with their own sources of legitimacy and their own measures of performance. The distinct tone of this approach is evident in the definition that my colleague, Yves Doz, and his co-author, C. K. Prahalad, give to corporate strategy as 'the dominant world view' among senior managers of the nature of the competition, the key success factors in sustaining a competitive advantage, the nature of the risk incurred, and the resource base on which they draw.[6]

The two schools of business strategy thinking – one more inclined to economics, and the other more sensitive to the political dimension – have been able to meet on a significant common terrain. As Doz and Prahalad put it, managers must be able to 'recognize the balance of the forces of global integration and local responsiveness to which a business is subject'.[7] The present from which senior managers start to consider their competitive position is the result of the inheritance from past policies, structures and performances. Senior managers must understand the history which makes their corporations as they are, in order to anticipate where they may lead them. The paths they take away from their original configurations have been analyzed by Christopher Bartlett of the Harvard Business School, and Sumantra Ghoshal of the London Business School and are illustrated in Figure 7.1.[8] It incorporates historical time, as it depicts the development of corporate strategy, as states negotiated the opening of markets in the decades after 1945.

Figure 7.1
CORPORATE STRATEGIES AND STATE STRUCTURES

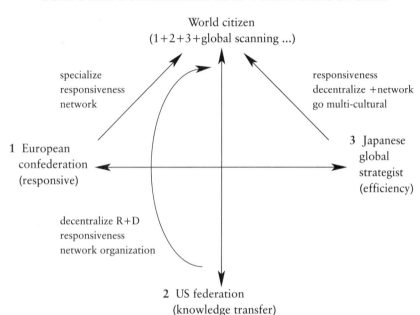

Source: C. A. Bartlett and S. Ghoshal (1989) *Managing Across Borders: The Transnational Solution*, Boston, Harvard Business School. Reprinted with permission.

The European decentralized federation

European corporations, such as Philips, Unilever or Nestlé, moved abroad in the early decades of the twentieth century, organizing in worldwide area structures. Local subsidiaries became highly independent of the parent company. Scale economies for the corporation as a whole were sacrificed in favour of servicing local tastes, and establishing sound working relationships with local governments. There was some sharing between the parent company and its units in terms of flows of information about research and development, appointments to senior positions, and the transfer of capital and dividends. Co-ordination mechanisms between parent and unit took the form of bureaucratic and budgetary mechanisms of control. Contacts between the units were limited. Such a structure was eminently suited to Europe's fragmentation in discrete national markets well into the 1980s, but proved highly vulnerable to cost pressures as markets opened and competition sharpened.

The US co-ordinated federalist

The postwar years were the era of US dominance, when GM, Ford, IBM, Coca-Cola, Caterpillar and Procter & Gamble became household names. US corporations operated abroad through relatively autonomous subsidiaries. Their key asset was the size and opulence of their home market. Overseas subsidiaries exploited products first developed there. They were not customized to local tastes, but competed on quality at competitive prices. Senior management kept research and development facilities in the US, and managed the transfer of skills and technologies through the life cycle of the product. But there were serious deficiencies in this method. Headquarters controlled the main resources, and left operations to the locals. Locals met glass ceilings for promotion to senior positions. Budgetary and bureaucratic controls from the centre suffered from upward creep, as did demands from local governments. In addition, US corporations, proved highly vulnerable to super-competitors from Japan.

Japanese global strategists

In the 1970s and 1980s the Japanese *tsunami* struck. The strategic intent of corporations such as Toyota, NEC and Matsushita was to achieve global dominance in their respective markets in order to fund the switch from competition on the base of low labour costs towards hi-tech, lean manufacturing systems. Such corporations treated the world as one market. Knowledge was developed and retained centrally. Their plants were scaled to produce mass standardized products, which were sold with aggressive price strategies. Integration between the central product division and each of the subsidiaries was achieved through top-down strategic plans and controls, the fostering of a strong corporate identity and through socialization of personnel. Subsidiaries were concentrated in a few locations. But such 'global strategists' were vulnerable to trade retaliation, consumer reactions to standardized products, and to glass ceilings for promotions of locals that were set very low in the organization.

The transnational corporate citizen

A transnational corporation, Bartlett and Ghoshal maintain, has to achieve all three virtues of local responsiveness, efficiency and knowledge management simultaneously. Its key feature is that it functions as an integrated network. Local units provide a source of skills, ideas and capabilities, and attain global scale by becoming the corporation's local champion for a product sold worldwide. It adopts flexible manufacturing techniques, and takes optimum choices with regard to sourcing of inputs, pricing and product design. This implies a very different role for headquarters, as all units must develop mechanisms for integration and co-ordination among themselves. Transnational corporations speak English as a common language, develop inclusive management networks, acquire a corporate-wide global scanning capability, and promote a common culture through incentives, corporate visions and leadership selection (see Box). In short, they become a learning organization in a permanent process of renewal.[9]

> What is required of business in the twenty-first century? 'You want to be able to optimize a business globally – to specialize in the production of components, to drive economies of scale as far as you can, to rotate managers and technologists around the world to share expertise and solve problems. But you also want to have deep local roots everywhere you operate – building products in the countries where you sell them, recruiting the best local talent from universities, working with the local government to increase exports.'
>
> Quoted from 'The Logic of Global Business: An Interview with ABB's Percy Barnevik', *Harvard Business Review*, March–April 1991.

The world trend to global markets requires large, diversified corporations to take the path to becoming transnationals. This means that the transformation strategies of the first three types involve different trajectories:

- The loose European federation has to have its units specialize while retaining their local responsiveness, transform relations between headquarters and local management, and develop global scanning skills or recruit skills worldwide.
- The Japanese-type global strategist must develop local responsiveness, decentralize and export the domestic skills for network relationships to its worldwide organization, and – the biggest challenge of all – become a multi-cultural corporation.
- The US-type centralized federation has to decentralize research and development, learn to be locally responsive and acquire the skills to manage a networked organization.

The model predicts the growth of highly flexible and competitive transnationals who treat the world as their oyster. As Bartlett and Ghoshal warn, this is no easy task, and above all depends on an inbuilt corporate capacity to tolerate a much greater degree of ambiguity in the organization while retaining vital control over far-flung operations. This entails senior management moving away from detailed strategies to clearly defining corporate purposes, to think in terms of managing a process rather than a structure, and to place people rather than systems centre stage. Ultimately, transnational corporations flourish if they build trust, the vital complement to inbuilt ambiguities in relations between interdependent units strung out across the world. *Transnationals become pillars of an open world order in which they have a crucial stake, and on which they depend but over which they cannot reign.*

The world trend to global markets requires large, diversified corporations to take the path to becoming transnationals.

National corporate regimes and corporate strategies

All major corporations, this line of argument holds, are converging on a norm, as they are driven to acquire the skills to succeed as transnationals. But they do so from their existing points of departure, as corporations with clear national origins and a web of subsidiaries nestled into their varied local landscapes. The task of senior management, Yves Doz and C. K. Prahalad argue, is that of strategic control and of the management of change, caused by competition in the markets and by the goals, policies and actions of governments. Analyzing the who, why and how of governments – which we presented in Chapter 4 – is, they suggest, an integral part of strategy formulation in a global business.

The question they ask is: what are the strategies of firms, given the nature of oligopolistic competition among few corporations in a particular branch and the variety of states in world markets? Let us answer this by looking at the different regimes prevailing in states as homes or as hosts to global corporations. States have three options with regard to foreign investment: they may favour direct investment, be hostile to it or prefer to sponsor international partnerships. Let us adopt this scheme, and apply it to the matrix presented in Figure 4.2 (see Chapter 4). The corporate population of different states is structured along two dimensions. As a reminder, the horizontal plane represents the degree of concentration in ownership, while the vertical axis depicts the degree of corporate concentration in terms of assets, sales and numbers employed. The Bretton Woods ideal sets the mythical, but crucial, universal standard against which corporate and state behaviour may be measured.

The 'Bretton Woods ideal'

Corporations invest in a country to the extent that they can benefit from factors of production – land, labour, capital and technology – that are competitively priced relative to alternative locations. In other words, *the attractiveness of location has much to do with reputation*. A 'Bretton Woods ideal' country, such as Ireland, is a favoured target for inward investors. Land is readily available for new plant. The government invests heavily in education at all levels. Capital is lightly taxed, and management skills can be learned by experience and through education. Ireland has the added advantage of being an old, established democracy. National corporations may remonstrate against the alleged privileges given to the foreign firms, but the government turns a deaf ear. They benefit in any case as subcontractors or as retailers of services. If inward investors wander to a new location, local jobs are lost to the government's displeasure. *But footloose corporations risk jeopardizing their reputation as good corporate citizens.*

A small business from a 'Bretton Woods ideal' country is content with exporting, until foreign governments threaten to impose duties or quotas. One option may be for our exporter to license technology, and earn income on the royalties paid. But the risk is that the licensee develops the technology, and in the longer term challenges our exporter on the home market. That is the experience of US and European corporations which licensed technologies to Japanese firms in the 1950s and 1960s, and paid the price in the coming decades in the form of greatly increased competitive pressures on their own markets. So our small firm exporter may decide to invest abroad rather than lose control over the firm's know-how. One step is to establish a foreign sales network in order to follow key home customers abroad. As the firm acquires knowledge about doing business abroad, its personal contacts there widen. Our exporter, say, is introduced by a friend to a local mayor. The locality is pleasant. A deal is struck to build a facility employing fifty people.

The Anglo-American shareholder system

In the Anglo-American shareholder system, there is a high degree of corporate concentration in some markets, and dispersed shareholding. Oligopolistic competition prevails and government takes a back seat with regard to corporate decisions on location. Foreign firms face little hindrance in setting up shop. Government is interested in inward investment because of the technology transfer, the jobs provided and the savings on foreign exchange as local production substitutes for imports. There may be some sensitivity when the inward investor bids to buy a national technology-rich firm, especially if it is a key subcontractor to the Ministry of Defence. There will be even more political resistance to purchase of local private corporations by foreign state-owned corporations, and foreign cross-shareholding conglomerates will not be allowed to list their shares – at least in the US – until their national accounts meet the transparency requirements of the regulatory authorities.

Corporate management is under permanent pressure to meet the demands of the shareholders for high returns on their investment. That means keeping profits up, even during a downturn in the national economy. Foreign investment enables the corporation to diversify its portfolio of assets, and become less reliant on the ups and downs of the business cycle in one country. But where senior management decides to locate a new activity is a more complex matter. Political or cultural preferences and affinities of senior management play their part. US foreign manufacturing investment is located in Mexico, Europe, the Gulf states or in ASEAN, where the US has significant political clout. Similarly, UK corporations invest primarily in North America and Europe. Another motive for location is to retaliate to competitor moves, or simply to go somewhere because others do so. *Such follow-the-leader decisions risk underestimating the dynamics at work in the host country.*

> *The home market is the launch pad for the conquest of foreign markets, and the domestic market is protected by all manner of means.*

German–Japanese corporate mercantilism

There is a high degree both of concentration in ownership and of corporate concentration. The domestic arena is highly regulated by legal norms or by custom. National ownership of major corporate groups is ensured through corporate cross-shareholding. Corporations own one another's shares, and share one another's boards. Inter-corporate links are tight throughout the chain of value creation, from the inputs to a production process, to the production itself, warehousing, marketing and after-sales. The home market is the launch pad for the conquest of foreign markets, and the domestic market is protected by all manner of means. The result is huge trade surpluses for the country, and cash flows for the corporations. Indeed, the reward for the prior investment appears only *when* foreign markets have been penetrated. This is national mercantilism's Achilles heel. The target country imposes tariffs, demands 'orderly marketing' accords, devalues its currency, or tries to loosen the clubbiness of corporate mercantilism through market-opening negotiations.

Inward investors have to negotiate their entry to the national corporate club, with which government is heavily involved in regulating oligopolistic industries, such as pharmaceuticals, telecommunications or foods. They cannot buy their way in through hostile takeovers because shares are tightly held and only a small proportion are traded. They must be patient until the club members decide to open their doors to the newcomer. Meanwhile, perpetuating unequal market access threatens to undermine political support abroad for open markets, as has been the case in Japan's trade relations with the US. In the longer run, home-based producers find their costs rise, so their members outsource a growing volume of activities and invest abroad. They disengage from their home base, and start on their journey to become world corporate citizens. But they do not readily disentangle from their corporate cultures the internal mechanisms and ways that were built into their previous procedures when they operated from the home base. *Corporations always carry two logos: their own, and that of their home state.*

French state-led capitalism

State-led capitalism by definition seeks to allocate national resources for national purposes. The government gives preference to local champions and protects large private or public corporations from takeover. It may promote alliances between inward investors and local corporations in order to maximize the benefits of national ownership. It may extend regulatory protection over fragmented industries, which it seeks to preserve from foreign competition. But such a system is unsustainable. Since major corporate investment decisions have to be agreed to by government, officials find themselves immersed in an ocean of financial, production or marketing and personnel details of industries ranging across the scope of business activities, and about which they know next to nothing. As one senior manager told me: 'Our pricing policies were regularly set at yearly luncheons. The prices for similar products depended on the quality of the wines consumed by ministry officials.'

State-led capitalism leans to trade protection, and tends not to welcome inward investors. But it cannot do without them because they bring access to technologies, management skills and foreign markets. Inward investors compete with national producers on their home markets, and this prompts national producers to retaliate by entering international markets via both trade and investment. The state finds itself torn between its old role and its new task of championing freer trade. Its ownership of large corporations also acts as a hindrance to foreign investment, as French corporations for years found in Germany. In the longer run, the state has to get out of the business of owning corporations in order to set their managements free to make their own decisions on location. In other words, state capitalism cannot sustain the policy of regulating foreign access to its home market, and having its own firms enjoy access to the markets of others. It must liberalize and privatize. *As state capitalism's corporations internationalize, so its domestic purposes and methods must undergo fundamental revision.*

Now an optimum world for a transnational corporation is one where states' policies towards inward investors seek to live up to the unattainable 'Bretton Woods ideal'. But states, as we have seen, are highly complex and individually unique entities, which may also be conceived of as learning organizations in a permanent process of renewal.[10] Their specific features, such as their laws or practices on corporate governance structures to give but one example, are ingrained in the texture of the firms which they foster. As states change over time, and their policies evolve, corporations adapt, and both alter the context within which the others operate. The propensity of states is to seek to protect their domestic arrangements by exporting them as non-negotiable items in international negotiations to establish regional or global norms. The result can only be agreement on international regimes, satisfactory to none, open to future amendments and replete with ambiguities. Meanwhile, corporations learn to flourish on the differences between the states, cast in their territorial mould, but also to demand less ambiguities in the international regimes – such as the WTO's stance on patents – which the states can agree on. This dialectical relation between corporations and states is inherent to the different types of corporate strategy:

- The European decentralized federation, modelled on the Dutch electrical and electronics giant Philips, adopted a strategy and structure which fitted postwar Europe's interdependent but fragmented market like a glove. Then, in the 1980s, Philips took a lead role in promoting the EU internal market legislation, as the creation of a large more integrated home market was a crucial element in its own corporate renewal strategy. Its corporate and political strategies were two sides of one coin.

- US corporations moved international along with US state policy to contain communism, and to underpin European, then Japanese reconstruction. When Japanese global strategists, from their protected home base, launched their drive in the US home market, US state policy took on a decidedly more unilateralist tone. It was Peter Peterson, president of the Bell and Howell company, which had suffered under Japanese competition, who helped to convince President Nixon that it was time to meet US trading partners 'with a clearer, more assertive version of new national interest'.[11] Japan's *tsunami* was a major cause of moving the US, as the pillar of the Bretton Woods fixed rate system, towards floating the dollar. Nixon's action created the present global financial regime.

Political transitions and corporate transformations

The years 1971–4 saw the transformation of Western regimes of trade and finance, coupled with the related adoption of '*détente*' towards the Soviet Union. There followed the spate of political transitions towards representative government around the world. The collapse of the Soviet empire transformed the world system of states. Meanwhile, corporations from their different legacies were challenged to become world citizens. All these four processes of transformation of world markets, the world state system, of states and of corporations, were simultaneous, interactive but non-synchronized. Let us look first at the transition of states from one form of governance norms to another, and then at the process of strategic transformation in corporations. We can start with some working definitions of regime types, to parallel our definitions of different national regimes for corporate strategies.

Regime types

A political regime is defined by its identity, and the regime's essence isolates its key attributes. The same can be said of a corporation, according to who controls and who owns it. The essence of representative democracy, for example, is that binding rules are made by elected representatives, who are ultimately responsible to the electorate through free and open elections. Its spread, as we have seen, is often associated with greater individual freedoms, wealth and international peace, though it is forcefully argued that without a prior evolution of a constitutional liberalism, which respects civil liberties and the rule of law and is predicated on the separation of powers between government institutions, democracy alone can degenerate into ethnic barbarism.[12] Hitler's rise to power, the terror around Africa's Great Lakes, and the massacres in the Balkans since Yugoslavia's disintegration are sober reminders that representative democracy is a frail creature.

The essence of communist party-states is to claim a monopoly over political power, economic resources and the truth. Initially, the party crushes all opposition, but as it tires of constant war against its own people, party rule transforms into a vast political market for preference and privilege. Eventually, it relies on performance, and when that fails, has few sources of legitimacy on which to draw. Authoritarian dictatorships differ. The dictator rules through the few in the name of the many. Secrecy is his code, and rumour substitutes for news. The few are responsible to the leader, and exercise power within formally ill-defined limits.[13] When the leader dies, so does the regime. Once dead, he cannot strike the living from the grave. That is a fact which the few anticipate, and make their preparations accordingly in readiness for the dictator's

Asking the age of the dictator is a preliminary question for an inward investor interested in knowing more about a country.

passing. *Asking the age of the dictator is a preliminary question for an inward investor interested in knowing more about the country where business is expected.*

Identifying when a regime transition is under way entails some definition of what is meant by change. A change of personnel in the government, or even a new nomenclature, does not mean that the regime is changing in essence. As the prince noted in Lampedusa's novel, *The Leopard*, about Sicily and the Italian *rissorgimento*, 'everything changes, so that everything may stay the same'. Let us define political change or transitions in states as involving a shift from one normative type of regime, or constitutional order, to another. Theoretically, four different types of regime – representative democracy, communist party-states, authoritarian dictatorships or monarchies, and theocracies – may seek to chart a path of transition in twelve different directions.[14] The shift from one to another means movement along different paths from differing historical legacies, and involves different tasks. Legacies crucially identify the path and the tasks that lie ahead for the transition to be fulfilled.[15]

Once a regime is embarked on transition to another normative identity, the process is too intricate and too contingent on a host of individual and collective decisions for anyone to be able to assert *ex ante* what the outcome will be. The best that can be done *ex ante* is for our inward investor to note the new incumbents' stated intent; draw up a list of tasks that lie ahead for that intent to be achieved; assess the alignment of personalities and the balance of interests; and judge the probable circumstances in the light of our analytical framework for business. Here is an ideal subject for scenarios: what are the driving forces at play? What are the certainties and the uncertainties involved in the situation? What would a business-as-usual scenario mean in such a case? Is the new leadership capable of exercising choice, and implementing it? What does a disaster scenario look like, and are serious efforts being taken to avoid disaster? What does a 'crazy' scenario – a totally unexpected outcome – look like? It is only *ex post* that the path of history looks predetermined.

The clock of political transition

But, *ex post*, we can study historical examples of regime changes, and compare the processes by dividing them into broad phases, and listing some of the regularities that tend to occur over the cycle of a transition. A starting point may be a reminder of our previous discussion where political choices in regime transitions result from the interactions between popular mobilization and elite expectations. It is the latter which weigh most heavily, and that indicate the future path to be taken.[16] That path is presented in the form of a clock, as in Figure 7.2, where we can imagine an hour hand travelling around its face. We should beware, though: our clock is only a device. It should not be allowed to trap us into forgetting our arbitrary division of time into segments, our assumption that individual paths are comparable, or that the time required for transitions and phases varies. Our clock is a metaphor – to mix a metaphor, it is a hat stand. Let us hang our hats and proceed.

Figure 7.2
TRANSFORMATION OF CORPORATIONS AND STATES

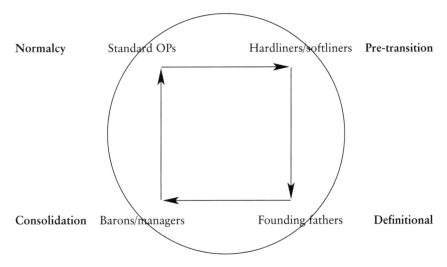

Normalcy	Standard OPs	Hardliners/softliners	Pre-transition
Consolidation	Barons/managers	Founding fathers	Definitional

Pre-transition

From midnight to three o'clock is the pre-transition phase.[17] This can last a thousand or more years, as in de Tocqueville's account of the French Revolution as accomplishing the task of the monarchy to create France.[18] Or we can choose a shorter period, such as the last years of the Franco regime or the two decades preceding the Soviet Union's implosion. *The proximate condition for breakdown of the old order is that the incumbent power is unable to resolve a growing list of problems.* A sure sign of trouble is the inability of the state to control money and credit, to accept corporate bankruptcies so risking bank overexposure, and to be particularly vulnerable to balance of payments crises and runs on the currency.[19] Two contending coalitions form, initially led by hardliners in the regime against any change, and softliners who argue the case for a dialogue with moderate opponents.[20] They deploy exclusive symbols and appeal to different mobilized factions within, or outside, the regime.

Definitional

At three o'clock the hour of decision strikes. The definitional phase lasts until six o'clock. Ruling elites must decide to resist dissent or make concessions. Either way, they – or their victors – make a declaration of strategic intent. The path they take depends on the predispositions of the leaders, the assessments they make about the future payoffs of concessions or suppression, and the balance of forces. It also depends on the participants' relation to the past, whether the losers can avoid punishment for the past and retain certain 'reserve domains' for the future (in the police, armed forces or state enterprises), and whether the eventual winners show moderation towards their former rivals, at the expense of sacrificing the expectations of their more militant followers. This phase is particularly delicate because it is characterized by an inrush of new participant groups to the arena of public policy, and because uncertainty is rife about the sustainability of what all know to be an interim situation.[21]

The definitional phase is characterized by a struggle between contending parties over the norms of the new regime. The moderates offer one set of proposals, which are not doomed a priori to failure. If they fail, the reign of the radicals is initiated, and the transition moves away from regime change to revolution. Whether or not this occurs is conditioned by three key factors. All parties, with few minor exceptions, accept the territorial boundaries and the ethnic composition of the state. The new constitution has to be inclusive, and voted for by an overwhelming majority. In Spain, and in South Africa, the existence of dissident ethnic groups to their new constitutions stored up problems ahead. Third, governments face crucial decisions over the sequence and character of reforms (see Box). After the constitution has been voted in, and the new norms become established, those who contributed to drawing it up become known as 'founding fathers'. In retrospect, they acquire charismatic reputations.

Consider the contrast of policy sequencing in Spain, Poland and Russia. In Spain the parties agreed in October 1977 to put major economic policy reforms on hold while they worked on the constitution. The result was a costly delay, with rising unemployment, inflation and indebtedness, but the benefit was a constitutional settlement that enabled sounder economic policies and compromises to be negotiated in the 1980s and beyond.

In Poland political reforms were put on hold until a new constitution was agreed, and an IMF-style stabilization-cum-liberalization programme was introduced in early 1990. By the mid-1990s Poland enjoyed rapid growth, helping to underpin the new constitutional order.

In Russia the new state, too, opted in January 1992 for an IMF-style policy package to stem hyper-inflation, but met stiff resistance from vested interests. In October 1993 President Yeltsin temporarily resolved the stand-off between the reformers and the old guard by bombing parliament, still the old Supreme Soviet, into submission. The new Russian presidential constitution was passed in December 1993. But Yeltsin fostered or became prisoner of a new, and grasping oligopoly, and the Russian economy continued to shrink.

Consolidation

From six to nine o'clock is the period of consolidation, when politics moves into more pragmatic channels. The excitement of revolution or of negotiating the new settlement abates. Compromisers and trimmers are in the ascendant, and the regime's personnel become a mixture of erstwhile radicals

Compromisers and trimmers are in the ascendant.

and relics from the old regime. When the silken threads of habit and tradition have been broken in revolution, people may be tempted to put on the iron chains of dictatorship.[22] If, by contrast, the moderates won out in the previous phase, the recently agreed settlement will have to be 'the only game in town'.[23] The close followers of the 'founding fathers' become 'barons' of the regime, which they help to consolidate by implementing the programme implicit in the constitution. For this, they need widespread support in society, acceptance of the rule of law, legitimate political procedures, a viable state bureaucracy and an economic settlement which people consider equitable.[24]

Normalcy

There is then a fourth phase, when the new regime acquires the features of an old regime. Standard operating procedures begin to prevail. Minds look backward to the past, now conceived of as a 'golden age'. A central question of public policy here is whether the inherited mixture of formal rules and informal constraints allows for a permanent renewal of bargains and arrangements such that people accept lesser stability in the short run in return for greater efficiency in the deployment of resources. The danger, as Douglas North argues, is that there will tend to be increasing returns to groups which have nestled into the fabric of the original settlement to preserve the existing constraints.[25] Mancur Olson suggests that such sclerosis is undone only by war, revolution, or free trade.[26] He quotes Thomas Jefferson: 'The tree of liberty must be refreshed from time to time with the blood of patriots and tyrants.' We are past twelve o'clock, and 'here we go again' around the clock towards a pre-transition.

Let us apply our analogy of the clock to two brief examples. The hour hand for Brazil in 1998 indicates seven o'clock. Arguably, the pre-transitional period began in March 1974 when General Geisel inaugurated a process of controlled democratization. His motive was to seek allies in civil society in order to regain control over the counter-terrorist forces. That process lasted for about two decades, as support for the military republic ebbed away, in the armed forces and among business. The military eventually yielded in the face of financial collapse and extensive popular mobilization. Drawing up a constitution took from 1984 to 1988. But corruption in high places and inflation continued until Fernando Henrique Cardoso as Finance Minister set the country on the path of market-oriented reforms. He was elected President in 1994. His task was not facilitated by the constitution's complexities, the fragmented political parties, the vast inequalities in society, the violence of everyday life and structural fiscal deficits.

The clock for China stands at three o'clock. When leader Deng Xiaoping died in February 1997, the country had recorded nearly two decades of economic growth. Agricultural reforms had revived the countryside, where upwards of 600 million people earn their living.

China was a favoured target for inward direct investment, with overseas Chinese business accounting for about 80 per cent of the total, and for well over 40 per cent of China's exports. The regime's challenge was to have the economy generate up to 500 million new jobs through to the 2020s. That meant deep reforms in the state and collective enterprises, which still accounted for three quarters of industrial output, and a massive overhang of non-performing commercial bank debt.

Deng's successors are determined, like him, to preserve the party's monopoly on power, while marketizing the economy. This means pushing for more efficiency, and risking mass unemployment when the gloss is off Asia's economic growth. If China is to introduce representative democracy to strengthen legitimacy and reduce dependence on performance, it will have to travel from three to nine o'clock, without imploding in the manner of the Soviet Union. This is the Chinese leadership's disaster scenario, and international investors can reasonably assume that everything is being undertaken to avoid it. But the experience of political transitions should tell them that there is a big gap between intent, if such intent there is, and outcome. If that is not the intent, the question remains whether a party-state can effectively supervise the move to a market system, where property rights, legal redress and civil rights are not ensured.

The clock of corporate transformation

There is a clear parallel between political transitions and corporate transformations. Neither is a permanent process, but proceeds in fits and starts.[27] Once a corporation embarks on the transformation of its strategy and structure – say from the European decentralized federation to a transnational corporation – the process, as in political transitions, is too intricate and too contingent on a host of individual and collective decisions for anyone to be able to assert *ex ante* what the outcome will be. The best that can be done is for management and shareholders to note the new team's stated intent; draw up a list of the tasks that lie ahead for that intent to be achieved; assess the alignment of personalities and the balance of interests; and judge the probable circumstances in the light of our analytical framework for business.

As in political transitions, it is theoretically possible for a corporate transformation to take twelve different paths from one of the four stylized strategies, illustrated above, to another. A decentralized European federation, for instance, can become a global strategist, just as a 'Bretton Woods ideal' exporter can develop rapidly into a US-type federation of units where the key attribute of management is to exercise control over the transfer of know-how. Which path corporations take – and in reality there are many more than in our simple stylized model – depends on personalities, corporate culture, the deployment of skills and capabilities, home and host country contexts, and above all on global political and market conditions. The idea that corporations are moving inexorably to a transnational model is a functionalist delusion, just as fallacious as the economics-drives-politics thesis which we visited earlier. *The real world of management is one where the future is open: effort, skill and a good dose of luck are required for original intent to be rewarded by successful outcomes.*

Here, then, is again an ideal subject for managers to use the technique of scenarios: what are the driving forces at play? What are the certainties and the uncertainties involved in the situation? What would a business-as-usual scenario mean in such a case? Is the new leadership capable of exercising choice, and implementing it? What does a disaster scenario look like, and are serious efforts being taken to avoid disaster? What does a 'crazy' scenario look like, one which at first glance lies beyond the bounds of respectable thinking – an oxymoron, if ever there was one?

Corporate transformation, like political transitions, entails a challenge to routine. In the case of a corporation, performance will have deteriorated for some time, and the signs of sclerosis will have been visible for anyone with eyes to see. Those signs include growing distance of senior managers from their own front-line experts, a proliferation of control procedures, and a declining level of commitment by people throughout the organization. In the case of a shareholder-driven corporation, a poor stock market performance is followed by pressure from shareholders. Business-as-usual becomes less and less defensible, and the limits of a moderate change to strategies or structures are soon revealed. It is the prospect of disaster, and a recognition by managers or shareholders that something must be done to avert it, that constitutes the first step. A 'crazy' scenario, one which seemed only a while ago to be unthinkable, becomes the new team's proposal to turn the corporation around.

Pre-transition

We are past midnight, and internal struggles within the organization have become more acute, as two opposing coalitions take shape. Hardliners favour business as usual, and look to reinforce existing capabilities rather than to develop new ones. They are internally concerned, backward looking, and their ears are closed to messages from frontline managers. In the words of Jack Welch, the Chief Executive of GE, they run an organization 'that has its face toward the CEO and its ass toward the customer'. The moderates are aware of the widening gap between corporate performance and that of competitors. Their initial inclination is to make incremental changes in policy, and to fiddle with the structure, without calling in question the inherited strategy. But as performance continues to be modest, radical voices start to be heard for root and branch changes in order to avoid disaster. Strategic drift worsens, until eventually the hardliners lose out in what amounts to a palace coup.

Definitional

At three o'clock a new CEO with a partly new team takes over. The crucial task is to provide a clearer understanding among the organization's stakeholders of why the organization is doing what it does. This requires the CEO to make a broad statement of strategic intent. The new strategic intent, and vision, redefine the norms which inform the corporation's future strategy (see Box on p. 172).

These ideas then have to be communicated throughout the organization, most effectively if one of the central ideas in the vision is that the organization has to become a thinking and learning organization, where innovative ideas can circulate freely and in all directions. With the Why? more clearly defined, the CEO can start choosing the Who? to have or not to have on the leadership team, and begin to address How? tasks will be newly defined and allotted. This may include divid-

Whirlpool, the US corporation, recognized in 1987 that if it stuck to the path it was on, the future would be neither pleasant nor profitable. On closer examination, it became evident that the business was becoming global, and that Whirlpool had to move accordingly. 'We could ignore this and die; we could wait for it to happen, then react; or we could control our own destiny and shape the industry', CEO David Whitwam said. In 1989 Whirlpool acquired N V Philips's European appliance business, and overnight moved to number one position in the worldwide appliance business. In an effort to build trust, and create a common vision of the future, Whirlpool brought 150 senior managers to Montreux, Switzerland, to spend a week developing global vision. These 150 people were then made responsible for educating 38,000 people around the world.

'The Right Way to Go Global', an interview with Whirlpool CEO David Whitwam, *Harvard Business Review*, March–April 1994.

ing units into smaller entities, simplifying reporting procedures, and making them more identifiable.

Consolidation

From six to nine o'clock the broad strategic design elaborated in the previous period is implemented. Big leaps are out, and incremental changes are back in again. The barons of the organization, associated with the charismatic leader who introduced the new strategy, are now implementing the changes elaborated in the previous period. The structure of the organization is slowly adapted to the new strategy, and the skills required are more widely disseminated. What those skills and tasks are depends on the corporation's legacy, its particular characteristics and on how both relate to the constellation of threats and opportunities. In general, the trend towards corporations becoming global citizens heightens their organizational complexity, in an environment full of uncertainties and risks. Much greater emphasis is placed on creating

The trend towards corporations becoming global citizens heightens their organizational complexity, in an environment full of uncertainties and risks.

trust and loyalty among people who can debate within a broadly shared vision. Much care is taken to ensure that the corporation is geared for future challenges, through development of worldwide scanning capabilities, heavy investment in research and development, and a high quality and cosmopolitan personnel policy. A key requirement is that the new strategy has sustainability built into it.

Normalcy

Past nine o'clock, *the key problem for corporations running successfully on what have become standard operating procedures is to ensure that the organization is capable of generating its own renewal.* There is a general awareness of sclerosis lurking close by. So managers are in permanent search for ways to keep momentum and to stretch the talents and ambitions of their people. A successful business finds itself pulled into the launch of new products, and expands its activities into new markets. The danger, of course, is that corporations imitate the British Empire, and acquire bits and pieces of the world in a fit of absence of mind. To avoid such over-stretch, mechanisms are introduced to select opportunities and to anticipate future contingencies. When necessary, extensive changes are introduced in line with the underlying principles of the corporation's strategy (see Box on p. 174). Knowledge networks are established, such as McKinsey's Knowledge Resource Pool, and corporate teams are built to enable the networked corporation to manage its subsidiaries in their many local contexts.

Conclusions

If corporations are driven to acquire transnational skills, and states are hustled towards some form of approximation to a Bretton Woods ideal, then the broad traits of the future are already recognizable. That future is identifiable as a One World, espousing the ideals of open markets and of market democracy. History, as it were, is at an end, and the only future that awaits us is one of growing prosperity and boredom, as the world is 'common marketized'. This is clearly not the world of our experience. Rather, it is an unattainable ideal, a useful fiction like our 'Bretton Woods ideal' country which sets the unattainable stan-

Since the merger in 1988 creating ABB, the engineering conglomerate went through three substantial restructurings, which helped raise operating margins from 3 to 7.2 per cent in 1998. In August Göran Lindahl, Percy Barnevik's successor, introduced the fourth. Country managers were now to report directly to main management, thereby speeding up decisions. Barnevik's matrix structure, where three members of the executive board responsible for regional management structures had shared operational responsibilities with the three executives heading its core businesses, was scrapped. The new structure is to operate in eight different core businesses, all of which will be represented on the new executive board. Elimination of one senior tier of management, said Lindahl, will provide 'greater speed and efficiency by further focusing and flattening the organisation'. It will also expose its divisions to closer investor scrutiny.

Financial Times, 13 August 1998.

dards for a world society of states and peoples who have to live together in the world as it is. The world in which corporate managers have to operate is rife with opportunities, conflicts and surprises. *The underlying assumption of a transnational future for corporations is that the economic, cultural, diplomatic and geopolitical conditions of the past, which facilitated the trend to a decentralized network of integrated units under a single corporate direction, will continue for the years, and even for the decades, ahead.*

That is a bold assumption to make. In the words of Ken Clarke, Britain's then Chancellor of the Exchequer, when speculation was still rife as to whether European monetary union would occur, 'It might happen, it might not – that's always been my view.' He thereby managed to sound prophetic, while saying absolutely nothing. That's probably why he's such a consummate politician. But at a different level Clarke's point is that the future is open and made by humans.

Local time holds its own exigencies, and there is no foregone certainty that the strains of adjustment to the whims of world time will not become too great to bear. Managers are all too aware of the volatility of expectations about the future. They are constantly concerned about the dynamics of change in societies and cultures, the swirl of events as world time's moods shift and change, and about the stability and predictability not just of the policies and goals of governments but of the regimes by which they govern or the wider international regimes of which they are a part. Indeed, international markets are a constant barometer tracking and shaping the world's exploration of its future. *Managers must permanently assess the multiple processes of political transition under way in the world, in the light of the transformations which they and their competitors are undergoing.* This hesitant exploration of probable futures lies at the heart of the difficulties inherent in deciding where, how and what to invest, and with what time horizons in mind. To this we now turn.

Notes

1 John Stopford and Louis Wells, *Managing the Multinational Enterprise*, New York, Basic Books, 1972.

2 Richard Schonburger, *World Class Manufacturing: The Next Decade*, New York, The Free Press, 1998.

3 James P. Womack, Daniel T. Jones and Daniel Roos, *The Machine that Changed the World*, Toronto, Collier Macmillan, 1990.

4 Michael Porter, *Competitive Strategy: Techniques for Analyzing Industries and Competitors*, London, The Free Press, 1980.

5 G. Hall and S. Howell, 'The Experience Curve from an Economist's Perspective', *Strategic Management Journal*, Vol. 6, 1985.

6 C. K. Prahalad and Yves L. Doz, *The Multi-National Mission: Balancing Local Demands and Global Vision*, New York, The Free Press, 1987.

7 Ibid., p. 30.

8 Christopher A. Bartlett and Sumantra Ghoshal, *Managing Across Borders: The Transnational Solution*, Boston, Harvard Business School Press, 1989.

9 Sumantra Ghoshal and Christopher Bartlett, *The Individualized Corporation: A Fundamentally New Approach to Management*, New York, HarperCollins, 1997.

10 Karl Deutsch, *The Nerves of Government*, Glencoe, Illinois, Free Press, 1963.

11 US President, *The United States in the Changing World Economy*, report by Peter Peterson (Assistant to the President for International Economic Policy), Vol. 1, 1972.

12 Fareed Zacharia, 'The Rise of Illiberal Democracy', *Foreign Affairs*, November–December 1997.

13 Juan Linz, 'An Authoritarian Regime: Spain', in Erik Allardt and Yrjo Littunen (eds), *Cleavages, Ideologies and Party Systems*, Helsinki, The Westermarck Society, 1964.

14 See Leonardo Morlino, *Como cambiano i regimi politici: strumenti di analisi*, Milan, Franco Angeli, 1980.

15 Juan Linz and Alfred Stepan, *Problems of Democratic Transition and Consolida-*

tion: Southern Europe, South America and Post-Communist Europe, Baltimore, Johns Hopkins Press, 1996.

16 Dankwart A. Rustow, 'Transitions to Democracy: Towards a Dynamic Model', *Comparative Politics*, April 1970.

17 G. O'Donnell and P. Schmitter, *Transitions From Authoritarian Rule: Tentative Conclusions about Uncertain Democracies*, Baltimore, Johns Hopkins University Press, 1986.

18 Alexis de Tocqueville, *L'Ancien Régime et la Revolution*, Paris, Flammarion, 1988 edition.

19 Stephen Haggard and Robert Kaufmann, *The Political Economy of Democratic Transitions*, Princeton University Press, 1995.

20 O'Donnell and Schmitter, op. cit. note 17.

21 See Yossi Shain and Juan Linz, *Between States: Interim Governments and Democratic Transitions*, New York, Cambridge University Press, 1995.

22 Crane Brinton, *The Anatomy of Revolution*, New York, Vintage Books, 1965.

23 Andreas Schedler, 'What Is Democratic Consolidation', *Democracy*, April 1998, Vol. 9, No. 2.

24 Juan Linz and Alfred Stepan, op. cit. note 15, pp. 7–15.

25 Douglas C. North, *Institutions, Institutional Change and Economic Performance, Political Economy of Institutions and Decisions*, Cambridge University Press, 1991, p. 99.

26 Mancur Olson, *The Rise and Decline of Nations: Economic Growth, Stagflation and Social Rigidities*, New Haven, Yale University Press, 1982, pp. 141–4.

27 E. Romanelli and M. L. Tushman, 'Organisational Transformation as Punctuated Equilibrium: An Empirical Test', *Academy of Management Journal*, Vol. 37, No. 5, 1994.

Chapter 8

CRAFTING CORPORATE STRATEGIES TO LOCAL CONDITIONS

Multinational corporations bestride the world economy. The largest 500, of which over 440 come from rich home countries, account for four-fifths of foreign direct investment and half of world trade. But in their search for growth they have to compete in the emerging markets of the poorer four-fifths of the world population. This is where the exponential growth in world demand lies. A vast consumer market of billions of people is developing rapidly, while the requirements for local production are likely to multiply. States want a slice of the corporate value chain, and corporations scour the world to select where to produce, assemble or sell. They face four questions: which activities should we select for a particular location? How should we screen the political geographies of the world? How can we compare different business conditions in distinct territories? And how should we structure corporate strategies in order to maximize our presence?

Which activities for a particular location?

The multinational's strategy is shaped by the particular characteristics of its industry: Nike and Reebok are driven by their search for low cost labour in footwear; Acer, the Taiwan-based personal computer maker, outsources components manufacturing around the Asia Pacific and has assembly plants in France, Italy and the UK near to its major markets; an oil corporation locates where it can find or exploit reserves in order to feed downstream outlets. It will also be influenced by the shifting conditions of world politics and markets. But as master in its own house, there are two particular aspects to a firm's decision on targeting a location as either a market for products or as a place to produce at any stage of the value chain:

1 It seeks the best location on offer. Different territories have distinct bundles of advantages and drawbacks. Selection entails making judgements about government policies and country resources. Managers must choose the type of activity in the light of the depth of corporate commitment to the market. A crucial feature of their decision is how to fit corporate operations to the particular features and potential of the country.

2 Location decisions must take account of the strategy already in place, and where the firm's present businesses are placed. An optimal strategy depends on having a clear definition of the firm's core competences (does the firm compete on cost, on quality, on technical skills? Does its core competence reside in technological know-how or in a bundle of managerial skills?). More pointedly, the firm must have clear ideas of what to expect from its factories.[1] Management must be prepared to spend much time negotiating within the firm about support for a new undertaking. A new or extended presence in a particular territory depends crucially on firm-wide flows of resources.

In previous decades multinationals treated emerging markets as places to sell old products.

In previous decades multinationals treated emerging markets as places to sell old products or as locations for the manufacture and distribution of old technologies. This flowed from a staircase view of the historical development process, whereby emerging markets would follow in the footsteps of those who preceded them. While emerging market customers, workers or managers cut their teeth on less sophisticated products and organizations, Western firms squeezed residual profits from sunset technologies. The general pattern was one of glass ceilings for local promotion, and central direction from headquarters.

Emerging markets were viewed as best explored sequentially:[2] the first stage involved the corporation arranging exports through an agent or by direct sales; the second stage had the corporation choosing between various forms of contractual relations, ranging from licensing technology to turnkey projects and contract manufacturing; stage three entailed direct investment through acquisition, joint ventures or the establishment of greenfield facilities. Stage four represented the corporation as designing its foreign entry from a global perspective. *That is where global corporations now start.* Stages have become options, each with its own advantages and disadvantages.

- Option one's advantage is that exporting avoids the cost of establishing more extensive operations in the host country. A firm can export to a particular territory indirectly through an agent, or use the time it takes to build up its own distribution network to learn about local conditions. The disadvantage is that exporting from one territory to another is vulnerable to exchange rate shifts, to changes in the importing country's tariffs, or that transport costs may simply be too high. Exporting in any event requires time and personnel. Strong relationships have to be established to secure the export channel, either with a local importer or with a trading company.

- Option two's advantage is that licensing a technology to a partner in the host country absolves the firm from the cost of developing a new market. It may not want to commit major resources to that market, and in any case licensing may be the only way to get around import barriers. The key to success is choosing the right partner. And there's the rub. Firms license their patents, know-how or trademarks to licensees in return for royalty payments, but they do not control their marketing plan. Nor can they prevent their partner from adapting the technology to become a fierce competitor. As Microsoft has found, even a patent strategy to restrict copying of software in China is of no use if the government cannot or will not co-operate effectively.

- Option three's advantage is that equity investment enables the firm to select the best location available, and to keep control over its own technology as well as the range of operations. The information and time required to establish this type of operation are much greater than in the other options, but the benefit is that the investor will acquire experience, and have access to a new pool of human resources. But it will also be much more exposed to political developments in the host country. This is the main reason corporations have to develop sophisticated political antennae in order to be able to ride the political rapids as well as possible.

One way for an equity investor to acquire the necessary knowledge in a host country is to establish a joint venture with a local partner. In China joint ventures have been a consequence of government policy to maximize the transfer of know-how to Chinese organizations, and to retain autonomy from foreign firms. The benefit for a foreign firm is that it buys into its partner's knowledge of the local market, while the local firm receives injections of technology, capital or managerial skills. But joint ventures tend to be problematical because the two partners follow different agendas, and as often as not have different expectations, stated or hidden. Consider the large diversified family groups in the India of the 1990s. With consumers more fickle, they enter into joint ventures with multinationals which they fear. But foreign investors complain that the Indian companies bring little to the deal, and dump them at the drop of a hat.[3]

Or an equity investor may form a strategic alliance with another corporation. Such arrangements occur mainly between industrial country corporations, when firms swap technologies and market access. Like joint ventures, these have boomed in the 1990s as corporations find that they can no longer compete alone, and need partners to share the fixed costs of developing products and processes.[4] And like joint ventures they are susceptible to breakdown if prenuptial arrangements are not thought through carefully. As in marriage, the partnership gets off to a reasonable start, assuming that the honeymoon is mutually agreeable. But, soon enough, both partners take a reality check and find that the other is not what it was cracked up to be. With disillusion, crisis and conflict set in. Either the partnership ends in divorce, and recrimination, or both agree to work out their differences and to reinforce affection with mutual commitment to a going concern.

Another way is for a foreign investor to acquire an existing operation. Our investor buys into local knowledge, skills or products and brands, and then is free to develop them. But such deals are not readily identified, and their potential has to be measured against alternatives. A considerable commitment is required to win over stakeholders, agree on an appropriate price and then fit the operation into a broader group strategy. Take the strategy of the Korean conglomerate, Daewoo, to make Central Europe the jumping-off stage for car manufacturing in

Europe. Poland, large, stable and centrally located, is the linchpin of its ambitious investment schedule to produce 570,000 units by 2000. It beat off rival GM by offering Poland's state vehicle maker, FSO, a three-year employment guarantee, a 70 per cent local content by 1998, and to keep Polish component suppliers under its wing. But its plans were upset by the Asian meltdown, allowing GM to discuss use of Daewoo's plants in Korea to build its own vehicles.

Establishing greenfield sites is often the preferred mode. The corporation ensures control over the technology, manages the operations, exploits economies of scale and scope and fits the activity into group strategy. Nonetheless, government relations loom large. Motorola, for instance, won government go-ahead in China to set up a wholly owned factory only when it decided not to withdraw after the Tiananmen Square incident in June 1989. Motorola's $120 million investment in a plant in Tianjin became operational in June 1993. The government insisted that Motorola cover its foreign exchange needs for imported components with sales of exports, thus requiring heavy investment in employee training to achieve high quality. In return, the Ministry of Post and Telecommunications (MPT) bought virtually all its paging and cellular systems. In the first half of the decade, Motorola was probably the most profitable telecoms company in China.

Perhaps one reason for corporations looking at stages as options for entry strategies to emerging markets in the 1990s was related to the demise of state socialism and the failures of import substitution. *After the Cold War's end, the risk of confiscation is limited because emerging market governments around the globe compete to attract foreign investors, and to sell off their nationalized industries.* Years of deficit financing to support consumption have starved the assets of much needed new investment. Only the prospect of world-class facilities is satisfactory to corporations scouring the world for new locations and markets. Total revenues from privatization rose from nearly $13 billion in 1990, when three-quarters came from infrastructure sales in telecommunications and power, to $156 billion in 1996, when mining, manufacturing and financial services accounted for well over half of total sales.[5] Foreign investors provided about 45 per cent of proceeds from privatization in emerging markets in this period. The main recipients were Latin America ($35 billion), Central and Eastern Europe ($17 billion) and Asia-Pacific ($14 billion), in that order. No doubt with the Asian meltdown, Asia-Pacific's share has risen.

Screening political geographies for market options

There are four corporate rules of thumb that have been applied in the past to selecting between political geographies. All of them depend in effect on management perceptions of the territory's potential and associated risks.

The first rule of thumb is the size of the market. In the 1990s ten countries have received three-quarters of total foreign direct investments in emerging markets. These are mainly middle-income countries, such as Argentina and Malaysia, or large and poor countries, like China, India and Indonesia. Local production there can achieve economies of scale, and reduce transport costs or customs duties. And break-even calculations rise the more that the firm commits to the market. But the rule of thumb on market size is flawed: Chile is by no stretch of the imagination a large market, yet it numbers in the top ten; China in 1997 received over ten times more inward investment than India, with a population of similar size and per capita income; as mentioned, Latin America and Central Europe received much larger amounts of foreign exchange in their sales of state assets than Asia-Pacific, suggesting widely divergent sensitivities to selling national assets to foreign owners.

The second rule of thumb is opportunism. Consider Michel Marbot, an INSEAD graduate, who had followed Gorbachev's desperate efforts at reform from his vantage point as a bank manager in Greece in the late 1980s. Married to a Pole, he decided as the course of events unfolded in Poland to try his luck there. He ensured solid backing for his enterprise in Paris, Brussels and Rome, while cashing in on his contacts in the Solidarity movement. In late winter 1989 he had his proposal ready on the table of the State Secretary in the Economics Ministry, who was only too glad to encourage the local mayor of Malbork in western Poland to sell him a viable pasta factory. Marbot offered no dismissals and a doubling of wages in return for three shifts and a tripling in productivity. He had President Walesa's wife open his business – named Danuta, after her. He is now Poland's Mr Pasta, and is considering expansion into China.

But other opportunistic investments have been less fortunate, like the Western firm I visited in Volgagrad which had not been operating for a month. Customs officials were holding up a convoy of trucks on the Ukrainian frontier, and were negotiating to keep the pasta, wine and cheese that Italian engineers in the plant had asked to be conveyed with the accompanying components from Italy. The deal was: you won't get your components if you don't surrender your pasta, wine and cheese. Deadlock ensued.

Customs officials were holding up a convoy of trucks on the Ukrainian frontier, and were negotiating to keep the pasta, wine and cheese that Italian engineers in the plant had asked for.

A third rule of thumb is market potential. Managers are concerned with the absolute size of the current market (small/large) and the market's future growth (low/high). This yields a handy matrix to serve as a guide to the entry mode and how much is committed to the new business over what time period. Next, the firm decides on its own sales potential, in the light of what is known about customers, barriers to entry, competitors, distributors and substitutes. Consider Marbot again. He made a back-of-an-envelope calculation that Polish customers would have less time and money to boil home made pastas, what with gas prices on the rise and a very competitive labour market. Potatoes were no substitute. Local competitors were not a threat, and the government would be likely to protect the domestic market. He started with a 20 per cent market share in pre-cooked pastas, invested in packaging, retrained ex-trade unionists as his marketing team, and is up around 40 per cent by 1998. Potential ultimately resides in the creativity of entrepreneurs.

A fourth rule of thumb is whether a country is judged to be stable. The past record on this score is not very good. Iran is the classic example. In the mid-1970s the Shah placed advertisements in the Western media announcing that Iran was on the way to catching up with

Germany as an industrial power by the 1990s. Western corporations duly sank a great deal of capital into the country. The US and British embassies, when asked, reported that the Shah's police had the Marxist radicals under control. They failed to report the alienation of the bazaar, and the hostility of the *mullahs* to his rule. Unfortunately, President Carter supported more power to the parliament, perhaps oblivious of the fact that the *mullahs* had supported parliamentary government in 1906 as the best way to control the emperor. Ayatollah Khomeini's memory had a longer reach. What the Iranian example teaches investors is the importance of learning about the history, culture and religions of the country where a major corporate commitment is made.

Rules of thumb are not adequate. As markets have developed and competition has toughened, corporations have found that they have to select the number of businesses and local markets that they service. With manufacturing operations requiring skilled labour and more sophisticated customers prompting close co-operation between product development and manufacturing, firms are scouring the world for appropriate locations. There are many tiny countries with rich human resources, and firms have some core and some non-core products. We can classify both countries and products as core and peripheral.[6] So the formal questions which corporations should be asking themselves relate the significance of the country's market to the level of corporate resources to be committed to it:

1 Which countries should we be in?
2 Which products should we be in?

To answer, we have to categorize target countries in a standardized manner in order to ensure the fit between corporate strategy, selection of location and the proposed activity. Such an approach also allows the corporation to think through the opportunities available around the world in a more formal way, and to cluster those country markets whose significance for it is low. And it requires plenty of co-operation and exchange of ideas between headquarters and subsidiaries.

Screening opportunities for target countries requires us to list a number of simple criteria and briefly record their likely impact on the firm's planned or existing operations. The criteria can be given notional values, to enable simple comparisons to be made between one country and another. Here is a proposed list:

- Size of the country in purchasing power: in 1995 only 12 of the 107 countries in the lower and middle income range had economies of over $100 billion, while Japan's economy alone nearly equalled all 107 together. The differences per capita were even more striking: the average per capita income of the 107 was just over $1,000, whereas that of the 25 high-income countries was nearly $25,000. So the implication for corporations is that if they sell to these countries the same types of products as they sell to rich populations, they won't sell to a large market. Conversely, if they think closely of the product's price-performance to the customers, they open up vast volume markets for utility products.
- Populations of 15–65-year-olds provide the present workforce and potential consumers. Of the 107 countries, 74 hold labour forces of under 10 million, though there are a cluster of countries with very large labour forces: China (709 million), India (398 million), Brazil (101 million), Russia (99 million), Indonesia (89 million), Bangladesh (60 million), Nigeria (44 million). But there are significant differences between them with regard to average age: Bangladesh, Nigeria, India, Indonesia and Brazil are young countries, while Russia and China are ageing fast. The implication is that labour is an abundant resource. But there is abundance and abundance. The next indicator will give some idea of how skilled labour is.
- The Human Development Index, introduced in the UN Development Programme in 1990, measures life expectancy, adult literacy and per capita income. As mentioned in earlier chapters, this index records a wide difference between the upper and lower ranges, but also provides a figure which states what the country has achieved in terms of development, and indicates what the future human potential is. Chile, for instance, numbers among the very highest on the index, though its per capita income places it in the lower middle income range.

I would also suggest the use of female literacy as a key indicator. The revolution in women's conditions around the world is one of the major developments of the twentieth century. But women's illiteracy is very high in parts of Africa, the Indian sub-continent and in many Middle Eastern countries. What this means is quite simply that about half of their population does not even have a foot in the modern world, which requires a modicum of literacy and numeracy. In those countries where women are literate, the country's potential is seriously augmented.

- Savings rates in most low income countries are below 10 per cent of national income, with middle-income countries averaging savings of 25 per cent. Savings indicate a collective choice between spending now or saving and investing for future growth. High savings rates, say in China, are a clear sign of a collective determination to postpone consumption and to work for the future. They provide an abundant pool of capital on which firms may draw for investment. If consumption is high, relative to income, as is the case in Latin America, India or Africa, then capital becomes scarce and therefore expensive. Financial institutions come under pressure to lend preferentially to privileged groups.

- Imports as a percentage of national income (GDP) indicates the country's growth potential for imports. In 1995, for instance, Nigerian imports equalled 29 per cent of national income, against 17 per cent in 1980, when the national economy was worth three and a half times more. This reflects the disaster which befell Nigeria when the oil price collapsed in 1986. Nigeria needs far more foreign exchange than it can lay its hands on. As a result, it runs large current account deficits, prompting the government to protect the domestic market and to raise exports. Another option is that the government may seek to cover the current account deficit by encouraging foreign equity inflows. If foreign investors are not interested, poor country debts rise – as they continue to do. Debts incurred in foreign currencies become very burdensome if the local currency is devalued: many more pesos or roubles have to be earned in order to repay the same amount of dollars or Deutschmarks.

- Foreign exchange is vital to emerging markets: if they do not have enough of it, they will not be able to buy the capital goods from the rich countries. In 1995, for instance, Nigeria had $15 per capita of foreign exchange reserves, compared to Japan's $1,566. Nigeria is typical of many countries which are over-dependent on a few primary products. Their economies ride the roller-coaster of world commodity markets, and are dragged into precipitate recession when prices fall and are launched back into boom when prices surge. For foreign investors, foreign exchange is a central consideration. Shortages will generally mean that the government attaches export provisions to any investment package, and is inclined to place import restrictions without warning. Physical infrastructure will tend to be poor, unless the government hands over infrastructure development to foreign corporations.

- Inflation rates have regularly been considerably higher in developing or emerging markets than in richer countries, though stabilization policies in the 1990s have tended to reduce the differential. This is a crucial area where corporate policy and government policy are particularly closely related. First, high inflation rates are generally accompanied by a capital flight of rich people into foreign havens: the foreign debt of Brazil, and probably of Russia, is equal to the funds held abroad by their rich citizens. Capital flight makes capital scarce at home, drives down the exchange rate, and hugely distorts the government's revenue sources. Second, the government cannot avoid having a policy on the exchange rate. Its options are: a currency board, like Argentina, when rises or falls in dollar reserves feed through directly into the money supply; a fixed rate, requiring abundant foreign exchange reserves; a pegged rate, providing an opportunity for speculators to anticipate when the next realignment occurs; and floating rates, when the currency finds its own value on the ocean of world finance.

The foreign debt of Brazil, and probably of Russia, is equal to the funds held abroad by their rich citizens.

The screening may proceed as in Figure 8.1. Screen one takes an initial look at all the target markets, or political geographies, and uses simple criteria, say the first three listed above. All are counted on a scale, and then weighed. Those we identify as an initial group of emerging markets, we take through to the second screen, when a

Figure 8.1
SCREENING OPPORTUNITIES FOR TARGET MARKETS

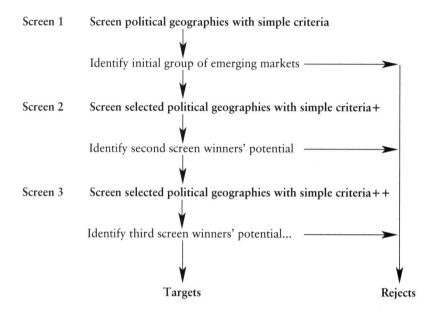

Screen 1   Screen political geographies with simple criteria

Identify initial group of emerging markets

Screen 2   Screen selected political geographies with simple criteria+

Identify second screen winners' potential

Screen 3   Screen selected political geographies with simple criteria+ +

Identify third screen winners' potential...

Targets   Rejects

couple of extra criteria may be added and the process is repeated. Screen three then selects the political geographies using all the criteria above. This approach enables us to reduce the number of countries we examine more closely to a manageable proportion. We catalogue the countries which we have rejected in three categories, and – if we wish to – come back to them later for re-examination.

Comparing different business conditions in distinct territories

Convention invites us to weigh the *political risk* of doing business in different territories. We look at risk[7] in terms of 'political unrest', and focus on management's uncertainty about host government actions that would destroy or limit the investors' ownership. This is termed *ownership or control risk*, for which insurance is available. But as an approach to assessing the political potential of doing business in a country, it is, to put it mildly, deficient. As one Lebanese businessman told me, *'my family has always done business here in peace and in war'*. In other words, potential and risk are two sides of the same coin. Let us, rather, use the clock analogy, which incorporates risk but takes a much longer-term view of both past and possible futures on a comparative basis, and let us also place our territories in the global context. Managers have to understand government intent, and to analyze the business context of their territories in the ways already touched on in earlier chapters.

The old method also deals with categories of *economic risk*, while failing to emphasize economic potential. *Operations risk* relates to host government policies effecting operations through import restrictions, local content regulations, tax changes or labour laws. *Transfer risk* relates to management's uncertainty about future government acts that may make it difficult to transfer payments, such as dividends and royalties, out of the country. Both require us to look at the deeper political and economic forces at work in our country, again in the world context, so that we have an understanding of why these events may or may not occur. If managers have no understanding of why events occur, they are bound to live in a permanent state of surprise. Their comfort is then to turn to gurus, who tell them to be 'optimistic' or 'pessimistic'. Examining the world as it is, is definitely not a recipe for spiritual fulfilment, but it is a prerequisite of sound business practice.

Associating both political and economic potential and risk yields a combined index, where we may compare one country's potential as a business location to another's. We ask a series of structured questions of each territory, with a view to establishing a profile of a country's potential and risk. (The Story Country Potential and Risk Assessment software is to be made available; visit www.StoryCPRA.com for details). For each question 10 is the worst possible mark, and 1 is top marks. The assessment requires teamwork, with local and corporate management participation. Indeed, analyzing the country's political and economic potential and risk is a prerequisite to assessing the potential and risk of a project. The latter requires a good idea of the plant's life expectancy in order to schedule plans for new investment in good time; a clear appreciation of fixed costs, of the minimum efficient scale and of whether or not flexible manufacturing techniques apply.

Our one-country profile can be compared to other country profiles, sharpening our sense of local conditions and of the varied opportunities available. We can then locate our evaluation of the country's potential on a grid. Both political and economic factors will impinge directly on different functional areas of corporate activity. We illustrate by choosing some questions from the politics and economics list, as in Figure 8.2.

Figure 8.2
EVALUATING COUNTRY/CORPORATE RISK AND
PERFORMANCE ON A COMPARATIVE BASIS

Political Assessment	Economic Assessment
1 The local regime Social structure Laws	4 Structures Labour availability/quality Capital, infrastructure ...
2 Extra-legal factors Corruption Civil war *Coup d'état*	5 Macroeconomy Budget, tax Monetary policy Subsidies
3 Global politics Diplomatic factors Geographic location Cultural location	6 External affairs Domestic/foreign protection Exchange, interest rates Commodity prices

The political regime

The norms, process and structures of the political regime is where we begin. The political regime impinges on business in multiple ways and requires us to develop a local and world capacity to deal with the governments in whose territories we are engaged. The manager must ask two key questions:

1 *Who are the key political players, what are the basis and extent of their powers, and what are their interests?* This requires drawing up a political map, with specific information about individuals and institutions, in national, regional and local governments. Non-governmental players may also be influential. We can fit our political map to a func-

tional map of managerial responsibilities (procurement, standards, wage setting, transport etc.) in order to be able to anticipate impacts of initiatives on key functions of our operations. We must also be aware that we can build or join coalitions to achieve our ends, but the converse is that government bureaux can also build coalitions in the corporation.

2 *How are government departments responding to changing circumstances?* One rule of thumb is that a corporation's bargaining power with the government erodes in value as it takes root in local soil, the costs related to exit rise and other firms enter the market. Motorola's privileged position began to erode in China as the 1990s progressed and Ericsson and Nokia challenged it in the cellular phone markets. Equally, firms should keep a wary eye on state–state relations. These cover a much wider spectrum than the more focused concerns of firms, but can directly effect corporate prospects. In 1992 France sold Mirage jets to Taiwan, greatly angering China. Beijing's retaliatory withdrawal of business from French companies cost Alcatel-Alsthom 4 billion francs (about $650 million).

Social structure

This measures the distribution of wealth and income, both geographically and across the population. It has a crucial impact on marketing strategy. Sharply demarcated social structures make markets narrower, and segmented. At the lower end of the income scale, the mass of the population is attracted by cheap and useful goods. Marketing managers will also want to know the approximate size of 'the middle class', in order to tailor their sales to its preferences. In India, for instance, Maruti-Suzuki sells India's most popular car for $10,000 (1995 prices), in the middle-income range. India has only some 7 million consumers with over $20,000 per annum, about 63 million with between $10,000 and $20,000 and about 110 million with $5,000 to $10,000, measured in purchasing power parities. The world's recorded champion of inequality, Brazil, has its richest 20 per cent hold 67 per cent of the country's total wealth, yielding a rich country market of 32 million with average incomes of $27,000.

Laws on labour and foreign investment

These laws are of direct concern to investors. Labour laws tend to benefit organized labour, as is the case in India. They often require investors to provide welfare services, and ensure skilled jobs for locals. And governments are schizophrenic about inward investment, as we have seen. But there are significant aspects of labour laws and of investment strategy about which investors must be clear, independently of what government policies or local social conditions may be. A crucial part of corporate calculations about a possible project (incorporating, for instance, the plant's life expectancy, fixed costs, minimum efficient scale, or warehousing and distribution factors) is an appreciation of available labour skills. Government subsidies come as a bonus, not as a prime reason for investing.

Corruption

Corruption is another direct link between politics in a territory and corporate policy. It is widespread and involves relations between governments, between corporations and governments, and between businesses. In general, the more political markets there are for licences, permits, exemptions, grants and tenders, the more opportunities there

Corruption is another direct link between politics in a territory and corporate policy.

are for bribery. Greed then greases the hinges of contracts. The agricultural economist George Moody-Stuart sums it up well in his remarks on corruption in emerging markets:[8] 'Five per cent of $200,000 is of interest to a senior official just below the top level; five per cent of $2 million arouses the interest of a top official (a state secretary, or a general director); five per cent of $20 million is a solid contribution for a minister and his staff; five per cent of $200 million awakens the interest of a head of government or of a president.' In hi-tech and arms trade, the percentages, he adds, rise to 20 or 30 per cent.

Global politics

Global business and global politics go together. Corporations are more than ever a target for world protest groups. One of the lessons that corporations learned from the 1970s was to take the lead in promoting worldwide standards, ethical codes and agreements on sustainable development. Lobbyists have meanwhile grown apace, with Greenpeace having offices in over thirty countries. Public opinion has been alerted to climate change, while trade unions and the media have become much more vigorous in revealing working conditions in emerging market 'sweat shops'. Both Nike, the US sportswear giant, and IKEA, the Swedish furniture manufacturer, initially denied reports that their contractors in cheap labour countries were their responsibility. Nike learned to change its tune when religious investors took an interest; it remains to be seen whether European firms, less vulnerable to shareholder activism, are as responsive.

The size of the labour force

This heads our short list of economic criteria. We are concerned at the relation between the growth in the size of the population and the growth in a measure of output. A much faster growth in output relative to population is recorded in a rapid GDP per capita growth, allowing for sharp rises in consumption and in savings. But the faster the population growth, the lower the per capita income growth. If population grows as fast as the economy, income remains static and little is left for people to save or to invest. The size of the labour force comes into play when we look at the age structure of the population: a large young population below working age in Africa, for instance, means that breadwinners have to feed and clothe more non-wage earners than their counterparts in older rich countries. They cannot save much, and their consumption is low. Poverty tends to be widespread, young people move to towns, and urban deprivation is widespread. A stagnant economy is a recipe for political violence.

Labour force quality

This is a central concern for investors. Firms such as IKEA or Nike go in search of cheap labour countries, when labour costs are a sizeable proportion of total costs in any particular segment of their activity. But wage levels tend to rise, and corporations find that government policies develop to induce them to invest in training, to sustain minimum standards or to fill quotas for ethnic groups. They may also be under pressure to upgrade their technologies. But once workers have been trained they will be motivated to search for better pay and prospects elsewhere. This is the experience of many investors in China who, like Siemens, have taken a longer-term view of labour costs in terms of mutual future commitments between employer and employees, looking to rising standards of quality and innovation. Motorola's Shanghai product development facilities have reached the corporation's world quality standards, with wage levels still far below those of rich countries.

Corporate structures

In emerging markets corporate structures often tend to be highly concentrated. Because resources are scarce, they are costly and unevenly distributed. Information does not circulate fluidly. The result is a tight coterie of public officials and corporate managers, who run the show. Insider networks ensure that outsiders, local or foreign, face restrictions on entry to local markets and, when they do join, do so on the terms of local insiders. Consider Motorola's efforts in Japan – not an emerging market, so much as politically under-developed – to enter the market for cellular telephony in the 1980s. After many years of effort Motorola allied itself with Toshiba to make microprocessors. Toshiba in return provided Motorola with marketing help in Japan. This facilitated Motorola gaining government approval to enter the market and to get radio frequencies assigned for its mobile communications systems. Once it had joined the insider group, Motorola was reported as dropping its previous public criticisms of Japan's trade barriers.

Capital scarcity and low savings

This combination is a chronic condition in emerging markets. Financial markets tend to develop privileged circuits accessible to insiders, paralleled by a network of financial boutiques lending at usurious rates to outsiders. Corporations operating in such conditions will have to operate with a minimum of payment delays, and learn, for instance, from Rallis, the Indian agribusiness group, which keeps a pile of signed cheques from its dealers in rural India. As soon as an order is shipped, it writes in the amount. Capital shortage will also be evident in the shortcomings of infrastructure, with frequent energy breakdowns, which oblige plants to cease production or that cause the refrigerators of middle-class households to warm up. Governments will have an incentive to adopt technological short-cuts, as in China where the Ministry of Post and Telecommunications and the armed forces sidestep the lack of expensive trunk lines, and use cellular telephony to bring outlying areas of the country into the modern age of communications.

Macro-economic policy

This is the point where capital shortage, government finances, financial circuits, corporate strategies and labour market regulations intersect. To keep taxes low, governments are tempted to issue bonds. In a relatively closed market like Brazil, India or China, this will push up the cost of borrowing for corporations. So the government may be tempted to print money, thereby inducing inflation. If government is beholden to specific interests in the country, it may try to offset the cost of inflation by imposing price or wage controls on products and workers. The government then wraps itself in a hopeless bind, stoking inflationary pressures with one hand and trying to dampen them with the other. Our investor is affected in every way: being visible, a foreign investor has to be 'squeaky clean' on tax payments; it may want to reduce the cost of capital by accessing global capital markets; it has to adjust its accounting to inflation; and it is directly affected by product or wage controls.

Foreign exchange markets

These are often a nightmare for foreign investors, and local corporations. It is never easy to predict the timing or the amount of a currency realignment. One way is for managers to track the nominal inflation rate (i.e. the recorded rate) relative to the nominal rate of a major trading partner. The currency will have to devalue for real exchange rates to remain constant. But this says only that a devaluation should occur; it does not say why the government resists devaluation, when the

Figure 8.3
INDICATORS OF A COUNTRY'S DEBT PROFILE

Growth of export ratio: A country which enjoys a continuous growth in export volumes is increasing its penetration of world markets. Can be averaged over several years. Countries with real export growth will probably be creditworthy. But they may also be under-consuming at home, or their corporations may be exporting at a loss.

Debt service ratio = interest and principal on external debt with maturity over one year/foreign exchange income in one year. It measures the payment for servicing the external debt over a time period in relation to total foreign exchange income. Debt service above 25 per cent indicates trouble ahead. This is because 25 per cent of export revenues go to debt repayment, and not to the purchase of needed imports.

Debt/GNP ratio = external public and private debt/GNP. Lenders are attracted by a high GNP. The ratio looks more at solvency (long-term problem) than liquidity (short-term financing).

Interest service ratio = interest payments over period n/exports of goods and services over period n. Focuses on the liquidity situation, while still excluding short-term external debt under one year. It is always lower than debt service. The difference between the two ratios shows the percentage of exports of goods and services needed each year to service the principal.

Reserves/imports = measures the country's ability to pay for its imports with current liquid assets. Normally expressed as a one-month average. Imports are measured as the average of the last six months. As long as reserves cover more than five months average of imports, liquidity can be considered as adequate. A one-month average means a critical situation that needs careful watching. This ratio looks at a country's short-term external liabilities, but omits interest and principal payments needed to service the external debt.

Liquidity gap ratio = one-year short-term debt, minus the balance on the current account. Estimates how a country manages its liabilities for the coming year. A rule of thumb is that a liquidity gap of 20 per cent can be covered through additional short-term borrowings. The higher the percentage of the liquidity gap ratio, the more difficult it will be to attain funds.

Current account/GNP ratio = $x\,(n-1)/y(n-1) + xn/yn + x(n+1)/y(n+1)/3$, where x = current account balance; y = GNP; n = current year. It covers the past, current and following year, and records the medium-term performance of a country's external situation in relation to GNP. The current and forthcoming years are estimates. A negative ratio forces a country to obtain outside funds or dig into reserves.

devaluation will come, what the amount of the devaluation will be or what the policy response of the government will be once the currency has fallen off its perch. So managers have to do the best they can. Another rule of thumb, then, is that managers track the government decision-making process, and their alarm bell rings as soon as a minister or central bank governor uses the 'N word' – 'never', as in 'We shall never devalue'. In practical terms, meanwhile, they can invoice in their own currency, they may contract by buying and selling at a specific price on a future date, or they can turn to religion for comfort. They can also keep an eye on the country's liabilities and assets as a guide as to whether or not the government will restrict transfers. Figure 8.3 provides some indicators.[9]

Structuring corporate strategies to maximize our presence in a host country

In this section we discuss what corporations can do rather than endure. Let's assume that we have analyzed a complete country profile, compared across country profiles, sharpened our sense of local conditions and of the varied opportunities available, and then located our evaluation of the country's potential relative to others on a grid. *The challenge is to do good business anywhere in the world because we are permanently thinking and learning how to operate to maximum effect in all conditions.*

Traditionally, corporate location decisions have been governed by corporate judgements and by me-too opportunism.

So, having looked at the constraints – the many factors and forces that impinge on our chosen operations in a target country or in a set of target countries – we ask ourselves what has to be done to open up the opportunities there. The aim of managers investing their corporations' money for the future is to consider tomorrow's prospects. Traditionally, corporate location decisions have been governed by corporate judgements about country size, potential and stability, and by me-too opportunism. Locations identified as those with high growth potential usually serve as the targets for large capital infusions, while the multitude of states in a low growth mode are way down the investment priority. This is the counterpart to the use of industry attractiveness and market share as indicators to make investments for the future. Businesses in high growth industries with strong market positions usually serve as the target for large capital infusion, while low growth sectors come at the bottom of the list.

Now there are some serious objections that can be made to this conventional approach. As my colleagues Chan Kim and Renée Mauborgne have argued,[10] it does not necessarily make sense to base future investment decisions on how well a business has done in the past. Changes in the business environment occur rapidly, and what was a formula for success in the past may no longer be for the future. In 1985 IBM's John Opel misread the tea leaves indicating that the market was moving the personal computer way, just as the established US news market providers failed to anticipate the entry of CNN. Both examples bear testimony to the attraction of business-as-usual thinking: historical patterns are assumed to serve as indicators for future potential. Tomorrow is just a bigger today. But we also know that the past is a fallible guide to the future: it is organizations and individuals which make the future, take initiatives and break new ground.

Then, there is the tyranny imposed on us by the language we use. Until the mid-1970s the name of the game had been growth, meaning the extension of capacity to meet what was assumed to be the onward and upward march of demand. The advanced industrial states then discovered the importance of sustaining economies which were flexible enough to adapt to changing consumer preferences, but the way this came to be expressed was in terms of the dichotomy between 'sunrise' and 'sunset' industries. You were meant to get into the first and out of the second. 'Sunset' industries, such as textiles, were clearly considered to be suited to developing countries. Italian manufacturers begged to differ and Italy took the lead as the world's hub for fashion. They developed network organizations like Benetton to snatch the lead in attractive designs and fabrics, offering customers style and quality at attractive prices. France's electronics champion Bull was 'sunrise', and government duly poured subsidies down its corporate throat to no avail.

My two colleagues' lesson for business leaders is clear: instead of adapting to pace setters you have to get your organizations to use innovation and value as the important parameters for managing your businesses, in whatever activity you are in. Adapting to pace setters is what emphasis on the competition tells you to do. You may want to benchmark against them, but that is only a necessary condition for keeping your corporate nose above water. As long as you seek to imitate or even make incremental improvements, you will be competing on price. Added value is the measure that consumers are ready to pay for innovative ideas. Hence their 'Pioneer–Migrator–Settler' map, as a way to assess companies' portfolios of businesses based on value innovation for the future. Settlers are businesses offering me-too value; migrators are businesses with value improvements over competitors; and pioneers are businesses that represent value innovations.

Corporate leaders must shift the balance of their future portfolio, say from the bottom right-hand corner of the map, where settler me-too activities are located, toward pioneers in the upper right-hand corner. That is the path to profitable growth. It is also the path that we must take on our combined index, as in Figure 8.4. Let us assume we place a number of target markets in the lower left hand corner, reflecting our view that country potentials are limited and risks are high for the territories we have examined. Our challenge is now to develop corporate activities in any geographic location which minimize the disadvantages of doing business there and maximize the benefits. We should aim to craft a corporate strategy for our target locations or markets which more than compensates for the difficulties of doing business there. *The corporate strategy maximizes the potential in the country and minimizes the risk, thereby moving us up to the top right hand corner of the diagram.* That means four things:

1 We have to devise policies which minimize or eliminate the general problems which we have just analyzed. For instance, we get round the problems of capital shortage by completing signed cheques from contractors as soon as deliveries are shipped. Or we have a no-corruption policy and are ready to live with a few lost contracts. We do not sell fresh vegetables, which promise to stay tasty as long as they are refrigerated, in a country where transport is unreliable and 'brown

outs', as power cuts are called in India, occur on a regular basis. But we may consider setting up a permanent corporate embassy in Delhi, with offices in key states, to shape the debate about opening up the Indian infrastructure to foreign investors.

2 We have to prepare to build into our strategy the factors which we consider for the moment we cannot alter. For instance, we conclude that the country for the moment has an endemically weak currency due to trade composition of exports, poor public finances, and social strains which regularly tempt government to buy off clienteles through printing money. We do not plan our manufacturing plant on the assumption of imported components (if we have to pay them in local currency); rather, we build up local suppliers, emphasize inflation accounting and develop a first-rate finance department to reduce our exposure to the twists and turns of gyrating interest and exchange rates. We make all employees aware that in such a context credits can turn into lethal debts overnight.

Figure 8.4
CRAFTING PIONEER STRATEGIES FOR DIFFERENT LOCATIONS

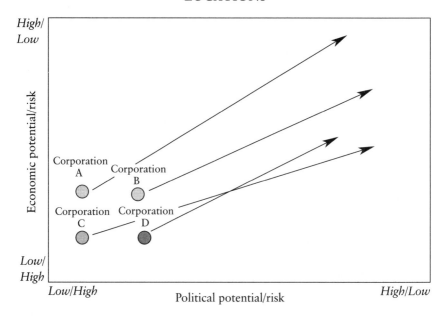

3 We have to maximize the advantages offered by the country. Let us say that the only asset the country has is cheap labour. Wages are very low, and so is productivity. There is a comparative advantage to be exploited in making simple, labour-intensive goods. Or a major advantage may be its geographical location, like Poland, which can be used to source components to our manufacturing units in the EU, or can serve as an export base into other CEE markets. Indeed, Poland has labour cost levels not dissimilar to Latin America, and below countries like Malaysia. But its social structure is relatively egalitarian, its population has numeracy and literacy levels equivalent to those in Western Europe, and after only one decade its political system is well entrenched.

4 Above all, we have to learn everything we can about the country's history, geography, peoples, government, literature and religion. If we don't know anything about the country, we find out who does and we ask to be taught by them. We won't know everything after a seminar lasting just a few days, accompanied by a visit to the target country, but we can learn enough in a short time to start asking reasonable questions. We can deploy our imagination in thinking about the type of goods which people with modest budgets may want to buy. Consider Walls ice cream's success in China, or Nokia's and Ericsson's success in China's cellular telephony market. Or the gargantuan appetite that Nigerians continue to show for Guinness, Ireland's inestimable dark, frothy beer. They are all accessible to local budgets, reasonably priced and serve a large market.

In other words, we go beyond being simply 'responsive' to local conditions; rather, we adapt our core competences to local conditions, and also creatively craft our corporate strategies to maximize the country's potential, and our own, and to minimize our exposure to the country's risks, whatever they are.

Conclusion

The conclusion is simple. Countries which have been initially labelled low potential and high risk may be considered in a new light. Corporate strategies have to be tailored to local conditions in order to maximize returns for the corporation and the country. So managers must seek to pioneer new ways of achieving a more satisfactory fit between a corporate strategy for any particular country and the present and future conditions which that country may be reasonably estimated as facing. Our method allows us to select among many territories where our scarce corporate resources may be deployed. But it also allows us to revisit our previous assessments, and to revise or confirm old judgements. We can also consider our activities on a comparative basis, and revisit them in the light of changing conditions; but we can be assured that we are always asking the same set of structured questions for which there will always be a host of specific answers.

Not least, we can become better world corporate citizens. We don't have to be somewhere because everybody else is there. Indeed, going to a territory which is off-track for others will probably earn us the local government's goodwill, and give us time to build up our local networks before the spin of fortune's wheel makes our location popular. We then benefit from first mover advantages. We can devise a corporate strategy for a location around laudable ambitions which the local government holds dear, such as China's or South Africa's emphasis on training. We can sell locally products which fit local tastes or that people learn to like. We should cherish our brand name, and learn from Nike's experience that world corporations are seen by the media and opinion as being responsible for what goes on in their contractors' factories. Denying responsibility is to forget that corporations are *de facto* accountable to their employees, their customers, their shareholders and to the broad public.

Only when we have worked through all these corporate details should we try to put future financial figures to our corporate project strategy. Otherwise, financial figures from the centre drive our local activities. That was Harold Geneen's method of controlling ITT's worldwide operations in the top-down world of nearly three decades ago. In the great transformation of the world economy in the 1990s and beyond, we have now entered a world driven by and predicated on the equal distribution of human capabilities around our globe. It is this that places us at the start of the history of the twenty-first century.

Notes

1 Kasra Ferdowes, 'Making the Most of Foreign Factories', *Harvard Business Review*, March–April 1997.

2 See Franklin Root, *Entry Strategies for International Markets*, Lexington, D. C. Heath, 1987.

3 'Mutual disenchantment', *Business South Asia*, 1 May 1996.

4 Yves Doz and Gary Hamel, *Alliance Advantage: The Art of Creating Value Through Partnering*, Boston, Harvard Business School Press, 1998.

5 Figures quoted in The World Bank, *Global Development Finance*, 1998.

6 John Stopford and Susan Strange, *Rival States, Rival Firms. Competition for World Market Shares*, Cambridge University Press, 1991.

7 S. H. Robock, 'Political Risk, Identification and Assessment', *Columbia Journal of World Business*, July/August 1971.

8 'Schwere Korruption in der Dritten Welt', *Kursbuch Heft*, 120/1995.

9 I have taken these from Thomas E. Krayenbuehl, *Country Risk Assessment and Monitoring*, Cambridge, Woodhead-Faulker, 1985.

10 W. Chan Kim and Renée Hauborgne, 'Value Innovation: The Strategic Logic of High Growth', *Harvard Business Review*, January–February, 1997.

Chapter 9

A SHORT NARRATIVE OF THE TWENTY-FIRST CENTURY

Looking back from our present vantage point in 2010, one of the surprising features of the past decade is the strength of the forces making for continuity in the world's development, as if they were predetermined by much that has happened since the 1950s. A large proportion of humanity has cast aside inherited attitudes that their fates are shaped by the gods, the elements or by chance, and have learned to take their futures into their own hands. The realization spreads, helped by travel, the media, communications and the operations of the world economy, that human capabilities are equally distributed. But with this realization comes also a greater awareness of the huge, and still widening, inequalities between people, and even more between ethnic groups and states. We have surely witnessed enough savageries this past decade to be more than concerned about the future, and the combined ability of the EU and the US to lead the world away from the many dangers which lie ahead.

As literacy and numeracy have spread, we have witnessed continuous improvements in productivity. Between 1995 and 2010, annual per capita income has grown in a range from 1.4 to 2.6 per cent. The rich countries, with the exception of Japan, where reforms were long delayed, have seen incomes grow by about 80 per cent over fifteen years ago. China's per capita income has grown about three times faster, as have those of many other poorer countries. But never has the world's income inequality been greater than now, and never since the late nineteenth century have the great cities of the US and of Europe so dominated the cultural life of the planet. Fashion, style and the arts parade before the sophisticated publics of London, Paris, Berlin, Amsterdam and New York. We are the fortunate participants in a golden age of Western civilization, without precedent in its scope, its variety and its appeal.

In this wealthier world the US is the dominant power. But it is no longer alone, as was the case nearly two decades ago, when the Soviet Union collapsed. The two world leaders – the US and the EU – are indispensable participants in any major negotiations. Their interests lie in sustaining an accessible and inclusive, rather than a borderless, world. One of the prime lessons learned from the Asian crash of 1997–8 was not to insist that poorer countries should adopt the type of financial market reforms which many Western countries were still having problems in implementing. Otherwise, many features of the 1990s agenda of 'globalisation' remain in place. Multinational corporations bestride the world. Governments make their territories as hospitable as possible to businesses. Poverty has receded for hundreds of millions of people, and their life expectancy has risen. All this has brought a cohort of problems, from pollution to an array of political troubles and international conflicts.

How has this all come about?

In the longer-term perspective, it is evident that there were two long cycles in the course of the twentieth century. The first lasted from the end of the First World War in 1918 to around the mid-1970s. Governments became responsible for their national economies, as state activities expanded. Demands for national self-determination fragmented the world market into an ever greater number of political units. Meanwhile, we witnessed the rise of the giant, diversified corporation, the development of

Sometime in the course of the 1970s the world embarked on a great transformation of the world markets.

mass consumer markets, and a sharp rise in living standards. Top-down corporate governance by managers and labour union leaders was duplicated politically by top-down decisions taken by politicians and bureaucrats. As long as they jointly delivered employment and prosperity, their leadership was tolerated.

Sometime in the course of the 1970s the world embarked on a great transformation of the world markets, the state system, the norms of state governance and the way that corporations were managed. This was the period of *détente*, when human rights became embedded in the unwritten constitution of the EU, and Portugal, Spain and Greece showed the way to what became a political contagion of transition towards representative forms of government around the globe. Meanwhile, the end of the cheap oil era accelerated the rise of the two champion export economies, Germany and Japan, confirmed the dollar as emperor on world financial markets, and kept the moribund Soviet economy alive for a further couple of decades. The crusade to roll back the state gathered force in the 1980s, while corporations felt their way towards operating as transnationals and the leading financial centres competed to end capital controls.

By the 1990s there was no doubt that the dominant trend of the decade was globalization. The US stood at the pinnacle of its world power, and its major markets were in Asia, where glorious prospects were predicted for the twenty-first century. US capitalism's interest in keeping the capitalist dynamo going at the end of the Cold War through the discovery of new frontiers was seen as coinciding with the world's interest in reducing world inequality. The vision was of a One World driving towards shared prosperity, democracy and better living conditions for all. Western corporations would pour technologies into the poorer regions of the world, where labour was abundant, cheap and talented. Global financial markets, no longer under political lock and key, would provide capital, ending the historical capital shortages of developing countries. Within a couple of decades there would arise a huge transnational market for consumers.

The World Bank's vision of the twenty-first century, current in the 1990s, encapsulated this ambition. Using purchasing power parities to measure the relative value of goods and services not traded on international markets, rather than national economies evaluated at market exchange rates, the World Bank elevated China to the world's second largest economy, larger than Japan, itself twice the size of united Germany, Europe's largest national economy. With Asia-Pacific annual growth rates expected to average 6 per cent, by 2010 the East Asian region was expected to account for 34 per cent of the world's total output – 40 per cent if South Asia were included – whilst Western Europe and the US would stand at around 25 per cent each. East Asia was expected to contribute almost 40 per cent of world trade, with Western Europe and North America respectively accounting for 37 per cent and 20 per cent. By 2020 the rest of the world, excluding the US, EU and Japan, would represent 67 per cent of the world economy. That is where the major markets of the world would be.

The conclusion was obvious: US and EU prosperity would rapidly come to depend on the prosperity of these regions. China and Japan would become alternative centres of power, once China had managed to implement further market reforms to sustain its rapid expansion, and when Japan had decided finally to implement the liberalization measures announced in 1986 by Haruo Mayekawa, the Governor of the Bank of Japan. Major changes in the global structure of wealth and power would occur within the coming two decades.

As we know, this prediction joined the many in history's graveyard of events which did not occur. But from our perspective of 2010, the prediction was erroneous on two scores. We can recognize its naïveté as derived from the economics-drives-politics school of flat-earth believers, particularly prevalent among the economics fraternity, joined by the one-fit-for-all brigade of Jeffersonian democrats, intoxicated, as Edmund Burke wrote over two centuries ago, with 'the wild gas of liberty'.[1] Fortunately, these fundamental errors of judgement did not prevent the world polity being configured around a great power society of two. On timing, its broad vision of Asian predominance is fifty years too early – quite a significant lapse of time as far as human affairs are concerned. In a nutshell, *the world's economic structure starts to swing on its hinges in the decade of the 2070s when Asia's per capita incomes – China's in particular – will start converging rapidly on the extraordinarily high incomes of the old Western world.*

Let us spin back in time, and review some of the driving forces which provided the momentum for this irreversible process toward the equalization of wealth, and the concomitant unequal distribution of power around the world.

1 Demographics: the trends shown in Figure 6.1 have continued, as the world population growth rates slow down, migration from the countryside rises, people become increasingly urbanized and demographic imbalances grow more pronounced. By 2025 the population

around the southern and eastern Mediterranean is likely to reach 360 million, just slightly smaller than the whole population of the new EU; sub-Saharan Africa will hold just under 1 billion, despite wars and disease, and South Asia will have reached the near 2 billion mark. That spells continued migrations of people in search of work to Europe in particular, and migration of capital – particularly to India, the transnationals' English-speaking El Dorado for the decade of the 2010s. It also points to a further growth in the ageing, rich world's pension assets, about 10 per cent of which are likely to be invested in emerging market assets.

2 Technology has long since netted the four corners of the earth. As the Federal Reserve Chairman told the US Congress in July 1998, 'the signs of technological change are all around us'. Since then, central bankers and 50 per cent of economists have come round to consider that the stream of new technologies has lifted growth rates in productivity. Global communications are denser and more far-ranging than ever. Progress in biotechnology has led to the discovery of genes which get cancers to eat themselves, but is prolonging the longevity of people, an increasing number of whom live well into their hundreds.[2] The first breakthroughs are promised within the next decade in nano-technologies for applications in surgery, and will no doubt be applied across the range of business activities. But the world is a more dangerous place as well: terrorists, criminals and prophets have ready access to the tools of modernity to spread their word and commit their deeds.

3 *Growth in global per capita incomes has been lifted by this stream of innovation in a range from 1.4 to 2.6 per cent, creating the golden age of the present decade in which the Western world is basking.* Never have the gaps between the rich and poor been greater, so that to many the enticing idyll depicted by the World Bank back in the 1990s of a rapid convergence of incomes by 2020 is a distant, forgotten dream. The World Bank's prognosis proved ludicrously wrong because purchasing power parities are a statistical illusion and because business is conducted in real dollars or Euros. The hype also led world markets in 1997–8 to overexaggerate the importance of developing country markets in the immediate future, and to undervalue their importance in the longer term. East Asia in the 1990s drew on foreign savings for just 0.5

per cent of its combined domestic product, so that the introduction of selective capital controls following the crash of that year helped to stabilize East Asian economies, and allow them to resume their growth by the turn of the millennium.

4 Co-ordinated efforts by the US and the EU staved off protectionist pressures when the world economy came perilously close to depression in 1998–9. With the help of multilateral negotiations in the World Trade Organization – established in 1995 after the conclusion of the Uruguay Round – tariff levels were lowered further to a meagre 1–2 per cent trade-weighted tariff for rich countries, 6 per cent for poorer countries (from 10–15 per cent in 1998) and 4 per cent average for the transition economies.

Among the cities with the worst air pollution, thirteen were in Asia.

This has helped strengthen regional trade in Latin America, and to a lesser extent in Asia. Much less progress has been made on multilateral accords on investment regimes, given the prominence of family ownership in most parts of the world and the related hostility to the sale of national corporations to foreign owners. *But the overall trend is clear enough: by 2020, the non-OECD world will account for 40 per cent of world imports.*

5 The environmental cost of the world's development was seen in the late 1990s as staggeringly high. Asia experienced shrinking forests, the spread of deserts, the silting of the rivers, floods and crop damages. That was when the World Health Organization reminded us that among the cities with the worst air pollution, thirteen were in Asia. In Egypt and India it was not difficult to predict that population pressures would further burden scarce water resources. And the continued long-term growth in demand for fossil fuels, particularly from the poorer countries, was expected to raise greenhouse emissions to unsustainable levels, while pushing up world oil prices. But the world has become much more sensitive since then to the cost of environmental abuse, while new technologies are making the world a cleaner place. The biggest breakthrough is the introduction of car engines run on hydrogen. Energy prices – and oil-dependent export countries – have collapsed.

6 Businesses compete in world markets, and seek to apply the latest technologies. This has tended to drive prices down, providing con-

sumers with an ever wider variety of products and services. Dissemination of information is instantaneous and free. In this context, creativity is the key to firms not taking the slide to being commodity suppliers. Corporations are scouring the world for talent, as success depends on technological advantage and on crafting corporate strategies to local conditions. Home and host country conditions remain distinct, but access and regulatory arrangements are more transparent than before. That has proved to be a further reason for recruitment in global corporations to be more than ever culturally mixed. As ever, the potential and risks of doing global business remain high, as world politics and markets are volatile. In particular, the general trend to prosperity is unevenly distributed, creating social and international tensions.

A global assessment for the coming decades

From our vantage point in 2010, it is easy enough to see what happened when world history turned on its hinges in the years of the great transformation between 1989 and 1992. Fortified by a combination of One World thinking, and a simple staircase, economics-drives-politics vision, the US administration, supported by the global agencies (the IMF, the World Bank, the WTO), steered financial markets towards a prolonged roller-coaster of boom overall, and bust here and there. It is as though the world economy was hitched to US manic-depressive mood swings, on the theme 'bound to lead' to 'bound not to lead'. The idea was to persuade poorer countries to open to trade and to capital flows, in return for an opening of Western markets to their products and for an encouragement of corporations to go global in a true sense. Worldwide liberalization was to be accompanied by promotion of democracy, and with democracy would come a great era of peace. This generous, liberal vision informed US post-Cold War policy, whose component parts were not readily compatible with one another:

● Making the world safe for democracy was an old ambition rooted in America's civil religion as 'the tree of liberty', to use Thomas Jefferson's phrase. In 1990 a world 'whole and free' seemed a realizable dream. The Western powers had the means to induce recalcitrant governments to co-operate. Both the EU and the US attached political conditions to trade agreements. Financial institutions made loans conditional on political change and institutional reform. But the complex process of managing regime changes meant that all sorts of political compromises would have to be struck, ones that were suited to local circumstances, to the interests of local elites and to the particular set of codes and aspirations of various interested parties. Politics was bound to prevail over concerns to encourage economic efficiency or financial market transparency. Besides, democracy, nationalism, religion and hunger for power, glory and privilege are never easy bedfellows.

- Ensuring an open world economy also expressed US experience. After the Soviet Union's collapse, the US was no longer politically prepared to absorb apparently unlimited quantities of Asian exports – 'no more Japans' became the watchword of US international economic policy. Countries with structural trade surpluses rooted in national systems of corporate mercantilism were a major source of dis-equilibrium in the world economy. Hence the global institutions' proposals for governments to adopt full currency convertibility and financial market liberalization. The formula seduced governments eager to attract foreign capital, but they proved less than enthusiastic about challenging the tangle of domestic deals which underpinned their power. By 1998 Asian elites, praised only eighteen months earlier for their farsightedness in running effective industrial policies, were being denounced as corrupt *caciques* in cahoots with crony capitalists. World time's inconsistency in moods is marvellous to behold.

- The US was, and remains, the dominant power in a dangerous world. This was the Department of Defence's justification for continuing to spend over $250 billion annually after the Cold War's end. US public opinion was flattered by the idea of American world leadership, and generally supported the Department's policy of preventing the emergence in Europe or Asia of any challenger to US primacy. Europe remains a protectorate within NATO's multilateral embrace, while China continues to focus on its economic and political transformation. But US public opinion and Congress are more than ever isolationist in mentality. America's many enemies in the Muslim world decided to encourage the trend by multiplying terrorist attacks on US lives and property, in the manner of the twin car-bomb explosions at the US embassies in Kenya and Dar es Salaam in August 1998. Like the death they dispense, modern weapons are great equalizers.

Before we proceed, it may be interesting for our readers to remember why the very dark clouds gathering on the horizon in 1998 were dispersed. They announced a major world financial meltdown. US savings had fallen to an unprecedented 0.6 per cent of national income, and Japanese interest rates were barely above zero. Financial markets, frightened by their own collective reaction to the Asia-Pacific crisis, panicked over Russia. A recently created hedge fund, graced by Nobel Prize winners, went bottom up, and concerns were widespread that the world economy was piling up debts. More seriously, governments had radically different views on bankruptcies, some emphasizing the importance of market clearance, but most more concerned to retain political support by their espousal of the 'too-big-to-fail' principle. The EU's single currency announced bank failures galore.

Favourable factors won the upper hand, but it was a close call. The US had moved to federal government surplus, and the widening trade deficit with Asia allowed the dollar to be gently devalued. Japan in particular muddled its way through to take in more Asian exports. The financial markets gathered their wits when they realized that the world mechanism was adjusting relative prices more abruptly perhaps than usual, and that the key to the world's future lay in the Western world keeping its markets open. Both the US and the EU leaderships did not need reminding, and faced down protectionist demands. The EU in particular proved more willing in the context of the Euro's introduction to allow firms and banks to become bankrupt.

Meanwhile, governments around the world realized, and began to act on their realization, that their efforts now had to be directed at creating political support for the more flexible market institutions which they had to introduce. *In retrospect, the key lesson from those years was the US's and EU's renunciation of one-fit-for-all formulas*. In particular, if countries wished to follow Chile's example and impose inward capital controls to reduce their exposure to the world financial markets, they were viewed as making a responsible decision in favour of political consent at the expense of some degree of economic efficiency. And if countries followed Malaysia's example, and slapped on outward capital controls, the new approach was to be sorry for the locals and for foreign investors trapped in the local market, but to allow other would-be imitators to learn from Malaysia's subsequent difficulties.

China

One area of the world where the politics, economics and security dimensions of US foreign policy have proved particularly difficult to reconcile is China. China was simultaneously a market opportunity, a political challenge and a long-term contender for the laurels of world primacy. The party-state remains in power, with managed elections introduced at provincial and city level as part of a longer-term strategy to democratize politics in China, provide stronger legitimacy to the introduction of market mechanisms, and remain on good terms with the US and the EU. Meanwhile, the party-state knows that world corporations consider China an indispensable opportunity. With the population growing by about 170 million every decade, migration from the countryside and the need to create 20 million new jobs each year, the government gives priority to growth. But its approach is exploratory rather than foolhardy. It steers China cautiously to more flexible structures, retrenching when conditions are judged adverse and speeding up when the opportunity is there.

Growth rates remain high, and living standards continue to rise. China runs a huge trade surplus and has amassed unprecedented foreign reserves. Capital controls have been eased, but not liberalized as Beijing does not want too close a link between domestic and world financial flows. Continued controls have not prevented the development of a large domestic capital market, fed by the high savings rates of households, and a modest government surplus derived from the hugely profitable operations of public service providers still in state ownership. The biggest of these is telecommunications operations, which nets up to 40 per cent of total government revenues. Though the Minister of Post and Telecommunications announced in 1997 that the government might be ready to open operations to foreign competition in 2010, there is no sign of this being achieved. One of the world news's fixtures this decade has been the discussion about when, how and whether China is to enter the WTO. China is in no hurry.

China's strategy is simply to grow into world power at its own pace and convenience. China is now number one importer of foodstuffs. This has boosted earnings for farmers from Australia, New Zealand and Argentina, as well as from the US and the EU. As predicted, about 90 per cent of the country's oil comes from the Gulf and the Caspian reserves, replacing brown coal as the prime source of energy for house-holds and industries. The stock of inward direct investment is second only to the EU and the US, and ever closer ties have been formed between the mainland and the overseas Chinese communities. Beijing is more closely involved with the governments of the Asia-Pacific, where the Chinese presence is extensive. There has been no precipitate boost in military spending, which would only scare neighbours, but neither has China abandoned its territorial claims. Indeed, the more that China develops, the more Beijing has had to assure neighbours of its peaceful intent.

In this, Beijing is neither deceitful nor wholly honest. Primacy not conquest is its longer-term, secular goal. The inevitable result has been to send China's smaller neighbours scurrying to Uncle Sam for protec-tion. Even so, China is swallowing the Taiwanese economy like a whale absorbs a minnow, while Chinese migrants continue to move into the open areas of Siberia. In the 2020s China will *de facto* dominate the Spratly islands and the surrounding seas. It is in the 2030s that we anticipate increasingly harsh debates in the US Congress about the pre-dictable and momentous shifts in the structure of world power towards this continent-civilization, now definitely double the size of the US economy and with the potential by the end of the twenty-first century to become seven times larger than America.

Japan

China's *de facto* emergence means that the US will be Asia's counter-balance well into the second half of the twenty-first century. Japan opted out in 1996, when it renewed the Cold War security arrangements with the United States. There had been a moment in the late 1980s and early 1990s when Japan seemed to be tempted to take charge of its own security. The experience of the US imposing a tax on Japan as its contribution to pay for the expense of a war against Saddam Hussein in 1991, on which opinion was at best lukewarm, opened Japanese eyes to how pathetically dependent they had become on the US. Tokyo seemed to hint on occasion that Japan might go nuclear if, as the world's second largest economy, it was not invited to take a seat as a permanent member of the Security Council. But the Japanese people were reluctant to have their troops sent abroad even under UN auspices, while China growled, made plain its displeasure and vetoed Japan's UN ambitions.

Japan's political paralysis was reflected in the perennial debate about its identity: was Japan an Asian state or an advanced industrial state? As an Asian state, Japan was bound to be reminded that its culture derived from China's, that it owed China apologies for the war of 1931–45 and that its future was best secured by deference to Beijing, while as an advanced industrial state Japan was bound to be pressured by the US to mend its mercantilist ways. The first was too humiliating to contemplate, the second too contentious to implement. In effect, Japan's prominence in the 1990s as Asia's giant – equivalent to 80 per cent of the Asia-Pacific economy – could be secured only by a true opening of its economy. Only by learning to live like Edwardian Britain off its overseas income could Japan hope to become the hub of a commercial, financial and cultural empire. That would mean running permanent trade deficits, and have the yen become a reserve currency in the manner of the dollar.

The challenge proved too great. There was the intellectual inertia inherited from the halcyon days of high growth, when Japanese corporations scattered competitors before them. Then, it seemed, bureaucrats, politicians and corporations managed public affairs well. Public attitudes were attuned to the portrayal of the rest of the world as essentially hostile, while hard work and high savings were seen as essential for survival of the Japanese people on their volcanic chain of islands. The vision of Japan as a 'global civilian power' – relaxed, cosmopolitan, innovative, slightly idle and agreeably decadent – was not comprehensible. Besides, liberalization entailed unravelling the many compromises on which the civil peace in Japan rested. Japan could not and would not alter. It was locked into trade surpluses, and had no option other than to lend its overseas customers the yen to buy the products it sold. Asia's workshop could not benefit by being the world's largest creditor.

It was therefore the prime cause of Asia-Pacific's financial meltdown in the course of 1997–8. Japan ran trade surpluses with Asia (with the exception of China) and, as the region's current account deficit with Japan widened, Japanese commercial banks lent in dollars. Foreign investment flowed to Thailand, Indonesia and South Korea. When the dollar rose in 1995, and China's yuan was devalued, Asia-Pacific's export boom to the US and the EU ground to a standstill. Japan's domestic markets were far too closed to take up the slack, while the continued funds from Japan's trade surpluses were being lent, almost given, to Asia-Pacific borrowers. Burdened with non-performing loans at home, a disappearing portfolio in Asia and exposure of Japanese investors in dollars on the US Treasury-bond markets, Japan's financial institutions' creditworthiness could be salvaged only by talking the yen down, in the hope of reigniting the export machine.

That was the magic moment in 1998 when the mantle of leadership in Asia began to shift from Tokyo to Beijing. Beijing rejected devaluation of the yuan as its contribution to stabilizing currency relations in Asia, conditional upon concerted US–Japanese efforts to stabilize the yen. Without the option of yet one more export boom, China's action and US compliance shifted the burden of adjustment much more squarely on to Japan: the only way to salvage Japan's financial system now was to start opening up Japan's nationalist cross-shareholding structures, prise control of banking away from the Finance Ministry, introduce much stricter bankruptcy regulations and further reduce the privileges of Japan's 'labour aristocracy' – in short to start on the path of domestic market liberalization about fifteen years late.

With the benefit of hindsight provided from our vantage point of 2010, the 1990s was Japan's lost decade. With a rapidly ageing population, and opting to continue the US security relationship as reinsurance against the prospect of China's rise, Japan missed the bus to world eminence. History passed Japan by, and the mantle has fallen to the EU.

Asia-Pacific

Japan's deficiencies were the main cause of the meltdown in the Asia-Pacific economy in 1997–8. One of the less memorable features of those years was world time's switch from lavishing excessive praise on the countries of the region to castigating them as run by 'crony capitalists'. All that the global financial system was being asked to do was to realign the overvalued currencies of four mini-South East Asian economies, equivalent to less than a third of the French economy, and to prompt some necessary corrections in the domestic arrangements of the Republic of Korea – the giant of Asia's developing countries. But once the language of 'crony capitalism' was in place, it did not take a genius to apply it generously to, for instance, Yeltsin's Russia. Further, the decline in Asian demand for commodity imports reduced revenues of commodity exporters in the Gulf, Africa, the Americas and Asia. Currencies duly adjusted.

Japan's deficiencies were the main cause of the meltdown in the Asia-Pacific economy in 1997–8.

In retrospect, the difficulties affecting the countries of Asia-Pacific in the late 1990s were a result of their previous successes. Japan had provided an example or model for many. The US imported the region's goods, underwrote its security and trade, and exported American 'can-do' attitudes. Governments came to base their legitimacy on growth, meaning the expansion of capacity and the race for market share. This transformed their societies, created aspirations, extended interdependence between highly diverse societies, inflicted severe environmental damage and prompted demands for political development. What the late 1990s revealed was that the old patterns of economic growth – over-dependence on the US markets, a still narrow range of export products and an emphasis on the simple expansion of capacity – were no longer sustainable. While Japan edged painfully towards opening its mind and economy, Asia moved fitfully to embrace representative government in order to ensure the political foundations on which adaptable, market societies depend.

One of the major successes of the first decade of the new millennium has been the way in which the many dangers that threatened to engulf the Asia-Pacific have been avoided. The countries of the region were more than ever at one another's throats in world export markets, migratory flows between them were considerable, and the Asia-Pacific boom had been notoriously accompanied by a surge in military expenditures. World time's vengeance on the wretched peoples of the region in 1997–8 lent credibility to the warnings that exasperated local populations would wreak terrible retribution on the region's Chinese minorities. Internal conflagrations risked spilling outwards into relations between the states. There were multiple territorial conflicts, all the more unsettling on account of expectations about changing power balances, fears of US disengagement and a multitude of boundary disputes.

One reason for Asia-Pacific's avoidance of disaster was the quality of leadership, which managed to steer Indonesia to more representative government, maintain a balance between the races in Malaysia, introduce a degree of honesty into Thailand's affairs, and consolidate the non-spectacular reforms of the 1990s in the Philippines. A second factor was that all Asian countries discarded the cruder forms of corporate or state mercantilism, while avoiding the full leap to Anglo-American-type financial capitalism, for which the cultural preconditions were absent. Third, the countries stuck to their longer-term objective of liberal trade and investment policies, but proved ready to impose controls on short-term capital movements. Fourth, bilateral diplomacy, completed by the loose multilateral regional organizations and supplemented by the US, managed to preserve the peace which most of the region has enjoyed since the end of the war in Vietnam in 1975.

The Republic of Korea has led the way as the example for modernizing Asian states. Since the Republic's membership of the OECD – the advanced industrial countries' club, based in Paris – the regulatory framework put in place has propelled the country past its initial state-centred capitalism, based on a combination of protectionism for the home market coupled with large corporate conquests of foreign markets. Financial market reforms have encouraged the unravelling of cross-shareholdings among the large corporates through the introduction of state-of-the-art accounting practices, the development of a large traded capital market, and the delegation of strict policing powers to autonomous regulatory authorities. Korean markets are wide open to foreign competition, and the very high standards of education at all levels underpin the country's expanding high technology base, as well as an open, confident democracy under the rule of law.

India

Resumption of a more sustainable expansion in Asia-Pacific has forced India, the world's largest democracy, to continue along the reform path initiated in 1991. The process entailed complex negotiations for favours across India's extensive political market. Growth rates lifted to around 8 per cent per annum – up two points over the previous decade – as the states competed to attract business, and India's comparative advantage in textiles accelerated its entry to the world economy. An unintended consequence of India's permanent public sector deficits was a financial market Big Bang in 2003, when nationalized financial institutions lobbied frantically to sell government debt. The highly publicized move gave a kick-start to a large, liquid capital market, enabling foreign and local investors to buy up poorly performing business houses, and India to finance over 80 per cent of the total $265 billion required to update its infrastructure. Foreign investment flooded in.

China has cast a lengthening shadow over India, which observes with concern the close but conflict-ridden relations between China and the US that have replaced Washington–Tokyo relations as the principal axis around which Asia-Pacific affairs turn. China continues to support Pakistan, and no solution is in sight with India over Kashmir. Despite India's improved economic performance, China's national economy in 2010 is three times greater than India's, up from over twice India's in the 1990s. India is an active lobbyist in Washington DC, and has acquired a solid reputation among US corporations as a place where good business can be done. Its main foreign policy thrust, though, is towards the EU, as a major market, a source of technology and a sympathetic listener to India's demands for permanent membership of the UN Security Council. Meanwhile, India has developed a considerable nuclear capability, and is much more assertive a player in world politics.

India holds the world's second largest Muslim population after Indonesia, and has not escaped the tremors and explosions which have wracked the Islamic world – which stretches from western Africa, along the southern and eastern Mediterranean littoral, extends into the Balkans, includes a growing immigrant population within the EU, and spreads across territories from Turkey to western China, down to the Gulf and out to the South-East Asian states of Indonesia and Malaysia. Only in Malaysia, Tunisia and to a certain extent Morocco and Jordan have special forms of Western-style 'market democracy' grown shallow roots. After the interim government of President Habibie, following the demise in 1998 of the Suharto family clan, Indonesia edged towards a managed multi-party regime under military tutelage. But China's priority there was for a law-and-order regime, capable of protecting the Chinese minority in the near decade of low growth following the rupiah's collapse.

The Middle East

The world's oil economy is still centred on the Middle East and the Gulf, which account for 65 per cent of proven reserves and about 30 per cent of total supplies. Caspian Sea gas and oil, developed during the 1990s, flows through the Gulf and the Levant, and overland to the Pacific. Iraq's re-entry into the market, renewed investment in Iran, the development of Russia's export potential, and the US interest in ensuring supplies closer to home in the Gulf of Mexico have helped to keep oil prices down, as have greater efficiency in fuel use and the introduction of car engines that run on hydrogen. Low oil prices have been a boon to energy-importing countries, and helped alleviate pressure on their balance of payments. But population-rich exporting countries, like Algeria, Indonesia and Nigeria, suffered. Low oil prices further stimulated demand for imports in the East Asian region, which has become equal to Europe as the world's largest importer, with its oil dependence rising to 90 per cent by 2020.

A central event of this decade has been the disintegration of what seemed in the 1990s to be a dominant US position in the Gulf. In retrospect, the 1991 Gulf war, won with such devastating speed by the US-led UN coalition against Iraq, turned out to be a pyrrhic victory. The US failure to stop the Israeli government building new settlements in the occupied territories alienated its most loyal allies. Weakened by over-dependence on one or a few commodities, and by their failure to develop regional trade, fragile regimes could not meet the needs of their urbanized, rapidly growing populations. A bloody struggle followed the death of President Assad in Syria; Saddam Hussein met a violent death in the putsch installing a nationalist junta; but both paled against the orgy of violence which engulfed Saudi Arabia when the old King was deposed, and the US troops were expelled. Saudi's new rulers summoned the community of Islam to expel infidels from Islam's holy lands.

Europe

The dramatic events described above prompted EU member states to bypass NATO and the transatlantic alliance. Four developments triggered the EU's changed position. First, Islamic minorities in EU member states could not integrate successfully, unless their sensitivities were taken into account with regard to developments in North Africa, the Middle East and the Gulf. Second, population growth of the southern and western littorals of the Mediterranean gave the EU a vested interest in seeking to promote a moderate Islam among its southern neighbours, which now account for 12 per cent of EU exports. Third, direct negotiations with Europe's main oil suppliers were all the more important, once the US had lost its privileged position. Fourth, Iran, Iraq, Libya, Algeria, Egypt and Saudi Arabia, following in Pakistani footsteps, are, or are on the way to becoming, nuclear weapon states. With nuclear weapons come delivery systems, capable of reaching deep into EU territory.

The EU is the counterweight to the US in 2010, so that the world is structured around a 'bi-gemony' between the two great powers, both sharing values of individual freedoms, representative government and market economies, but differing significantly in terms of domestic structure. The US is a federation, whose founding fathers ensured a separation of powers between legislature, executive and judiciary. Centralizing tendencies won out over states' rights in the American Civil War, in the New Deal and with the rise of the imperial presidency. The EU is much more of a confederation of states, networked ever more tightly among themselves and with multiple ties to the rest of the world. The member states participate in the EU's subversive machinery with its federal ambitions to remake the EU along US lines. This permanent stimulation of national adhesion to and resentment against 'Brussels' is the central political tension within the EU.

The EU's economy accounts for a massive 35 per cent of the world economy, with a population of over 400 million people, or 5 per cent of the world's. Turkey is in the customs union and the Ukraine has an association accord, so that an extensive definition of the EU yields a population in excess of 530 million (55 million in the Ukraine, 80 million in Turkey). Per capita income averages $40,000 (at 1995 prices). Enlargement of the EU of 15 was launched in July 1997, when the European Commission spelled out the market democracy requirements for membership, and the farm policy and budgetary reforms needed to accommodate the entry of eleven new member states from Central and Eastern Europe, including Cyprus and Malta. Negotiations were completed in December 2009, the length of time being prompted by member states' domestic inhibitions, electoral timetables, competing EU agendas and applicants' foot-dragging. The new EU of 26 is scheduled to open shop on 1 January 2012.

Other aspects of the EU's geopolitics are falling into place as this huge polity grows into its natural space. The EU provides two-thirds of Russian foreign exchange earnings, and launched a Russia bond on the Euro capital markets in 2005, as part of a Marshall Plan deal whereby the Russian government agreed to focus, under direct EU tutelage, on building a state subject to the rule of law. Russia's terrible downward spin out of communism into the mafia state of the following decade saw its economy shrink to 5 per cent of the French (with nearly three times the population) when the rouble collapsed in August 1998. Similarly, the EU modified its miserly Euro-Med accords of 1995 with twelve Mediterranean non-member states, promising industrial free trade by 2010, and grasped the nettle of the urgent need to accelerate economic growth among southern neighbours through a Nordic alliance which conveniently overrode protectionist interests in the southern member states.

Africa

Europe's biggest challenge lay in sub-Saharan Africa, accounting in the 1990s for 10 per cent of world population, but with only 1 per cent of the world trade and GNP, and dependent on the EU for two-thirds of its foreign exchange earnings. Hopeful 1960s visions of a decolonized Africa were replaced by grim despair. Africa's pre-colonial structures were undermined by the slave trade; decolonization undermined the precarious European structures in place; Cold War rivalries militarized the successor states; kleptocracies and ideologues multiplied. The EU's Lomé Convention trapped African producers in quotas; imposed local content regulations on prospective African manufacturing competitors; EU fishing boats sucked African waters dry of fish. In the 1980s the fragile African economies collapsed under high oil prices and foreign debt. Per capita incomes shrank, as IMF medicine men applied 'structural adjustment' programmes, discreetly supervised by the US Treasury.

With apartheid ended, South Africa's new administration had a crowded agenda: it was confronted with the tasks of creating a 'rainbow' nation and of galvanizing the economy, which represented half of Africa's and received over 90 per cent of the continent's inward direct investment. The challenge was for the economy to generate 1 million new jobs per annum. But South Africa's government could not convince world corporations to invest there in a major way, and export earnings were hit by the Asian meltdown of 1997–8. Job creation and growth were restricted, and it was only in 2005 that the EU linked its Marshall Plan to Russia to a separate, simple plan for South Africa. The South African government agreed to joint supervision with the EU of South African monetary and fiscal policy, against 50 billion Euros for South Africa's foreign exchange reserves. For the last five years South

African growth has averaged 8 per cent a year and foreign investors are pouring in.

The rise of the EU and the Euro

In retrospect, it is clear that 1999 marked the end of the world's transition out of the Cold War structures to the new structure which is shaping the first half of the twenty-first century. In January eleven countries in the EU had their bond markets, swollen by decades of government deficits, converted into Euros. National currencies, still circulating for retail purposes, were pegged at a fixed price to the Euro. European corporations and governments could now finance their needs by recourse to a capital market the size of the US, and in the knowledge that currency relationships were fixed. In 2002 the retail industry also converted to the Euro, and in 2003 the second Blair government held a referendum on whether or not the UK should join 'Euroland'. The Australian-American media mogul, Rupert Murdoch, needed access to EU satellite television markets, and ordered his clutch of UK newspapers to back Blair. The referendum was won by Blair with an 80 per cent majority in favour.

The UK pro-vote had been helped by the boom which accompanied the Euro's introduction. The French, German and Italian economies had entered the Euro in good shape, at least as far as corporate performance was concerned. The boost to corporate confidence provided by the Euro brought forward investment projects, high rates of unemployment began to edge down, and consumer spending rose. Mobile capital moved into the Euro out of higher-risk emerging markets and pushed up the exchange rate of the Euro to the dollar, thus helping the rest of the world's exports. Unwittingly, the EU took over the role of world locomotive, as the US economy slid from the top of its prolonged boom. Protectionist voices shouted louder about unfair competition, but the Commission was not listening. With the UK playing a supportive role while out of Euroland, and a vigorous role once in it, the Euro rapidly developed as the world's second reserve currency.

There had been much speculation prior to 1999 about which type of financial system and corporate governance structures – French, German or Anglo-American – the EU would move towards. There had been three scenarios:

1 The Continental states would move rapidly to Anglo-American-type corporate finance, given the stimulation from a large, liquid capital market, populated by financial institutions searching for corporate winners. Shareholders and consumers would become the two kings of corporate strategy, to which managers would have to defer in a highly competitive US-type market.

2 The Continental states would not change corporate governance structures, predicated on national cross-shareholdings and on the search for market share over profit. Governments would still consider trade surpluses to be virtuous, and national labour market structures would remain much as before. The only change would be the greater facility afforded to corporations in raising funds on the Euro-capital market.

3 Some middle ground would be achieved: corporate managers would have plenty of incentives to raise capital in order to finance the intensive investments required to supply a market of 350 million people. Financial institutions would demand much higher returns for shareholders than in national capital markets; but the traditions acquired of shareholder patience, existing national labour laws and taxation differences would provide the basis for an EU-wide social–liberal compromise.

By 2010 the new Europe-wide social–liberal compromise is tilted heavily the Anglo-American way. This has been achieved with much weeping and gnashing of teeth, as the European economy began to restructure out of its national inheritances. Fortunately, the destruction of jobs as inefficient activities were closed down was more than compensated for by the creation of jobs in the high-growth sectors of Europe's technology-driven economy, more amenable to green concerns. People move to jobs, and no longer wait for politicians to bring subsidized jobs to them. Government expenditures are balanced by buoyant tax revenues due to higher growth. The EU's older and longer-living population saves more, and invests in unit trusts. Corporations and family firms have unlocked their non-traded shares, providing a further boost to the capital market. Mega-hostile takeovers have become frequent, and a Europe-wide managerial culture is developing, quite at home in the EU's multinational polity.

The EU's rapid development provided the world economy with an alternative liquid capital market and reserve currency to the dollar. The countries of Central and Eastern Europe converted their central bank reserves to Euros as soon as the currency was introduced, and Russians stopped using the vanishing rouble, preferring to hold Euros. Oil, commodity and tropical product imports to the EU were invoiced in Euros. The Gulf, Middle East and North African states converted half their reserves to Euros, as did the countries of South America – except

> *The EU's rapid development provided the world economy with an alternative liquid capital market and reserve currency to the dollar.*

for Mexico and Venezuela, which stayed with the dollar – and the countries of the Asia-Pacific. China, interested in promoting a multipolar world in order to reduce the overwhelming presence of the US, was one of the first to acquire Euro central bank reserves. India followed suit. As part of the EU–South Africa package, sub-Saharan Africa moved into the EU-Euro-Africa zone, where African reserves were held in Paris, London and Berlin.

The world flow of funds has altered considerably from those distant days when the dollar reigned supreme and the world economy beat to the combined pulse of domestic US demand, the price of oil and the Japanese savings rate. The EU is the world's trading emporium, fed by its many Mediterranean, Atlantic and North Sea ports, and tied overland to India and China with the reopening of the old silk road, closed down by Russia's emergence in the eighteenth century. It is the indispensable market for suppliers from all over the world. Australia and New Zealand have negotiated association agreements with the EU – a development greatly accelerated by the Asian meltdown of 1997–98 and Indonesia's subsequent travails. World corporations are based in the main in the world's two central markets, making transatlantic corporate ties and investments the core area for the transnational global economy. Asian corporations cannot afford not to have a presence in the US and in the EU.

The EU is also the world's largest foreign investor. In the 1990s the pecking order for emerging markets was Asia-Pacific, Latin America and Central Europe. But European corporations began to plan their operations on a pan-European basis, preceding the slow pace of EU enlargement negotiations by nearly two decades. CEE countries were stable, reasonably well managed, with well-educated populations, and close to home markets. European investors led the field in Brazil, the Andean countries and in the southern cone. Both the CEE and Latin America, including Mexico, have recorded 5–6 per cent per annum growth rates, and have per capita incomes ranging from $6,000 to $14,000. Industrial trade has grown rapidly from both regions. And European corporations also lead the field as inward investors in the expanding markets of East and South Asia. That was already the case in the late 1990s for both China and India, and the trend has been confirmed since then.

Old international organizations have been weakened by the EU's rise to world eminence. This transformation in world affairs had been visible during the Uruguay Round of trade talks in the GATT, between 1986 and 1993, when the negotiations on farm products, cultural goods and trade in services had been decided between Americans and Europeans. As the world's prime services exporter, it pushed for global liberalization. As soon as the Euro was introduced, the EU's clout rose sharply in the IMF and the World Bank, so that the negotiations initiated almost immediately on the new international financial order became a bilateral affair. The US sought through a variety of channels to have discussions launched in an extended G7 group, to which a number of emerging market leaders would be added. The Europeans went along with this, because they dominated numerically, while G16 discussions, after a polite *tour de table*, replicated the *de facto* US–EU bi-gemony.

Security and defence

NATO also underwent a subtle transformation. As long as the Western European states saw their security in national terms, a European security policy proved impossible to shape. Military production had been

excluded from the Treaty of Rome, and the joint production and procurement facilities in NATO had never been developed. The result was
US domination of the European military market, with Europe's
national producers searching for sales outside Europe. In the 1990s US
dominance as Europe's protector seemed confirmed. But two developments altered this state of affairs. The first was the widening gap
between EU concerns and US actions in the Middle East and the Gulf;
the second was the realization that the advent of the Euro transformed
the EU's military-industrial base. An EU security policy was required to
prevent the EU being swept into mindless militarism by business-
driven defence lobbies, in the manner of Kaiser Wilhelm in the
Germany of the 1890s.

The catalyst for an autonomous EU security policy was provided by
the spread of nuclear weapons to Europe's south, fears in Germany,
Poland and the Baltic states over Russia's unpredictability, and the
change in attitudes to NATO in the US Congress. President Clinton
had managed to salvage Atlantic relations from breakdown over the
Balkans in 1994, but in hindsight it is clear that he fought a rearguard
action against a Congress, and a US public opinion, that grew ever
more isolationist in mentality. At the end of the twentieth century, this
mentality was strengthened by the surge of imports into the US when
emerging market currencies devalued on a trade-weighted basis by 50
per cent, by the puncturing of the belief in an Asian El Dorado, the
challenge of the Euro, and the Muslim world's widespread hostility to
US interests. Above all, the hi-tech security strategy of the Department
of Defense indicated a go-it-alone view of the world.

Given the very different sensitivities of European and US public opinion to events in the world, it was not surprising that the EU should side-
track NATO and develop its own security framework. That framework
defines the EU's security area as stretching to Russia's China frontier,
southwards to the Gulf and the Cape of Good Hope, the Mediterranean, its southern littoral, and out to the Canary islands and the mid-
Atlantic, up to Greenland. There is a European armed force, composed
of national secondments. Like-minded states may take initiatives
without asking for the participation of all. The European Council must
sanction policy and 'conduct' operations. Major European arms manu-

facturers produce on a more transnational basis, and can provide the necessary hardware. But the US President remains the commander-in-chief of NATO forces, and of NATO nuclear weapons, and the US supplies hardware to European troops deployed on alliance business.

In other words, the Atlantic bargain has been renegotiated by sleight-of-hand. In 2010 the US remains in effect the most cohesive and powerful entity on the globe. The EU is larger and more diverse. Both regulate their mutual concerns and differences in the institutional framework built up over the past sixty years. Their symbiosis is strengthened by the structured organization of artistic, sporting and academic exchanges and meetings, by their mutual penetration of each other's economies, by their shared values and preferences. They stand unchallenged as the world's leading powers, confident that market democracy is the best way forward for a world still pregnant with violence and hatreds, and torn by cries for revenge at imagined and experienced humiliations.

There are numerous threats, some familiar and others only faintly visible over the horizon. Familiar are the traditional bands of anti-Americans in Europe and anti-Europeans in the US. Their composition changes as different issues come and go, but so far they have not been able to break out of their national compounds – though, in Europe, racial supranationalism has been resuscitated from Hitler's unknown grave by the creation of a European *Grossraum*, and by violent confrontation between Islamic militants and Catholic revivalists, fighting for Christianity's holy lands in Europe. Racists in the US are fond of citing Thomas Jefferson, a slave owner, to the effect that 'the tree of liberty must be refreshed from time to time with the blood of patriots and tyrants. It is its natural manure'. But they are continually undermined by Afro-American triumphs in world sports.

The global civilization

Ten years hence will see even greater world prosperity, with the Euro–Atlantic alliance achieving unprecedented predominance. Arrogance rooted in a conviction of natural superiority over others is one of the unpleasant characteristics which enables the EU and the US to keep their crazies in their respective compounds, spitting out their venom and hatred. But by 2020 the rising importance of the rest of the world will be recorded in the interest taken by business in emerging markets, while by the 2030s China will have started to eclipse the US and positively dwarf Japan. Europe will have found a new mission to heal Africa, draw in Russia, negotiate an ever deeper *modus vivendi* with Islam, reach out to Latin America and help maintain balance within the US.

The US stands at its apogee, but the next decades are Europe's. Thereafter, China is destined to take its place in the sun. Meanwhile, world time has to be tamed, and local time reconciled to a world civilization. The capitalist revolution, unleashed by the great transformation in world affairs in 1989–92, is in full swing, and shows no sign of abating. The world is duly politicized and business is more exciting, but also more risky, than ever. It is more than high time – the clock stands past twelve – for the great planetary debate to open to create a world civilization of civilizations.

Postscript

'Funny,' I remember thinking as I woke up, 'generally, I tend to take a more sober view of human affairs. What was that ludicrous statement that Henry Brailsford, the historian, made in the summer of 1914 about Europe, and the role of socialist parties in educating the public about the value of fostering an integrated Europe? Something about there being no more wars among the six Great Powers.'

I went down to breakfast, and looked lazily at the headlines: 'Germany Exits from Euro: Unemployment at Record Levels.' Better turn to the sports pages. Ah, now this *is* news: 'England and Scotland contest football's World Cup Final.'

Notes

1 Quoted in Conor Cruise O'Brien, *The Long Affair: Thomas Jefferson and the French Revolution 1785–1800*, London, Pimlico, 1998.
2 William Schwartz, *Life Without Disease: The Pursuit of Medical Utopia*, University of California Press, 1998.

INDEX